Flexibility in Climate Policy

Flexibility in Climate Policy
Making the Kyoto Mechanisms Work

Edited by

Tim Jackson, Katie Begg and Stuart Parkinson

Earthscan Publications Ltd, London and Sterling, VA

First published in the UK and USA in 2001
by Earthscan Publications Ltd

ISBN: 1 85383 706 7 paperback
       1 85383 705 9 hardback

Typesetting by PCS Mapping & DTP, Newcastle upon Tyne
Printed and bound in the UK by Creative Print and Design Wales, Ebbw Vale
Cover design by Yvonne Booth

For a full list of publications please contact:
Earthscan Publications Ltd
120 Pentonville Road, London, N1 9JN, UK
Tel: +44 (0)20 7278 0433
Fax: +44 (0)20 7278 1142
Email: earthinfo@earthscan.co.uk
http://www.earthscan.co.uk

22883 Quicksilver Drive, Sterling, VA 20166–2012, USA

Earthscan is an editorially independent subsidiary of Kogan Page Ltd and publishes in
association with WWF-UK and the International Institute for Environment and
Development

A catalogue record for this book is available from the British Library

Library of Congress Cataloging-in-Publication Data

Jackson Tim.
   Flexibility in climate policy: making the Kyoto mechanisms work / Tim Jackson,
Katie Begg, Stuart Parkinson.
      p. cm.
   Includes bibliographical references and index.
   ISBN 1-85383-705-9 (hardcover) — ISBN 1-85383-706-7 (pbk.)
   1. Climatic changes—Government policy. 2. Greenhouse gases—Government
policy. 3. Climatic changes—International cooperation. 4. Greenhouse gases—
International cooperation. I. Begg, Katie. II. Parkinson, Stuart. III. Title.

QC981.8.C5 J32 2000
363.738'75526—dc21
                                                                    00-046596

Contents

List of Figures, Tables and Boxes

Figures

Tables

Boxes

Acronyms and Abbreviations

AIJ	activities implemented jointly
BOD	biological oxygen demand
°C	degrees Celsius
CCAP	Center for Clean Air Policy
CDM	clean development mechanism
CEA	cumulative environmental assessment
CEE	Central and Eastern European countries
CEF	Czech Environment Fund
CEGB	Central Electricity Generating Board
CER	certified emission reduction
CH_4	methane
CO_2	carbon dioxide
CO_2e	carbon dioxide equivalent
COP 1	first Conference of the Parties to the UN FCCC (Berlin, 1995)
COP 2	second Conference of the Parties (Geneva, 1996)
COP 3	third Conference of the Parties (Kyoto, 1997)
COP 4	fourth Conference of the Parties (Buenos Aires, 1998)
COP 5	fifth Conference of the Parties (Bonn, 1999)
COP 6	sixth Conference of the Parties (the Hague, 2000)
CZK	Czech crowns
db	decibel
DETR	UK Department of the Environment, Transport and the Regions
dr	discount rate
DPSIR	driving forces, pressure, state, impact, response
DSM	demand-side management
EAES	environmentally adapted energy system
EB	executive body
EBRD	European Bank for Reconstruction and Development
EC	European Commission
ECE	UN Economic Commission for Europe
EEA	European Environmental Agency
EEK	Estonian kroons
EIA	environmental impact assessment
EIS	environmental impact statement
EPA	US Environmental Protection Agency
ERU	emission reduction unit
EU	European Union
EVA	Energieverwertungsagentur (Austrian Energy Agency)

FCCC	UN Framework Convention on Climate Change
GATT	General Agreement on Tariffs and Trade
GDP	gross domestic product
GEF	Global Environmental Facility
GHG	greenhouse gas
GJ	gigajoule (= 10^9 joules)
GW	gigawatt (= 10^9 watts)
GWP	global warming potential
ha	hectare
HFC	hydrofluorocarbon
HFO	heavy-fuel oil
IEA	International Energy Agency
IPCC	Intergovernmental Panel on Climate Change
JI	joint implementation
km	kilometre
kW	kilowatt (= 10^3 watts)
kWh	kilowatt hour
LRTAP	Long-Range Transboundary Air Pollution
m	metre
MADA	multi-attribute decision analysis
maf	moisture and ash free
mg	milligramme
Mt	million tonnes
MtCe/y	megatonnes of carbon equivalent per year
MW	megawatt (= 10^6 watts)
MWh	megawatt hour
N_2O	nitrous oxide
NGO	non-governmental organization
NO_x	nitrogen oxide
NPV	net present value
NUTEK	Swedish National Board for Industrial and Technical Development
O&M	operation and maintenance
ODA	official development assistance
OE	operational entity
OECD	Organisation for Economic Co-operation and Development
PCB	polychlorinated biphenyl
PFC	perfluorocarbon
PJ	petajoules (= 10^{15} joules)
PM	particulate matter
PPPs	policies, plans and programmes
QELRC	quantified emission limitation and reduction commitment
R&D	research and development
SBI	subsidiary body for implementation
SBSTA	FCCC Subsidiary Body for Scientific and Technological Advice
SEA	strategic environmental assessment
SEK	Swedish kronor
SF_6	sulphur hexafluoride

SIA	social impact assessment
SIDA	Swedish International Cooperation Development Agency
SO_2	sulphur dioxide
STEM	Swedish National Energy Administration
t	tonne
tCO_2	tonnes of carbon dioxide
tCO_2e/MWh	tonnes of carbon dioxide equivalent per megawatt hour of output
UK	United Kingdom
UN	United Nations
UNDP	United Nations Development Programme
UNEP	United Nations Environment Programme
URF	uniform reporting format
US	United States
USIJI	US Initiative on Joint Implementation
V	vanadium
WMO	World Meteorological Office
Zn	zinc

About the Contributors

Peter Bailey has been a Research Associate at Stockholm Environment Institute since 1992 and also a Research Fellow in the Department of Sociology at the University of York since 1997. His areas of expertise include the application of technologies for air pollution abatement, environmental policy analysis, environmental modelling, environmental economics, energy economics, public participation techniques and social aspects of environmental management and policy.

Dr Katherine Begg has been involved in environmental problems associated with the energy industry for a number of years. She worked on the acid rain problem while at the former Central Electricity Generating Board (CEGB) and was the UK expert on the effects of pollutants on materials, and then the UK delegate to the UN ECE experts on electricity and the environment. She is currently a Research Fellow at the Centre for Environmental Strategy at the University of Surrey and has worked on accounting and accreditation issues for activities implemented jointly (AIJ) under the UN FCCC for the last three years. Her current interests are in designing modalities for joint implementation (JI) and the clean development mechanism (CDM) – in particular, in relation to the sustainable development and baseline aspects of these mechanisms – and in energy modelling and decision analysis.

Professor Michael Chadwick is an environmental biologist who worked in the Universities of Wales, Khartoum (Sudan), Cambridge and York. Latterly he has been Director of the Stockholm Environment Institute (1991–1996) and Director of the Leadership for Environment and Development Programme in Geneva (LEAD-Europe). His academic interests were mainly in the ecology of difficult ecosystems, such as deserts and industrial waste sites. From his work on the restoration of waste from the coal industry, he developed a more general interest in the environmental impacts of phases of fuel cycles. Much of this work was concerned with models that attempted an integrated assessment of environmental systems from waste emissions, to their transport, deposition, impacts and cost-effective abatement. He now works as an environmental consultant from 3 Skipwith Road, Escrick, York, YO19 6JT.

Dr Gary Haq has been a Research Associate at the Stockholm Environment Institute since 1997. He has undertaken a number of research projects, some of which have been funded by the African Development Bank, European Commission, the Swedish Environmental Protection Agency and the Swedish International Cooperation Development Agency (SIDA). His main areas of expertise include environmental impact assessment, strategic environmental assessment, climate change, transport, air pollution and sustainable development issues.

Dr Tiit Kallaste is a Senior Research Fellow at the Stockholm Environment Institute – Tallinn, Estonia – where he is Director of the Climate Energy and Atmosphere Programme. He has been the national coordinator of several UNEP and the Global Environmental Facility (GEF)-granted international programmes devoted to the research of global climate change issues at the local level. He was also involved in the Estonian Country Case Study on Climate Change Impacts and Adaptation Assessments. His current research interests lie in the area of joint implementation of pilot-phase issues such as baseline construction, host country's institutional enhancement, emissions trading and capacity-building. Other interests include energy efficiency, energy taxation and renewable energy.

Professor Tim Jackson holds the chair in sustainable development at the Centre for Environmental Strategy in the University of Surrey. He has previously held research posts at the University of Western Ontario (Canada), St Andrews University, South Bank University, the University of Lancaster and the Stockholm Environment Institute. He has contributed research, consultancy, advice and teaching to a wide range of institutions and organizations, including the World Bank, the United Nations Environment Programme (UNEP), the United Nations Development Programme (UNDP), and the European Commission. His research interests include climate policy, renewable energy, ecological economics and environmental philosophy. He is reviews editor of the journal *Climate Policy*.

Klemens Leutgöb has worked since 1994 as a consultant with Energieverwertungsagentur, the Austrian Energy Agency. He previously studied economic and social sciences at the Johannes Kepler University in Linz and held research fellowships at the Technical University, Vienna, and the Open University, Bratislava. His key qualifications are in the area of investment calculation and financial engineering, and he has been involved in a number of projects related to energy efficiency projects in Central and Eastern European countries. He recently carried out a comprehensive analysis of the instrument of joint implementation from the point of view of the Austrian climate protection policy (on behalf of the ministry of environment).

Poul-Erik Morthorst is a Senior Research Specialist in the Systems Analysis Department at Risø National Laboratory. He holds a Masters degree in economics from the University of Århus and has been with Risø since 1978. Poul-Erik Morthorst's main activities cover general energy and environmental planning, evaluation of policy instruments for regulating energy and environment, development of economic, environmental and technical models, and the assessment of the economics of renewable energy technologies, especially wind power. He has participated in a large number of projects within these fields and has extensive experience in international collaboration.

Dr Lise Nielsen has a Masters in economics and a PhD from the Department of Economics, University of Copenhagen. She joined the Systems Analysis Department at Risø National Laboratory in 1995 and held previous positions in the Danish Ministry of Finance and at the Department of Economics, University of Copenhagen. Her work at Risø relates to economic regulation of energy and environment – including analysis of Kyoto instruments and renewable energy certificates – and macroeconomic modelling of energy and environment.

Dr Stuart Parkinson is a research fellow at the Centre for Environmental Strategy at the University of Surrey, UK. He has a Bachelors degree in physics and engineering, and a PhD in environmental modelling. He has been working in the area of joint implementation for three years, first on the European Commission-funded project: Accounting and Accreditation of Activities Implemented Jointly, and currently on a UK government-funded project: Evaluation of Clean Development Mechanism-Type Projects in Developing Countries. This work has included energy-systems modelling. He has worked for industry, academia and NGOs.

Foreword

Research on criteria and methods to integrate equity, efficiency and effectiveness within European and global climate policies can provide valuable inputs to policy-making and to public debate on policy choice. The project Accounting and Accreditation of Activities Implemented Jointly, which provided the basis for this book, was part of a group of projects supported by the Research Directorate-General of the European Commission with the aim of identifying those criteria and methods. This, in turn, was part of a broader effort to improve the research/policy interface, taking into account the European Union effort to provide leadership in fostering policies and agreements to mitigate climate change.

One of the key insights arising from the project was the identification of multiple objectives underlying the Kyoto mechanisms. While economic efficiency is usually referred to as the main argument for these 'flexibility mechanisms', other important objectives are also at stake. These include inter and intragenerational equity, North–South relations, and the ability to deliver environmental improvement (for example, reduction of greenhouse gas emissions). This insight has important implications for the actual formulation of the mechanisms: what might seem at first to require a purely technical definition of issues, such as baselines and accreditation rules, turns out to hinge on a broader range of criteria. Technical robustness needs to be coupled with economic and administrative feasibility, with political priorities and with social acceptability.

The fact that this situation is not peculiar to joint implementation (JI) but relates to the whole climate policy issue makes the case even more interesting. The JI case, discussed in detail in this book, illustrates clearly what forms the trade-offs between potentially conflicting objectives tend to take. This book also demonstrates what alternative methods can offer in terms of transparency, verifiability and so on.

The project started before the Kyoto Protocol was agreed upon and it was completed afterwards. This meant that, as is often the case for research endeavour aiming at policy relevance, Tim Jackson and his team worked in a context of intense negotiation leading to continual changes in policy and language. One of the successes of the project was that, instead of developing a sort of 'moving target' syndrome, the team managed to keep a clear research focus while taking into account the changing circumstances of pre- and post-Kyoto climate policy.

As a consequence, it is expected that this book will be of direct interest and use to a wide range of stakeholders in the climate debate, including: policymakers, non-governmental organizations, business representatives, and researchers interested in the formulation and implementation of climate policies both at the international level, and also at the local level – where projects are actually carried out. Ultimately, it is to be hoped that this contribution will help frame the debate in such a way as to ensure that environmental effectiveness is not forgotten when assessing economic efficiency, and that equity is taken into account when discussing whether technically efficient and effective options are also socially sustainable.

Dr Angela Liberatore
Research Directorate-General
European Commission

Preface

As this book goes to press, climate policy is still reeling from the breakdown of the political negotiations at the sixth Conference of the Parties (COP 6) to the United Nations Framework Convention on Climate Change (FCCC). Amongst the decisions which should have been – but were not – taken at that meeting were several which relate directly to the operationalization of the so-called 'Kyoto mechanisms': joint implementation, emissions trading and the Clean Development Mechanism (CDM). These mechanisms were a vital ingredient in the negotiations which culminated in the Kyoto Protocol in December 1997 and are seen by many as critical to the political success of the Protocol. Yet as this book demonstrates, their operationalization has always been and (in the light of recent events) clearly continues to be fraught with difficulty; and must be negotiated, if at all, within a minefield of potentially conflicting objectives.

The book itself evolved from a study (Jackson et al, 1999) supported by the Research Directorate-General (formerly known as DGXII) of the European Commission (EC) within the framework of the Human Dimensions of Environmental Change research area in the Environment and Climate Programme. The broad aim of the original study was to examine the concept of 'joint implementation' as an institutional instrument relevant to the 'fair and efficient abatement of greenhouse gas emissions'.

Introduced formally into the language of the FCCC in 1992, the phrase 'joint implementation' originally referred to a generic family of institutional mechanisms which would allow parties to the convention to engage in cooperative (bilateral and multilateral) implementation of their commitments. Such mechanisms, it was argued, would serve the interests of economic efficiency and allow for a greater flexibility in meeting the aims of the convention. Joint implementation has subsequently taken on a much more specific meaning, usually referring to the project-based mechanism introduced in article 6 of the Kyoto Protocol; but the objective of this mechanism is, once again, to contribute a certain kind of flexibility to international climate policy.

In keeping with the conceptual aim of the EC study, this book approaches the evaluation of project-based 'flexibility mechanisms' from a broad perspective, taking into account a wide range of technical, economic, environmental, social and ethical factors; and recognizing that international policy instruments operate under multiple objectives. It undertakes a careful analysis of a number of case study energy sector investments located in Eastern European countries. Using these cases studies as illustrations, the book confronts some of the difficult issues associated with the Kyoto mechanisms: the dangers of counterfactual baselines, the incentives for gaming, the 'openness' of the CDM, the potential for leakage, the problems of complexity and uncertainty, and the practicality and political acceptability of flexibility mechanisms. In the process of addressing these issues, the authors develop a unique approach, in which streamlined assessment procedures are combined with institutional safeguards in order to balance the demand for practical mechanisms with the environmental objectives of the Kyoto Protocol.

The analytic work at the core of the book is based on the case studies examined in the EC project. Consequently, the lessons for climate policy developed in this book are most directly applicable to project-based flexibility mechanisms of the kind reflected in the case studies. Specifically, it is to this context that the phrase joint implementation now usually refers. However, many of the lessons arising from the book are relevant to joint implementation in the wider, generic sense envisaged in the FCCC. In particular, this book has clear implications for the design of the CDM and for emissions trading, as well as for joint implementation in the narrower sense.

Almost a decade of intense negotiations contributed to the signing of the Kyoto Protocol. Subsequent discussion of the operational modalities of the Kyoto mechanisms has been no less intense. With the collapse of the COP 6 negotiations in the Hague, a satisfactory resolution of the outstanding questions concerning these modalities must realistically be expected to take some time. However, it will continue to occupy an absolutely critical place in the ongoing climate negotiations. The development of flexibility within global climate policy is thus an ambitious, demanding but extremely timely task. It is towards that task that this book is dedicated.

Tim Jackson, Katie Begg and Stuart Parkinson
University of Surrey, Guildford
November 2000

Acknowledgements

This book is based on a study supported by the European Commission's Environment and Climate Programme 1994–1998 (Human Dimensions of Climate Change Programme), contract number ENV4-CT96–0210. We are particularly grateful for the inspiration and support of Dr Angela Liberatore, who was then the DGXII liaison officer responsible for the project.

We would also like to thank the numerous individuals and organizations who made this study possible through valuable contributions of knowledge, time and critical evaluation of the work during its earlier stages. Thanks are due in particular to: Toomas Pallo, Jürgen Salay and Sune Westermark for their contributions to the EC project; to Catrinus Jepma, Axel Michaelowa, Fanny Missfeldt, Liam Salter, Martin Wietschel and Thomas Zylizc for their critical role as peer reviewers; to Jiri Spitz of VUPEK and Poul-Erik Grohnheit of RNL (Denmark) for tuition in the use of the EFOM-ENV model; to the staff at SEI Tallinn (Estonia) and Alice Sedmidubsky from EVA (Austria) for their invaluable help in arranging site visits; to the plant managers, engineers and administrative officials who succeeded in making our site visits both informative and pleasant; to NGO representatives Petr Hlobel and Kalev Sepp, and representatives of the environment ministries in Estonia and the Czech Republic, for their generosity in taking the time to discuss these issues from a host country perspective; to Beth Hickman for analysis undertaken during a summer placement at the University of Surrey; and to Joe Flynn at the University of Surrey for his patience in managing the financial complexity of a project of this nature.

Beyond Joint Implementation: An Overview and Summary of the Argument

T Jackson, K Begg and S Parkinson

Introduction

The signing of the Kyoto Protocol in December 1997 was the culmination of a decade of protracted and often heated political negotiation, and over four decades of scientific research on the subject of global climate change.

Concern over the impacts of human activity on the global climate can be traced back over 100 years. As long ago as the 1890s, the Swedish Nobel Prize-winning chemist Svante Arrhenius drew attention to the possibility that anthropogenic emissions of certain gases could change the composition of the Earth's atmosphere and thus affect the climate (Arrhenius, 1896). The science of climate change received very little attention for the next 50 or 60 years, but in the last four decades of the 20th century a significant international effort was made to achieve a better scientific understanding of the complex interactions between concentrations of atmospheric gases and the global climate.

Sparked by a series of dry summers in the US, and fuelled by rising environmental awareness, concern over the global climate reached a new level during the late 1980s, and resulted in the establishment of the Intergovernmental Panel on Climate Change (IPCC). Set up under the auspices of the United Nations Environment Programme (UNEP) and the World Meteorological Office (WMO), the IPCC was charged with providing governments with authoritative assessments of the state of knowledge concerning global climate change. The IPCC's first assessment report published in 1990 communicated the findings of three working groups: one on science, another on impacts and the third on responses. Accepted by the international community at the Second World Climate Conference in November 1990, this report laid the foundations for the United Nations Framework Convention on Climate Change (FCCC), which was signed at the UN Conference on Environment and Development (commonly known as the Earth Summit) in Rio in June 1992.

The 'ultimate objective' of the FCCC, as set out in article 2 of the convention, is to stabilize greenhouse gas (GHG) emissions 'at a level that would prevent dangerous anthropogenic interference with the climate system'. However, the convention itself established no legally binding commitments by any of the parties to limit or reduce their emissions of GHGs.[1] Rather, its aim was to provide an umbrella for negotiating such reductions in the future. It laid down the principles under which such commitments might operate, and the political framework within which negotiations might proceed. For example, the FCCC established a strict timetable of future negotiations.

The first Conference of the Parties (COP 1) to the FCCC was held in Berlin in 1995, a statutory year after the convention came into force. One of the principal aims of COP 1 was to review the adequacy of the commitments laid down under the convention. After considerable negotiation, the meeting concluded that the existing commitments were inadequate and set out an agreement (the Berlin Mandate) to begin a process which would, *inter alia*, 'set quantified emission limitation and reduction objectives within specified time-frames'. This was the process which would lead, in less than three years, to the signing of the Kyoto Protocol at the third Conference of the Parties (COP 3) in December 1997.[2]

The principal success of the Kyoto Protocol was in establishing quantifiable commitments by the industrialized nations – the so-called Annex I countries – to limit and reduce their greenhouse gas (GHG) emissions. The aggregate aim of these commitments is to reduce emissions of a basket of six GHGs[3] from the Annex I countries to at least 5 per cent below the base year[4] level during the *commitment period* from 2008 to 2012.

This achievement might appear slight in view of the longer-term commitment to stabilize concentrations of GHGs in the atmosphere. Nonetheless, there were points during the negotiations when even this level of commitment appeared unlikely. In fact, it is almost beyond doubt that the Kyoto agreement would never have been achieved at all had it not been for the incorporation into the protocol of certain *flexibility mechanisms* – mechanisms which would allow parties to meet their commitments in part by actions carried out abroad, rather than at home, if such a course of action proved economically efficient.

The ground for introducing such mechanisms had been laid within the FCCC. Specifically, article 4.2(a) allowed parties to the convention to 'implement...jointly' their commitments to policies and measures designed to mitigate the threat of climate change. So it was that the concept of joint implementation (JI) entered the institutional language of climate policy.

In the context of the FCCC, JI is generally taken to mean bilateral or multilateral investments in GHG emission reduction or sequestration projects carried out between parties to the convention. Typically, a *donor* country provides investment funds towards the implementation of an emission reduction or sequestration project in a *host* country, in exchange for emission reduction *credits* to be held against its own emission reduction targets. In principle, it has been argued, this kind of arrangement should allow for greater cost-efficiency in meeting global targets, since abatement action can be taken first where it is least costly to do so.

From the start, however, JI has been a contentious concept – so much so that a pilot phase designed to test the concept was only agreed (at COP 1 in Berlin) after the name had been changed to activities implemented jointly (AIJ). The Kyoto Protocol, although retaining the concept, has abandoned the language of joint implementation altogether.

Nevertheless, flexibility was a key ingredient in the success of the Kyoto Protocol. A number of mechanisms were introduced within the protocol that bear a close family resemblance to the idea of JI. These mechanisms were critical in gaining the acceptance by certain parties of quantified emission limitation and reduction commitments (QELRCs). The negotiating position of the US, for example, was against accepting any specific reduction targets at all in the absence of flexibility mechanisms (Grubb et al, 1999). For better or worse, flexibility has become a central pillar of international climate policy in the wake of Kyoto.

In spite of their political importance, the operational details of the Kyoto flexibility mechanisms remain largely undefined. Considerable political pressure is now building to get the protocol ratified and into force before Earth Summit 2002. But this is unlikely to happen without the implementation of all the Kyoto flexibility mechanisms.

In order to facilitate the early entry into force of the Kyoto Protocol, the fourth Conference of the Parties (COP 4) in Buenos Aires in 1998 agreed a detailed plan of action, including a strict timetable for making decisions about the outstanding issues. Under this plan of action, the sixth Conference of the Parties (in the Hague in November 2000) was charged with taking decisions on all the flexible mechanisms incorporated within the Kyoto Protocol. The failure of COP6 to reach agreement has inevitably delayed this timetable. Full-scale international emissions trading may not be in operation for a decade.

It is clear from these remarks that the negotiations which are currently taking place, and which will continue to take place over the forthcoming months and years, are vital to the success of global climate policy and to the effectiveness of the Kyoto Protocol. In particular, the success of the protocol is likely to depend upon appropriate resolutions to the open questions still surrounding the operationalization of flexible mechanisms. In the wake of the breakdown of negotiations at COP6, its lessons are more critical than ever. It is towards an examination of these same issues that this book is directed.

Summary of the Argument

It has proved tempting to portray JI as a straightforward mechanism for delivering flexibility to global climate policy. Proponents of JI have pointed out that, from an environmental perspective, a reduction in GHG emissions in one place is as good as a reduction in any other place. Accordingly, they argue, it makes sense to reduce GHG first where it is least costly to do so. An argument from economic efficiency is clearly important both in terms of the explicit aims of the convention, and in terms of the politics of international negotiation. However, a single-minded allegiance to this principle is misleading for three very important reasons.

Firstly, JI does not really define a single institutional mechanism at all. Rather, it describes a broad idea which encompasses a range of different mechanisms. Each of these individual mechanisms is constructed differently, operates at different scales and under different conditions, and involves different actors, different operational modalities and different incentive structures. No single evaluation of this spectrum of mechanisms is to be trusted. Each must be evaluated on its own merits.

Secondly, climate policy operates under multiple objectives. Principally, of course, the Kyoto Protocol reflects a climate-related environmental objective: reductions in GHG emissions. The argument from economic efficiency, although important, must operate within the constraints of this overarching environmental objective. In addition, however, it should be noted that a number of other objectives inform global climate policy. For example, the concept of equity is introduced explicitly into the language of the FCCC, and imposes quite specific limitations on climate related interventions. In addition, climate policy labours under a host of other international pressures, including non-climate related environmental objectives, technology transfer imperatives, trade liberalization policies, and bilateral or multilateral cooperative alliances. Furthermore, it is clear that climate policy mechanisms are likely to be redundant if they do not satisfy certain criteria of practicability. In short, JI operates in a multi-objective decision-making context. Generally speaking, it will not be possible to satisfy all the underlying objectives simultaneously, and typically trade-offs will emerge between conflicting objectives. It is vital that these trade-offs are identified explicitly and addressed within the policy-making process. The evaluation of JI mechanisms against a single objective (such as economic efficiency) is inherently flawed.

Finally, it emerges that JI labours under an almost intractable epistemological problem, namely: the irreducible uncertainty arising from the counterfactual baseline against which emission reductions and costs are measured.

The baseline is an estimation of what would have happened in the absence of the JI intervention. This baseline is essential for any determination of the emission reductions and the costs associated with the intervention. Furthermore, these two variables are precisely those required in order to determine whether or not JI is environmentally effective and whether or not it is economically efficient. And yet the fundamental reference point for measuring both emission reductions and costs is counterfactual. It refers neither to what is happening, nor to what has happened, nor even to what might happen in future. Instead, the baseline is an estimate of what would have happened if the intervention had not taken place – an assertion which is impossible, in principle, either to verify or falsify. What makes matters worse is that the indeterminacy of the baseline provides significant incentives for gaming by those involved in the buying and selling of emission reduction credits. Consequently, it is impossible to determine, with any real conviction, the exact extent to which a particular JI action reinforces or compromises the objectives of the convention.

In the light of these three fundamental features of JI, it is tempting to ask whether there is any realistic prospect of designing flexibility within global climate policy. Given the critical role flexibility has played in negotiating consensus under the Kyoto Protocol, however, such a prospect urgently needs to be explored. In this book we pursue an approach to the evaluation of JI which is founded on three main pillars.

Firstly, this book undertakes a detailed assessment of a number of case studies. These case studies are taken from pilot-phase investments by Western nations (primarily Austria, Denmark and Sweden) in energy sector projects in Eastern European nations (primarily the Czech Republic and Estonia). These projects are evaluated by calculating the emission reductions associated with the project and the incremental costs of these reductions.[5] This evaluation requires the establishment of an appropriate baseline. It is a primary contention of this study that the counterfactual nature of baselines introduces an element of irreducible uncertainty into these accounting procedures. Rather than pre-select a single baseline, therefore, each project is assessed against a variety of credible baselines for each project. Therefore, the results of the case study analysis are presented as a range of values for emission reductions and costs, and calibrated as far as possible against the associated uncertainties.

Next, this book advocates the adoption of specific institutional measures for managing the uncertainty and complexity associated with JI, and for limiting the incentives for gaming where these exist. In particular, it is possible in some circumstances to adopt certain streamlined assessment procedures, for instance by standardizing baseline types according to specific project criteria. However, it is necessary to combine these streamlined procedures with certain institutional safeguards (for example, limited crediting lifetimes, baseline revision, partial crediting, monitoring and verification protocols) in order to maintain an appropriate balance between underlying objectives.

Finally, each *package* of streamlined procedures and institutional safeguards can be evaluated against the underlying objectives – for any specific context – using a holistic multicriterion evaluation framework. The final chapter of this book illustrates how this kind of evaluation could work. Typically, different packages will perform differently against the underlying objectives. Some will perform well against the criterion of environmental effectiveness, but may be cumbersome to operate and therefore turn out to be unattractive to investors. Others may be more attractive to investors but offer high incentives for gaming and hence compromise the environmental objectives of the protocol. Others again may perform well in terms of GHG emission reduction but have adverse local environmental or social impacts and thus compromise host country equity.

This book argues that designing flexibility within climate policy relies on being able to identify explicitly the conflicts between underlying objectives and to make appropriate trade-offs between them.

Chapter-by-Chapter Synopsis

This book is divided between conceptual analyses of flexibility, quantitative analyses of specific projects and illustrative analyses – based on these case studies – designed to show how flexibility might be operationalized. The following subsections provide brief summaries of each of these individual chapters.

The Language of Flexibility

The language associated with the use of flexibility mechanisms has changed several times during the course of recent negotiations. These kinds of linguistic shifts are confusing in policy terms. Chapter 2 attempts to categorize different flexibility mechanisms according to a variety of defining characteristics, including the scope or scale of the trade, the actors involved in the arrangement, and the degree to which these actors are, or are not, bound by emission targets under the Kyoto Protocol.

Generally speaking, the term joint implementation is now usually taken to refer to the transfer of emission-reduction units for project-level investments in Annex I host countries under article 6 of the Kyoto Protocol. However, it is shown in Chapter 2 that there are strong similarities between emissions trading mechanisms and joint implementation. It is also clear from this analysis that the clean development mechanism (CDM) introduced in article 12 of the protocol – in which Annex I donor countries invest in emission-reduction projects in non-Annex I host countries – also defines a form of joint implementation. The two project-level flexibility mechanisms defined by articles 6 and 12 of the Kyoto Protocol provide the focus for the subsequent analysis in this book.

What emerges most clearly from this chapter is that joint implementation does not define a single institutional mechanism at all. Rather, it covers a multitude of operational forms. Each of these has different defining parameters, and each of them will have different operating characteristics. In particular, each of them is likely to perform differently against the range of objectives against which flexibility might be evaluated.

Objectives of Joint Implementation

The principal justification for introducing flexibility mechanisms within climate policy has generally been the argument from economic efficiency. However, as we have already made clear, there are several important objectives that inform global climate policy. Chapter 3 discusses the three most important objectives under which flexibility mechanisms operate.

The overriding environmental objective of the convention (and indeed the Kyoto Protocol) gives rise to two main considerations. The first of these is the question of *additionality*: the problem of ensuring that JI projects do, in fact, lead to real, measurable reductions in greenhouse gas emissions. The second is the broader environmental and social context of energy-sector investments. Clearly, it would be wrong if actions to reduce GHG emissions were to lead to increases in other non-climate related environmental and social impacts.

A part of the rationale for keeping a careful eye on the local environmental and social aspects of JI projects is a concern for equity, particularly since this applies to the interests of the host country. Chapter 3 discusses the question of equity in some depth and argues that host country equity is most likely to be at risk where institutional capacity is low, where environmental regulations are likely to be lax and where access to capital and resources is poor. This suggests that principles of equity are most likely to be breached in non-Annex I host countries, or in Annex I host countries with transitional economies, and highlights the need for appropriate institutional safeguards in these cases.

The economic objective is the most frequently expressed rationale for incorporating flexibility within climate policy. However, a robust evaluation of the extent to which this objective is achieved in a particular situation is far from straightforward. The starting point must be clarity in the analytic framework. In particular, we need to establish appropriate concepts of cost and cost-effectiveness with which to judge the economics of specific JI projects. Furthermore, Chapter 3 points out that a number of problems stand in the way of a simplistic extrapolation from principles of market efficiency. Principal amongst these problems is the question of the counterfactual baseline.

The Baseline Question

Assessment of both environmental effectiveness and economic efficiency requires an evaluation of the emission reductions and costs associated with JI projects against an appropriate baseline. As we have already noted, this baseline is counterfactual. It describes neither what has happened nor what will happen, but what would have happened in the absence of the JI project – an eventuality which is inherently indeterminable. It may be possible to establish more or less credible or defensible hypotheses about this counterfactual context. However, it is epistemologically impossible to verify these hypotheses, even in retrospect. Nor is the situation necessarily improved by employing complex models or increasingly data-intensive assessment procedures.

In the light of these difficulties, Chapter 4 discusses a number of different approaches to constructing appropriate baselines for JI projects. These include project-specific baselines, a 'default-matrix' approach, benchmarking procedures, investment analysis methods and a systems model approach. Chapter 4 also sets out some of the critical elements associated with the construction of credible baselines.

Ultimately, however, none of these methods is capable of reducing significantly the uncertainty associated with the counterfactuality of the baseline. In the light of this problem, the remainder of the book sets out a quite specific structured approach which attempts to negotiate the complexities and uncertainties arising from the counterfactuality of the baseline. This approach has the following three steps:

1   We specify a range of baselines against which the selected projects can be assessed. These baselines are constructed according to the guidelines set out above for project-level baselines. The results of our analysis of case study projects are presented as a *range of values* for emissions reductions and costs (Chapter 7) and are calibrated, as far as is possible, against the associated uncertainties (Chapter 8).
2   We examine (Chapter 9) a variety of institutional measures which are designed to manage both the operational complexity and the epistemologi-

cal uncertainty associated with JI, and show how these measures can be combined into operational packages which provide both a degree of standardization and the implementation of certain institutional safeguards.

3   Finally, we show (in Chapter 10) how the use of a multi-attribute decision-making context allows us to evaluate each package of measures against the underlying objectives discussed in Chapter 3.

Case Study Projects

The broad-based conceptual analysis in this book is complemented by an extensive evaluation of real case study joint-implementation projects. Not all of these case study projects have been classified as AIJ projects under the FCCC pilot phase. However, all of them involve investment by a donor country in emissions reduction in a host country and are, in principle, of the same form as those defined under the AIJ pilot phase.

Chapter 5 describes the selected projects, and the donor–host combinations involved in them. The chosen projects are all energy-sector investments by Western nations in Central and Eastern Europe. The donor countries were Austria, Denmark, Sweden and the US. The principal host countries were the Czech Republic and Estonia. For the most part, these case studies have been concerned with the conversion of heating boilers from heavy fuel oil or coal to biomass or natural gas. The study has also examined two electricity supply projects (wind farms), one gas-fired cogeneration (combined heat and power) project, and one demand-side efficiency project in the heat sector.

A number of general lessons about the evaluation of projects have been learned during the course of this study. Firstly, it is clear that there are large variations between apparently similar plants. Incomplete project descriptions and practical difficulties in acquiring the relevant data meant that site visits were an essential prerequisite of the evaluation process. Even with skilled country personnel making repeat visits, the evaluation database remained incomplete in certain respects. This experience led to the formulation of a number of conditions which might be imposed on the eligibility of joint implementation projects for crediting purposes:

- An irreducible minimum of reliable and appropriate data should be available for the project to be eligible for credit under the protocol.
- Guidelines should be established for the acquisition of this key data; technical, environmental and social data are required; initial surveys should provide a focus on whether such data are likely to be available in order to make the inclusion of the project feasible.
- Procedures for collecting such data should be set up at the design and approval stage and should include output monitoring.
- Verification and ground-truthing should provide checks on details of projects.
- The sustainability of fuel sources should be demonstrable.
- Care should be taken in defining the system boundaries of the project.

Environmental and Social Aspects of Joint Implementation

Chapter 6 discusses the non-climate related environmental and social impacts of JI projects. These impacts are important not only in terms of the broad environmental objective of the FCCC, but also in terms of ensuring that host country equity is not compromised.

Determining whether or not JI actions incur non-climate related environmental or social benefits or disbenefits is, however, no easy task. All interventions in the energy sector are likely to have some kind of environmental and social impact. A number of methodologies have been developed to try and assess these impacts. In this chapter, we have outlined the basic principles of several of these methodologies, including: environmental impact assessment (EIA), strategic environmental assessment (SEA), social impact assessment (SIA), and approaches based on various models, system boundaries and evaluation procedures.

This chapter also reports on an attempt to engage in a limited retrospective environmental impact assessment of the selected case study projects. This task proved difficult, partly because of problems in attaining sufficient data. Nevertheless, it was possible to make some limited assessment of changes in various impact categories between the JI project and the baseline. For instance, no significant change was observed in impact categories related to water, land use, soil, visual impact, noise, forestry, energy consumption and socioeconomic aspects. Positive changes (benefits) associated with the JI projects included: significant reductions in sulphur dioxide (SO_2) and nitrogen oxide (NO_x) emissions – by at least an order of magnitude in certain project types; and reductions in particulate emissions for conversions from coal to gas or biomass. The main disbenefits from the case study projects included: some increases in carbon monoxide emissions for conversions from oil to biomass; increases in waste production for oil or gas conversions to biomass; and increases in transport requirements for some oil to biomass conversions. In certain cases, it has been clear that environmental or social benefits which are deemed secondary in terms of the aims of the FCCC have, in fact, been the principal motivation for local involvement in the projects.

The discussion in this chapter highlights the need for a practical methodology for the environmental and social assessment of JI projects. It also points to the need for a consistent set of procedures through which this methodology can be incorporated within the approval procedures associated with the Kyoto flexibility mechanisms.

Accounting for Emission Reductions and Costs

Chapter 7 presents and applies the accounting framework used to analyse the performance of the chosen case study projects. It defines and explains four critical accounting variables: the total emissions reduction achieved by the project over its lifetime; the specific emissions reduction (per unit of energy output); the incremental cost of achieving the reduction; and the specific incremental cost (per unit of emission reduction). This accounting methodology is then used to analyse the chosen case study projects.

In line with the discussion in Chapter 4, we define a range of possible baselines against which to analyse the projects, and thus present a range of

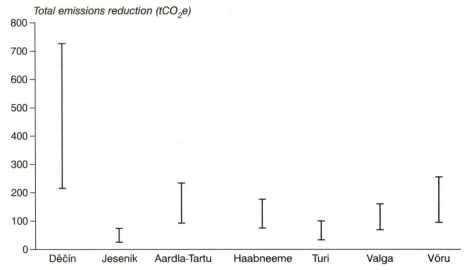

Figure 1.1 *Emissions Reduction for Case Study JI Projects*

values for each of the critical accounting variables. In this way, we make explicit the irreducible uncertainty introduced by the counterfactual nature of the baseline. In particular, for the project types studied, we derive ranges of values for the emissions reduction associated with the project (Figure 1.1). For simple heat-supply projects, the uncertainty is found to be around ±45 per cent, whilst for cogeneration and electricity supply projects this rises to ±55 per cent and ±60 per cent respectively. This increase is due to the particular difficulty in defining the displaced emissions in a complex system: the electricity network. For the heat-demand projects, the uncertainty is found to be lower, at approximately ±35 per cent. This is due to the shorter technical life of the project, allowing less variation in the baseline. The variation in the value of the specific incremental costs of the projects is also found to be large (Figure 1.2).

A number of the case study projects investigated in this study had been officially registered with the FCCC secretariat as AIJ pilot projects. As such, reports were produced by the project implementers estimating the emissions reduction associated with the project. As a result, Chapter 7 carries out a comparison between the officially reported values and those derived here. For four heat-supply projects, where Sweden was the donor country and Estonia the host, the official estimate had been at the low end of the range derived here. For the cogeneration project, where the US was the officially reported donor and the Czech Republic the host, the official estimate had been at the high end. While this is a small sample, it nevertheless highlights the importance of consistent procedures for estimates of emissions reduction.

A key conclusion of this chapter is that the uncertainty associated with the baseline increases the further the baseline is projected into the future. It is in light of this conclusion that later chapters argue for revising baselines, and limiting the lifetime over which credits can be issued. A further conclusion of

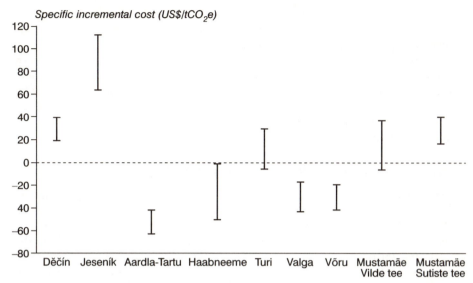

Figure 1.2 *Specific Incremental Costs for Case Study JI Projects*

this chapter is that the specific emissions reduction can be used as a basis for baseline standardization. This issue is revisited in Chapter 9.

Uncertainty and Sensitivity Analysis

Chapter 8 undertakes detailed uncertainty and sensitivity analyses of the chosen case-study projects with respect to these different forms of uncertainty, and discusses the implications of the analysis.

Some uncertainty is related to the counterfactuality of the baseline, and the implication of this uncertainty for evaluating critical variables was addressed through a scenario analysis in Chapter 7. Further sources of uncertainty include project-performance uncertainty, measurement uncertainty – related to the accuracy of technical or financial data on the project – and background uncertainty, which refers to the variability in technical, economic, social, environmental or political factors influencing the analysis. For example, considerable variability in the values of the critical accounting variables may be introduced as a result of the application of different discounting procedures. In fact, this is identified as an area where standardization is important.

This chapter attempts to quantify variability in results associated with each of these different forms of uncertainty. Using stochastic simulation, the chapter estimates the combined uncertainty due to all these sources for the Estonian heat-supply projects and identifies the relative importance of each type of uncertainty. Typically, the total uncertainty in estimates of emission reductions was found to be very high, in the order of ±60 per cent. However, this could be reduced to around ±40 per cent if monitored data (rather than feasibility data) are used as the basis of assessing critical accounting variables. Since the measurement uncertainty is assumed to be small, it is argued that the remaining uncertainty (around 40 per cent) is mainly a result of the counterfactuality of the baseline – comparable to that found in the previous chapter for heat-supply projects. One of the contentions of this study is that this uncertainty needs to be managed by putting in place appropriate institutional safeguards (Chapter 9).

A further investigation carried out in this chapter is a comparison between estimates of the critical accounting variables derived at the *project level* (where interaction between the project and the wider system is considered negligible) and at the *system level* (where such an assumption is not made). This analysis concludes that, for small-scale projects, the extra effort needed to carry out a system-level analysis is not justified.

Institutional Measures for Managing Joint Implementation

Given the complexity of JI, it is perhaps not surprising to suggest that its success or failure is likely to depend heavily upon the institutional framework under which it operates. Defining an appropriate institutional framework is, however, no easy task. The broad aim of such a framework is to facilitate the operationalization of JI in such a way as to meet the underlying objectives of environmental effectiveness, equity and economic efficiency. In particular, institutional measures are required for the following specific purposes:

- the management of uncertainty;
- dealing with complexity;
- limiting gaming; and
- creating appropriate incentive structures.

Chapter 9 describes a range of institutional measures that can be employed in these various tasks. Some of these measures have already been incorporated, in some form, within the mechanisms of the FCCC. For example, the early crediting mechanism – which is designed to create incentives for investment in developing countries – already forms a part of the institutional context set out under the CDM in the Kyoto Protocol.[6] Other measures (such as baseline revision, standardization, limited crediting life and partial crediting) are still very much in the process of discussion and negotiation within the context of the FCCC.

In view of the significant uncertainties associated with JI project evaluation, and the incentives for gaming which these uncertainties present, this chapter proposes an approach to the operationalization of JI which combines the use of standardized assessment procedures with the introduction of specific institutional safeguards. It should be noted, however, that the standardization we propose is always assumed to be project- and country-specific.

Four standardized baseline types are formulated. Type 1 baselines make simple assumptions about the plant which has been replaced and the *separability* of the JI project from the rest of the energy system. However, they compensate for this simplicity by using a short crediting life. Type 2 baselines also assume separability but include more complex assumptions about the timing of replacement plant over a longer crediting life. Type 3 baselines adopt an average mix for situations where the replaced plant is difficult to define explicitly, and again incorporate the possibility of revising this mix to account for unforeseen changes in technology over time. Type 4 baselines are based on an assessment of a small number of projects of a given type.

The use of such standardization procedures has the advantage of reducing the potential for gaming by JI participants, but does not altogether eliminate the risk of compromising the environmental objectives of the convention. To reduce that risk, Chapter 9 suggests a number of possible institutional safeguards. These include:

- the use of project-approval criteria and verification procedures;
- a supplementarity cap;
- limited crediting lifetimes and/or baseline revisions;
- the use of monitored operating data (rather than feasibility data) for crediting purposes;
- monitoring and verification of existence, operation and output;
- partial or discounted crediting;
- environmental and social assessment.

Typically, it has been argued, the operational form of a particular JI situation should be defined by a *package* of measures which includes a combination of standardized assessment and institutional safeguards. Each package (and each situation) is likely to perform differently with respect to environmental effectiveness, equity and economic efficiency, and must be evaluated separately to determine their success or failure in meeting these objectives.

Evaluation of Joint Implementation Options

This study has analysed specific case-study JI projects in considerable detail. It has also analysed the institutional, technical, economic, environmental and social context in which these investments are made. In the light of this analysis, a rather specific view has been formulated as to how JI may be best operationalized. The fundamental basis of this perspective is the assertion that JI operates in the context of multiple objectives. Operationalizing JI depends, we argue, upon providing a holistic framework within which multi-attribute decision-making can occur, on evaluating carefully the critical components of that framework for individual JI options, and on identifying explicitly the trade-offs which arise between different objectives in each case.

Policy-making in a multi-attribute context such as this must typically concern itself with the problem of making appropriate trade-offs between underlying objectives when selecting and evaluating appropriate operational forms. It is our contention that the appropriate way to proceed in this situation is to engage in a structured approach to the design of flexibility mechanisms which recognizes the existence of multiple objectives, and explicitly identifies the trade-offs which occur between them.

This task is, however, rather complex. Firstly, it requires us to define individual *operational forms* of JI. Essentially, this must be done by specifying values for a number of operational parameters such as the project type, the actors involved, the extent of commitments under the protocol and so on. Next, we need to evaluate these individual operational forms of JI against each of the underlying objectives. Finally, we need a means of integrating these judgements within a consistent and coherent policy context.

Although this study set out to evaluate JI as a fair and efficient instrument for abating greenhouse gas emissions, it has become clear that no such overarching evaluation is possible. Each combination of institutional procedures in each situation must be assessed on its own individual merits against a range of underlying objectives. The objective of Chapter 10 is to set out one possible approach to this task.

The chapter defines eight illustrative operational forms of JI – which we call *JI options* – by selecting sets of values for the operational parameters which might be typical in the context of bilateral energy-sector investments under the Kyoto Protocol. It then illustrates how a particular *decision-analysis* methodology might be used to evaluate these options according to the evaluation criteria based on the objectives defined in Chapter 3. Finally, Chapter 10 discusses a proposal for defining an operational framework for JI in which the minimum requirements are met in terms of environmental effectiveness, equity and economic efficiency.

Conclusions

Flexibility mechanisms have become a vital ingredient of climate policy since the signing of the FCCC in 1992. They have achieved a particular significance in the wake of the Kyoto Protocol. Without flexibility mechanisms in place, there is a danger that the protocol may not be ratified by all the necessary parties. If, however, institutional frameworks are put in place which allow parties to pursue economic efficiency at the expense of environmental effectiveness, there is a clear risk that Kyoto targets will not lead to real emissions reductions and the objectives of the FCCC will be compromised.

Ultimately, the acceptability of JI depends upon being able to design institutional mechanisms which achieve an acceptable balance between multiple objectives. The lessons from this study suggest that this balance is possible under certain conditions. The procedures and methods detailed in this book demonstrate that, for certain project types and situations, it is possible to design flexibility mechanisms which combine a degree of standardization with appropriate institutional safeguards, and thus find ways of managing the complexity and uncertainty associated with JI.

Importantly, however, these mechanisms do not seek justification purely from the argument for cost-effectiveness. Indeed, the discussion in this book suggests that such a justification is not even possible. Designing flexibility mechanisms to meet the range of underlying objectives inevitably means imposing certain kinds of institutional safeguards. In addition, it may be necessary to restrict the application of the mechanisms to certain kinds of projects – for instance, those for which uncertainty can reasonably be managed and the opportunities for gaming are not too high. Each of these kinds of restrictions involves intervention in the market for projects, and threatens to undermine the supposed efficiency of the market mechanism. Nonetheless, such interventions are essential if the environmental objectives of the FCCC are to be fulfilled and the principle of equity respected.

In summary, the work presented in this book provides a clear warning to policy-makers against making hard and fast generalizations about the efficiency of flexibility mechanisms. The seductive premise that JI automatically represents an economically efficient means of achieving an environmental goal is not sustained by a closer examination of the philosophical, technical, social, economic and institutional complexity involved.

Designing flexibility within global climate policy remains a complex and demanding task in which there are few short cuts and no easy gains. Nonetheless, the analysis in this book suggests that it is possible to design appropriate safeguards within joint implementation and the CDM. This possibility offers the hope for bilateral and multilateral investment strategies which could make a responsible contribution to the goal of mitigating climate change.

The Language of Flexibility: Operational Forms of Joint Implementation

T Jackson, K Begg and S Parkinson

Introduction[1]

Given the prominence of the concept of joint implementation (JI) during the five and a half years between the signing of the Framework Convention on Climate Change (FCCC) in June 1992 and the third Conference of the Parties (COP 3) in December 1997, it is surprising at first sight to find that the Kyoto Protocol contains no explicit reference to 'joint implementation' at all. Nor does it mention the phrase 'activities implemented jointly' (AIJ). There are, however, numerous references to the transfer or trade of emission reduction credits. By a strange contrast, the FCCC contained no explicit reference to emissions trading at all, but couched any consideration of flexibility issues entirely in the language of joint implementation.

In this chapter, we examine the political and institutional reasons behind these apparently trivial linguistic anomalies. We discuss, in particular, the relationship between JI and the concept of emissions trading, and set out a characterization of JI which reveals a number of different operational forms for flexibility mechanisms. We conclude by drawing some important lessons about the appropriate institutionalization of these concepts within the context of global climate policy.

Institutional Background

The concept of emissions trading was first proposed as a general mechanism for pollution policy by Tietenberg (1985), and was introduced specifically in the context of greenhouse gas (GHG) emission reductions in *Negotiating Targets* (Grubb, 1989), published some three years before the signing of the FCCC. Between the publication of that influential report and the Earth Summit, considerable effort was made to incorporate the concept of emissions trading into the FCCC.

Those efforts were obstructed by a sharp division of views on emissions trading. Advocates argued that emissions trading would allow for improved cost-effectiveness and flexibility in reducing GHG emissions. In support of the argument from cost-effectiveness, they pointed out that the costs of reducing emissions vary widely between countries, and that the least expensive route to emissions reductions would be to implement first those options which are least expensive, irrespective of geographical location. Opponents to emissions trading argued (variously) that such arrangements would reduce the incentive for donor countries to take domestic action; compromise the sovereignty of host nations, their ability to harness indigenous resources and develop their own markets; increase the transaction costs of achieving emissions reductions; and ultimately undermine the objectives of the convention. An additional obstacle to global emissions trading was the highly political issue of devising an initial allocation of permits.

In the event, the failure to reach agreement on these issues led to the omission of any language in the convention explicitly referring to emissions trading. Instead, the terminology of joint implementation was introduced as 'enabling language' to allow for the future development of trading type mechanisms. Almost immediately, however, it became apparent that the change in terminology had not eliminated the underlying conflict of views (see, for example, Jackson, 1995). In fact, at one point the term joint implementation became so problematic that the attempt to introduce a pilot phase – in which bilateral investments could be made (without credit) for the purpose of testing the concept – only survived by changing the terminology, yet again, to refer to investments during this pilot phase as activities implemented jointly (AIJ).

The existence of conflicting views on JI and AIJ prior to Kyoto may have been one reason for excluding explicit reference to it in drawing up the protocol. There were already enough inflammatory elements in the negotiations. Arguably, the problematic nature of the JI terminology may even have drawn some of the adverse criticism away from the emissions-trading terminology, and allowed the latter to re-enter the institutional language. From a historical perspective, JI and emissions trading were quite clearly references to very similar kinds of mechanisms. In the intervening five years, however, the two terms had increasingly come to be seen as separate mechanisms, although the distinguishing line between JI and emissions trading was seldom explicit and often blurred. Thus, for example, Bohm (1997) published the results of a 'thought experiment' in which a hypothetical trading arrangement between four Nordic countries was investigated. The report was entitled *Joint Implementation as Emission Quota Trading*.

More recent characterizations tend to accept that JI and emissions trading now refer to different mechanisms, but accept that there are similarities between them, and that the differences are largely defined by institutional factors. For example, Woerdmann (2000) argues that JI and the CDM show more promise as flexibility mechanisms than as emissions trading because the counterfactual baseline is made explicit under these project-based mechanisms. Emissions trading, on the other hand, could end up as a mechanism for trading counterfactual 'hot air'.

Whatever the truth behind this confusing terminology, it is clear that there are, in fact, a number of different kinds of mechanism which could, in principle, loosely be characterized as flexibility mechanisms, but which bear different characteristics depending upon a number of factors. In the next section, we unravel some of these distinguishing factors.

Classification of Flexibility Mechanisms

The purpose of this section is to characterize different kinds of JI-type mechanisms according to three specific factors: namely, the presence or absence of overall emission constraints on the actors involved in the arrangements, the institutional status of these actors with respect to the convention, and the physical nature of the trade in which actors are engaged.

Closed versus Open Flexibility

Firstly, there is an important distinction between *closed* and *open* flexibility instruments. Closure, in this respect, refers to arrangements in which both parties are subject to clearly specified emission *caps* or – in the terminology of the Kyoto Protocol – quantified emission limitation and reduction commitments (QELRCs). In these circumstances, it is possible to identify total emission allowances, and therefore to define a closed market in a clearly tradeable commodity amongst different partners. When both donor and host are bounded by QELRCs, the incentive to ensure that the trade realizes concrete emission reductions is increased, and the likelihood that trading arrangements compromise the objectives of the convention is reduced. In principle, in these circumstances JI is essentially equivalent to an emissions trading regime (Barrett, 1994).

By contrast, openness in the context of flexibility instruments refers to a situation in which the host country has no emission cap.[2] In these circumstances, the host country has no emissions allowance, and so the structure of allowance trading is less clearly defined. Nevertheless, if the credits can be transferred from host to donor and used by the donor against its own emission reduction targets, then there may well be incentives on both sides to engage in the trade. The host country would benefit from investment funds in specific market sectors (such as the energy sector); the donor would benefit from accredited emission reductions from the project.

The problematic element in open JI arises from the fact that there is no restriction on emission levels in the host nation. Transfer of emission-reduction credits to the donor nation will reduce the amount of abatement carried out in the donor nation. But the investment may not lead to real, lasting emission reductions in the host nation. For example, there is a clear incentive for both nations to 'talk up' the baseline against which emission reductions

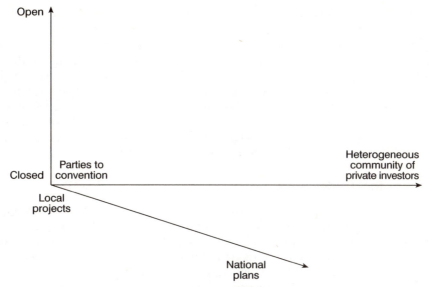

Figure 2.1 *Schematic Representation of JI*

might be measured (see Chapters 4 and 9). In the worst case, large-scale implementation of open JI arrangements could compromise the objective of the convention to reduce global greenhouse gas emissions.

Institutional Status of the Actors

A critical issue in defining JI-type arrangements lies in specifying the kinds of actors involved in the transaction. Trading arrangements have been discussed at various different levels. Quota trading is the term which has most often been used to apply to trading at the level of parties to the convention. Thus, the actors involved in the transaction would, most often, be individual national governments. One government – the donor – would agree to compensate another government – the host – in exchange for an increase in its own emission allowance at the expense of the emission allowance of the host. This is the type of arrangement envisaged, for example, by the Nordic experiment cited above.

As we have already noted, one of the main advantages claimed by proponents of JI-type arrangements is the ability to deliver flexibility in meeting targets. In this view, it is envisaged that trading arrangements could take place between any number of different kinds of partners – not just between national governments, but between national governments and private investors, between local or regional authorities and foreign governments, or between municipalities and a wide variety of different kinds of private investors. Thus, the scope of JI-type arrangements ranges from direct bilateral agreements between individual parties to the convention, to the establishment of a broad-ranging, heterogeneous market of private traders.

In reality, there may not be as large a distinction between these different kinds of arrangements as appears at first sight. For instance, even if trading is allowed within a heterogeneous trading community, it is likely that authorization will nonetheless be required from a legally accredited national body. Conversely, even if the trade occurs as a bilateral agreement between two governments, the host country must then ensure that domestic emission reductions meet the agreed target. There are a number of mechanisms for ensuring this. One of these would be to put in place a domestic permit system which would implement heterogeneous trading internally (see, for instance, Fleming, 1997). Nevertheless, for the purposes of classifying the kinds of JI-type arrangements which might be envisaged under the convention, the distinction between different kinds of actors is a useful one.

Nature of the Trade

Finally, it is useful to distinguish the nature and scale of the investments implied by the envisaged trades. These can range from individual project-level investments – for instance, investments in specific energy technologies – to national policy plans for GHG emission reduction. Clearly, there is some correlation between the types of actors engaged in trade, and the types of trade in which actors are engaged. For example, investments in national policy plans are only likely to be made in the context of quota trading between national governments. On the other hand, a wide range of different kinds of actors, including national governments, municipalities or private traders, could, potentially, invest in specific projects at the local level.

Schematic Representation of Joint Implementation Characteristics

Figure 2.1 provides a schematic representation of these different characteristics of JI-type relations in terms of a three-dimensional *JI space*. This representation is at best illustrative, and omits a number of potentially important institutional factors within JI-type arrangements, such as the extent to which credit is shared between donor and host, the degree of monitoring and verification of investments, and the degree of institutional competence of host and donor parties. Nevertheless, it is a potentially useful way of identifying the characteristics of different JI-type arrangements and of classifying specific proposals for flexibility mechanisms in terms of these characteristics.

Figure 2.2 illustrates how some of the arrangements proposed prior to the Kyoto Protocol might be situated within this three-dimensional representation.

As noted above, when both parties are subject to emission caps (closed JI), the arrangement essentially reduces to a form of emissions trading. Thus, the plane of the diagram which constitutes the 'floor' of JI space in Figure 2.2 is characterized as emissions trading. The particular form of emissions trading envisaged by the Nordic experiment (quota trading) is closed, takes place between individual parties to the convention, and is implemented at the level of national plans. It can, therefore, be located at a quite specific point in the representation space. In contrast, pilot-phase AIJ operates at the project level. As originally conceived (in the absence of any established emission targets for the

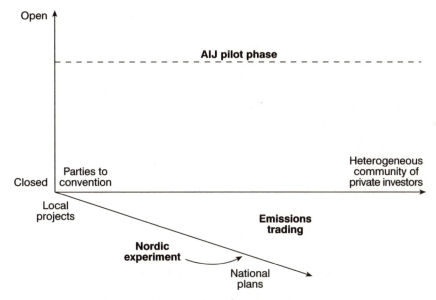

Figure 2.2 *Examples of JI-Type Arrangements*

parties), it is essentially an open form of JI. AIJ could, in principle, be implemented by a range of different types of actor, ranging from national governments to individual private investors. Thus, pilot-phase AIJ appears in the representation as a horizontal line at some distance above the horizontal axis.

Although the scope of this representation is illustrative, a number of useful conclusions can be drawn. Firstly, it is clear that the terminology of joint implementation could be used, and indeed has been used, to refer to a fairly wide range of different kinds of arrangements, each with different characteristics. Some of these different arrangements have little in common with one another – at least in terms of the characteristics represented here. On the other hand, it seems reasonable to suggest that there is an overlap between some of these JI arrangements and the concept of emissions trading. In the sense of the characteristics represented here, emissions trading can be seen as a special case of JI.

Next, it is perhaps worth asking whether there is any subset of the characteristics for JI/trading arrangements which is more or less desirable than any other. From the point of view of environmental security, it could perhaps be argued that the best arrangements are those which are closed and implemented at the project level, but legitimized directly between parties to the convention. Such arrangements would lie close to the intersection of the three axes in JI space. Closure would, at least to an extent, reduce the scope for emissions leakage, which might compromise the objective of lowering global emissions.[3] Implementation at the project level would ensure that real, concrete measures were put in place to reduce emissions. The direct involvement of parties to the convention would ensure appropriate accountability.

On the other hand, one of the virtues which JI-type arrangements are deemed to possess is that of flexibility in achieving the goals of the convention.

There are certainly individuals who would argue that this flexibility is best achieved by involving a broader community of actors and, in particular, by motivating private investment to engage in JI-type investments. At least some of those who hold this view also believe that the full benefits of this flexibility will only be achieved by opening the market for such trade to countries without QELRCs (in other words, to implement open JI arrangements; see Jepma, 1998a). This area of JI space is clearly disjoint from the area close to the origin. It becomes apparent, then, using this form of representation, that there are certain inherent trade-offs between conflicting objectives in designing appropriate flexibility mechanisms. This is a theme to which we return in the concluding discussion, and which informs much of the following analysis.

Finally, it is instructive to inquire how the various flexibility mechanisms introduced into the Kyoto Protocol may be characterized within this representation. This is the subject of the next section, in which we also provide a more general discussion of the implications of the Kyoto Protocol for JI.

Flexibility Mechanisms in the Kyoto Protocol

In spite of the absence of language specifically referring to JI, it is clear that the Kyoto Protocol incorporates a variety of different mechanisms which might loosely be characterized as joint implementation. In fact, there appear to be at least three distinct types of JI envisaged within the protocol, as described in the following sections.

'Joint Fulfilment'

Articles 3 and 4 introduce the possibility that parties may jointly fulfil their commitments under the protocol. Thus, individual parties can group together and form *bubbles* within which the total agreed quantified emission limitation and reduction commitments (QELRCs) from the participating countries are met. In theory, this procedure could allow for a country-level quota-trading system as envisaged, for example, within the Nordic experiment. No explicit mention is made, within articles 3 and 4, of financial exchange within the bubble; but there is clearly nothing to stop parties from negotiating related financial transfers. On the other hand, the allocation of emission reductions within the bubble could equally be negotiated on a political basis – as happened, for example, within the proposed burden-sharing arrangement in the EU's pre-Kyoto negotiating position (EU, 1997).

Transfer of Emission Reduction Units

Article 6 of the Kyoto Protocol allows for the transfer and acquisition, between the parties to the protocol listed in Annex I of the FCCC, of emission reduction units (ERUs) from projects which reduce anthropogenic emissions or enhance sinks of greenhouse gases.[4] Although not explicitly described as joint implementation, this kind of arrangement is essentially equivalent to *closed, project-level joint implementation* as envisaged previously. It is worth noting that, in spite of the earlier characterization (see Figure 2.2), some pilot-phase AIJ would now belong to this class of JI. This would be the case, for example, for pilot-phase AIJ between Western and Eastern European partners. Arrangements which, when set up, were open, would now be classified as closed because the participating countries are now subject to QELRCs. Furthermore, these arrangements foresee the transfer of emission reduction credits in one direction as a result of a financial transfer (an investment) in the other direction. In other words, as well as being JI, this arrangement also defines a form of trading under a specified emissions cap.

It has been argued by many that closed JI between parties who are both subject to QELRCs is far less open to abuse than open JI – in which the host country is not subject to QELRCs. The reason for this is that, in the former case, both countries operate under an emissions cap as specified by article 3 (and Annex B) of the Kyoto Protocol. By calculating actual emissions inventories during the commitment period in both host and donor country, it is possible to ensure that JI/trading arrangements do not lead to direct emissions leakage, and that the overall objective of the protocol is met.[5] In this situation, it is argued, the legitimacy of baselines is less critical, and the need for approval, certification, monitoring and verification procedures is less important. In other words, it is argued that streamlined institutional procedures may be appropriate in this context, at least from the immediate perspective of the convention.

At the very least, the success of closed JI arrangements requires that donor and host nations both satisfy themselves that they are able to meet their commitments under the convention. In particular, donor countries will need to assure themselves that invested funds generate real, measurable returns in terms of emission reduction units. They will also require guarantees that these emission reduction units provide legitimate credits against their national inventories during the relevant commitment period. On the other hand, host countries will need to satisfy themselves that investment projects lead to real, measurable emission reductions in the commitment period. These countries will need to ensure that the price at which they sell emission reduction credits to donors (or, equivalently, the number of emission reduction credits which are transferred to the donor for a given investment) reflects the full cost of achieving the additional emission reduction.

In other words, even though the need for procedural safeguards at the level of the convention as a whole appears less urgent, both host and donor must implement appropriate safeguards at the national level if the trade is to be robust, and to qualify legitimately under the accounting procedures of the convention. In particular, baselines remain an important part of the procedural elements of JI-type relationships – albeit at the national level rather than at the level of the convention.

These issues are of particular importance where there are differences in institutional capacity between donor and host nations. When both countries have a similar level of technical and financial expertise, there is a good chance that one can spot if the other is *gaming* or *cherry-picking* in relation to JI investments.[6] But when the host country has a lower level of institutional capacity – as may be the case for certain Central and Eastern European hosts

– then there is an increased danger of trades which compromise international equity. In the long run, such compromises will have impacts on the success of meeting the objectives of the convention, and it may be advisable for the convention to impose suitable procedural safeguards even in the case of closed trading arrangements.

Some such safeguards are already envisaged under article 6 of the Kyoto Protocol. For example, article 6.1(b) lays down a provision regarding the *additionality* of projects (see Chapter 3), and article 6.1(d) states that such projects should be 'supplemental' to domestic policy. At the moment, neither additionality nor supplementarity are clearly defined, and both terms require clarification if they are to be meaningful. As we discuss further below, the requirement of additionality demands an appropriate procedure for determining what would have happened if the project had not been implemented. This, in its turn, requires the elaboration of baselines in both host and donor countries.

The question of supplementarity remains, at the moment, entirely undefined. It is clearly important to rectify this. In particular, in ensuring that the accrual of emission reduction units is supplemental to domestic action, it would be advisable to specify precisely how much (what percentage) of its reduction commitments a party could satisfy through the accrual of emission reduction units from other Annex I countries. In principle, this level of activity could, and perhaps should, be different for different countries. For instance, countries which have a lower carbon intensity, and for whom further domestic reductions are more costly or more difficult to achieve, might reasonably be allowed to satisfy a higher proportion of their commitments through transfer of emission reduction units than countries with a higher carbon intensity and a larger potential for domestic reductions.

Finally, it should be stated that, even where safeguards are set in relation to JI/trading between parties, both of whom have QELRCs under the Kyoto Protocol, there remain some possibilities for emissions leakage. These occur because the global system is not yet closed with respect to GHG emissions. Thus, one of the ways of reducing domestic emissions of greenhouse gases is to export polluting processes to countries which have no emission cap and to import the associated products. There are several possible ways round this problem. These include the following:

- closure of the global system with respect to greenhouse gas emissions;
- revision of emission accounting procedures to include the emissions *footprint* associated with all domestic consumption rather than just domestically based activities; and
- the imposition of a comprehensive framework of environmental and social safeguards on global investments markets.

None of these options is entirely straightforward. The first implies getting developing countries on board and signed up to QELRCs under a (revised) protocol; and the second implies substantial – and methodologically complex – revisions of existing inventory procedures. Of the three options, the third may turn out to be the most feasible even though it clearly runs counter to the prevailing trend of liberalization and free trade. This highlights the importance of implicit relationships between the Kyoto Protocol and other trade agreements such as the General Agreement on Tariffs and Trade (GATT), the failed Multilateral Agreement on Investment and any future investment or trade agreements that may follow in their wake.

The Clean Development Mechanism

Article 12 of the Kyoto Protocol defines a clean development mechanism (CDM) through which Annex I countries can obtain *certified emission reductions* (CERs) as a result of project activities carried out in non-Annex I countries. The CERs accruing from such activities may be used to contribute to compliance with QELRCs under article 3 of the protocol. This arrangement is broadly similar to what was previously envisaged as *open, project-level joint implementation*. So, for example, AIJ between EU member states and any developing country could be construed as falling under this category. However, the extent to which the CDM will actually mirror existing AIJ projects depends heavily on the institutional arrangements under which the mechanism is eventually set up.

As pointed out above, and discussed in more detail in Chapter 9, this situation is significantly more complex, more uncertain and more open to abuse than closed JI. Typically, the difficulties include:

- an increased reliance on counterfactual information (baselines);
- an increased potential for gaming both by host and by donor with respect to baselines;
- greater uncertainty in outcomes;
- reduced incentives for the host country to avoid cherry-picking by the donor;
- reduced incentives for domestic action by the donor;
- an increased potential for emissions leakage;
- a risk of compromising the development of the host energy system and sustainable development path by haphazard investments;
- a potential for any adverse social or environmental effects of projects to be multiplied.

In this case, the need for procedural safeguards is increased over the closed case and there is less opportunity for streamlining of institutional procedures, even on a sector- or project-specific basis. Some such safeguards are already included in article 12 of the Kyoto Protocol. For example, it is implied that certification procedures must be carried out on transferred emission reductions. The mechanism is subject to supervision by an executive board, and projects are subject to independent auditing and verification. It will be important to ensure that appropriate institutional arrangements are set in place to meet these increased requirements.

In addition, article 12.2 of the protocol indicates that the purpose of the clean development mechanism is, in part at least, to assist non-Annex I parties to achieve sustainable development.

Emissions Trading

In addition to these three JI-type mechanisms, article 17 is an enabling clause allowing Annex B parties to participate in emissions trading schemes according to rules, principles and modalities yet to be defined. Article 17 once again invokes the concept of supplementarity of emissions trading with respect to domestic action.

There are a number of difficulties associated with the concept of emissions trading, including the process of initial allocation of permits, the question of supplementarity, the problem of ensuring that equity is maintained, issues of transparency, liability and compatibility, and effects on international competitiveness (UN FCCC, 1998).

Amongst the most serious of these difficulties is the so-called *hot air* problem, which is illustrated most clearly by the situation in which Western donor nations attempt to purchase emission reduction credits from certain Eastern European nations. The problem is that, to all intents and purposes, emission reductions greater than those required under the protocol have already been achieved in some of these countries as a result of structural changes in the economy since 1990. Thus, any transaction in emission reduction credits is essentially empty of environmental benefit, counter to the intention of JI and the objectives of the convention. Some authors have argued that this problem is significant enough to devalue the potential for emissions trading and favour project-based JI mechanisms, such as those provided under articles 6 and 12 (Woerdman, 2000).

In spite of these difficulties, a number of countries have already begun to investigate the feasibility of national emissions trading schemes, and the European Commission has just given its backing to a proposal by Denmark to create the EU's first national greenhouse gas emission trading scheme.

Schematic Representation of Kyoto Flexibility Mechanisms

Figure 2.3 illustrates how the different flexibility mechanisms envisaged within the Kyoto Protocol are represented within the three-dimensional JI space.

Several points are worth noting. Firstly, the enabling language of article 17 refers to the emissions trading floor of JI space. The specific form of trading envisaged by article 6, which we characterized above as closed project-level joint implementation, constitutes the horizontal axis bounding one edge of the emissions trading floor. The bubble concept under which parties may jointly fulfil their commitments under the protocol lies at a specific point on the axis perpendicular to the plane of the page – in essentially the same place as the Nordic experiment in Figure 2.2. The CDM is a horizontal line in the plane of the page some way above the horizontal axis – in essentially the same place as the AIJ line in Figure 2.2.

In spite of the changes in language, therefore, there are clear similarities between mechanisms proposed under the Kyoto Protocol and mechanisms which have been put forward and argued over previously. In particular, aside from the fact that AIJ pilot-phase projects could not formally claim credit for emission reductions, the structural characteristics of the CDM are very similar to the pre-Kyoto concept of AIJ.[7] Specifically, the CDM allows Annex I

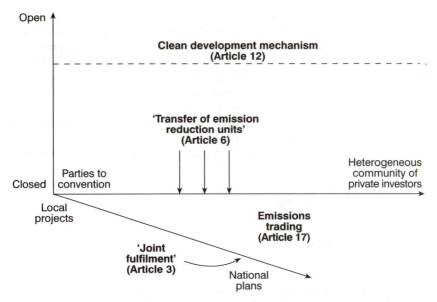

Figure 2.3 *JI-Type Arrangements in the Kyoto Protocol*

countries to invest in emission reduction activities in countries without QELRCs. As pointed out earlier, this form of JI has been, throughout, the most contentious of the flexibility mechanisms discussed. This is mainly because of the potential for abuse of host countries with underdeveloped institutional capacity, the absence of incentives for the participating parties to avoid gaming, and the problem of global emissions leakage. These were among the difficulties which hindered the incorporation of the concept of emissions trading within the FCCC during the run-up to the Earth Summit in 1992. They also constituted a part of the difficulties which have dogged the progress of JI since that time.

It may be cynical to suggest that it is for these reasons that the name of the mechanism has been changed yet again. Grubb et al (1999) relate an amusing anecdote concerning the horror on the faces of the Kyoto delegates when a Canadian representative pointed out the obvious association between the CDM and AIJ, almost scuppering the acceptance of the CDM and jeopardizing the signing of the protocol. Clearly, however, a name change will not in itself resolve the difficulties associated with implementing such a mechanism. The CDM may for a while enjoy fresh kudos as a new policy concept. But if the underlying conflicts are not explicitly recognized and appropriately addressed, then the honeymoon is likely to be short.

Conclusions

It is clear from the analysis in this chapter that JI does not define a single institutional mechanism at all. Rather, it covers a multitude of operational forms, each with different defining characteristics. For the most part, JI now tends to be used mainly to refer to the implementation of real, local projects, rather than more extensive regional or national plans. In other words, it tends to be used to refer mainly to investments lying in the plane of the paper in Figures 2.1 to 2.3. Yet, even once this simplification has been made, there remains a variety of operational forms which JI-type arrangements could take.

In summary, the following points have been made. Firstly, it has been pointed out that the terminology of JI has been used to cover a wide range of different institutional arrangements for increasing the flexibility of meeting commitments under the FCCC. Secondly, each of these arrangements is characterized by different features, which include:

- the degree of closure or openness of the participating parties with respect to emission reduction commitments under the convention;
- the type of actor engaged in the trade;
- the scale of the activity engaged in.

In addition, it has been pointed out that there are clear links between the concept of JI and the concept of emissions trading. Indeed, JI was originally introduced into the FCCC as 'enabling language' to allow the incorporation of emission trading arrangements at a later stage. Furthermore, it is clear that JI and emissions trading have been the subject of considerable political wrangling because contentious elements arise in both concepts. Finally, shifts in institutional language may have side-stepped some of this political wrangling. However, contentious elements remain within the Kyoto flexibility mechanisms and are only likely to be resolved by explicit recognition of the conflicting objectives which underlie JI.

Generally speaking, the term JI is now usually taken to refer to the transfer of emission reduction credits for project-level investments by Annex I donor countries in Annex I host countries, under article 6 of the Kyoto Protocol. However, it has been shown in this chapter that the CDM introduced in article 12 of the protocol – in which Annex I donor countries invest in emission reduction projects in non-Annex I host countries – also defines a form of JI. These two forms of project-level JI provide the focus for the analysis in the rest of this book. The implications of the analysis remain relevant generally, however, for the design of flexibility in climate policy.

3

Objectives of Joint Implementation: Towards a Multicriteria Evaluation Framework

T Jackson, K Begg and S Parkinson

Introduction

The most-often cited motivation for the use of flexibility instruments in climate policy comes from the theory of market efficiency: by opening up opportunities for investors to exploit the cheapest emission reduction options irrespective of their geographical location, it is argued, the overall costs of achieving a given level of emission reduction will be minimized. In spite of this fact, the starting point for an assessment of joint implementation (JI) must be the overarching environmental objective to stabilize greenhouse gas (GHG) concentrations in the atmosphere at levels that would prevent dangerous anthropogenic interference with the climate system. This environmental objective is clearly at the heart of the Framework Convention on Climate Change (FCCC), and flexibility mechanisms only assume any justification at all within the context of this objective.

However, article 3 of the FCCC requires that parties be guided in pursuing this aim by the principle that 'policies and measures to deal with climate change should be cost effective, so as to ensure global benefits at the lowest possible cost'. Flexibility instruments such as JI are intended – in part at least – as a mechanism for achieving cost effectiveness. In addition, article 3 requires that parties proceed 'on the basis of equity and in accordance with their common but differentiated responsibilities and respective capabilities'.

It is immediately apparent that JI mechanisms operate in the context of multiple objectives which include at least: the environmental goal of achieving real reductions in GHG emissions, the social goal of protecting or enhancing equity and the economic goal of cost effectiveness in meeting environmental targets. Additional objectives which are either explicit or implicit in the FCCC include specific policy goals, such as the diffusion of technology to less industrialized countries, and more general operational goals, such as the need for practicable mechanisms which can be easily implemented. It might also be argued that additional goals from outside the objectives of the convention – such as the liberalization of trade and the expansion of global markets – are influencing policy within the convention.

The principal objectives, however, are those relating to environmental effectiveness, equity and economic efficiency, and the following subsections examine each of these major objectives in turn.

Environmental Effectiveness

The environmental goal of the FCCC is mainly enshrined – for the moment at least – in the quantified emission limitation and reduction commitments (QELRCs) negotiated under the Kyoto Protocol. As a result of these negotiations, Annex I countries will be committed to limiting or reducing their annual emissions of GHGs during the commitment period (2008–2012) by specified percentages over base-year emission levels.[1] Since these commitments, on their own, will not meet the overall environmental goal of the FCCC, there is every possibility that further emission reduction commitments will be necessary by Annex I countries in the future. In addition, it seems clear that levels of GHGs in the global atmosphere will not be stabilized without action being taken to slow down the rate of growth in GHG emissions from non-Annex I countries, although at the moment no such commitments are placed on these countries.

In principle, JI is just a mechanism to achieve this environmental objective as cost-effectively as possible. In reality, however, we have seen that JI defines a number of different operational mechanisms and involves a number of contentious issues. Amongst these contentious issues is the claim that, in certain circumstances, JI could actually impede the underlying environmental objective of the FCCC.

A particularly clear example of this possibility is provided by the case in which an Annex I donor country invests in emissions reduction activities in a non-Annex I host country. In return for this investment, the Annex I country is credited with a *relaxation* of its own emission reduction target. In theory, this relaxation is offset by the fact that the non-Annex I host country now emits fewer GHGs than it would have done if the JI investment had not taken place. But if this reduction is not real (for instance, because the accounting mechanism is not reliable), then the environmental objective is not served.

In practice, the Kyoto Protocol attempts to ensure that flexibility measures do not compromise the environmental objectives of the convention by imposing certain conditions on the use of specific mechanisms. Thus, for example, building on criteria defined under the activities implemented jointly (AIJ) pilot phase, article 12 of the protocol specifically requires that actions taken under the clean development mechanism (CDM) should achieve 'real, measurable and long-term benefits related to the mitigation of climate change'. Furthermore, article 12.5(c) of the protocol insists that certification of these

CDM activities can only proceed on the basis of emission reductions that are 'additional to any that would occur in the absence of the certified project activity'.

Generally speaking, closed JI – between two Annex I countries – offers more security in terms of the environmental objective of the convention than open JI, because both host and donor country are subject to QELRCs. We have already noted, however, that certain kinds of host countries, particularly those with lower institutional capacity, may find themselves at a disadvantage in terms of meeting QELRCs as a result of engaging in JI. This may compromise the environmental objectives of the convention if, as a result of JI, the host nation fails to meet its commitments. Perhaps in recognition of this possibility, the language of *additionality* is also invoked under article 6, which defines project-level JI for Annex I host countries.

Thus, the concept of additionality appears as a crucial safeguard in institutional attempts to protect the environmental objectives of the FCCC. Depending on how it is operationalized, it may also affect the underlying goals of economic efficiency and equity. At the moment, however, the concept remains largely undefined in operational terms. In fact, its operationalization is closely related to the problem of counterfactuality, an issue which is addressed in considerable detail below. In the meantime, it is perhaps worth summarizing some of the attempts to define and operationalize additionality in relation to JI.

Operationalizing Additionality

The concept of additionality in relation to JI was first introduced at the first Conference of the Parties (COP 1) in 1995, in the context of approval criteria for pilot-phase AIJ projects (Decision 5e/CP.1). The term was taken, at that time, to refer to two specific requirements relating to a JI investment. Firstly, it was argued, such projects should be additional in the sense of achieving real reductions in greenhouse gas emissions, over and above what might be expected in the absence of the projects. Secondly, the investment in JI should be additional to investment normally channelled through official development assistance (ODA), or required within existing commitments under the FCCC. This latter type of additionality has sometimes been called financial additionality.

Confusingly, the term financial or investment additionality has subsequently been used in another sense, namely to refer to the additional costs associated with a JI project (costs over and above those associated with a project undertaken at the economic margin under the normal conditions of the market). Although this suggests that JI projects should be more costly than the market choice, such projects would also be expected to yield higher emission reductions than the market choice. Thus, the additional investment in the JI project could be offset against the value of emission reduction credits achieved by it, and these credits would ensure that the project was attractive to investors. The World Bank has used this definition in their investment additionality and behavioural model (Heister, 1999).

It is important to note that this is a theoretical model. The World Bank uses the model to justify the requirement for financial additionality on the grounds of cost effectiveness. It is also clear that considerations of additionality may have significant implications for host country equity (see below). However, in practice, additionality in this sense is not sufficient to ensure cost effectiveness. It is now well known that energy markets are distorted in various ways, and that certain kinds of emission reduction options are not implemented, even though they are cheaper than the marginal technology. Barriers to implementation include (IEA/OECD, 1997):

- technology;
- legalities;
- policy;
- financing;
- market;
- knowledge/information;
- institutions.

For this reason the International Energy Agency (IEA) and the Organisation for Economic Co-operation and Development (OECD) have proposed a *barrier removal* method to test for the additionality of projects. They suggest that a project is additional if it can be demonstrated that:

- Institutional, financial, technological or informational barriers exist which inhibit the implementation of AIJ projects and would not be removed under circumstances in which there is no incentive to reduce greenhouse gases for an investor.
- These barriers do not have the same effect for the baseline project.
- The design of the AIJ projects effectively addresses these barriers.
- The financing of the AIJ-related part of the project is additional to ODA financing or existing commitments under the FCCC.

The US Environmental Protection Agency (EPA), on the other hand, has suggested that there are several tactical approaches to the operationalization of additionality within the convention. Carter (1997) categorizes these approaches in terms of six options:

- option 1: the development of narrow categories of projects which are deemed, *a priori*, to be additional;
- option 2: the definition of additionality as overcoming project-specific barriers (as above);
- option 3: the measurement of additionality from quantitative sector-specific guidelines by using system models;
- option 4: specific sets of additionality guidelines;
- option 5: assessment of additionality on the basis of a combination of the options described here;
- option 6: limiting efforts to determine additionality in favour of taking measures to restrict JI through measures such as discounting, limiting the lifetime of JI or limiting the scope of JI.

The first of these options would largely be used to ring-fence specific technologies – such as renewable technologies – for JI investment. One of the problematic aspects of this procedure is that it undermines the argument from cost effectiveness. If JI consists of implementing particular technologies irrespective of cost, then it can no longer operate as a mechanism for achieving a least-cost path for emissions reductions. Another difficulty is the assumption that particular technologies remain ineligible for this kind of protection over long periods of time.

Option 2 refers to the IEA/OECD approach discussed above. Option 3 can be interpreted in two ways. According to one interpretation, a project is deemed additional if it is not already planned in the national baseline in a particular country. There are several problems with this particular definition of additionality. In the first place, it assumes that something that is planned in the baseline projection for the country would, in fact, be realized. It also assumes perfect knowledge of the timing of the investment and any alternative investments. Finally, it suggests that something which is not planned is better for the country and the environment. Option 3 can also be interpreted as meaning that a project is additional if it reduces emission levels below a certain benchmark level, where the *benchmark* is defined according to certain sector-specific standards. This interpretation may have advantages in terms of ease of operability. However, without checking the specific circumstances of a particular project, the use of benchmarks can give rise to incorrect assessments of real emission reductions, and misleading assumptions about the additionality of the project.

Option 4 refers to an approach developed within the US Initiative on Joint Implementation (USIJI), which adopts two concepts of programme additionality and emissions additionality. Programme additionality means that the project should be specifically developed because of the USIJI. Emissions additionality deals specifically with the basis for the emissions reduction compared to the baseline or what would have happened in the absence of the project. This considers barriers, requirements in the host for emissions reduction and the difference between the project and prevailing technologies in the host. Option 5 suggests the possibility of combining two or more of the options discussed here.

Underlying all of these options, to a greater or lesser degree, is the problem of determining the counterfactual context against which additionality should be judged. As we have already indicated, and shall discuss further below, this problem is crucial to the operationalization of JI.

Option 6 offers a tactical alternative to the problems associated with additionality. Essentially, the suggestion here is that the problems associated with baseline determination, and other forms of uncertainty associated with JI, are best managed by limiting the application of JI and imposing institutional safeguards. These ideas were first attributed to Fritsche (1994) and others at early international negotiations on JI.

Environmental and Social Impacts of Joint Implementation

Before leaving the question of the environmental objectives underlying JI, it is worth noting that the convention does not limit its environmental concerns to those associated with climate change. Article 3 of the Kyoto Protocol, for example, requires that parties should strive to implement their commitments 'in such a way as to minimize the adverse social, environmental and economic impacts', and a concern for the environmental and social impacts of mitigation projects is also explicit in article 4.1(f) of the FCCC. This is further enshrined in article 12.2 of the protocol, which states that the CDM should assist developing countries in achieving sustainable development.

This study contends that potential environmental and social impacts of JI projects should be explicitly recognized. It will not generally be sufficient to consider only emission reductions with respect to GHGs. Project assessment should strive to include the wider environmental and social impacts of energy-sector investments. It is possible that, in some cases, there will be trade-offs between GHG emissions reductions and certain other environmental or social impacts. In other cases, there may be synergistic benefits – with reductions in specified emissions leading to additional environmental or social benefits. In both cases, however, there is a need for transparency in recognizing such costs and benefits.

This implies the need for an assessment methodology capable of determining what the additional environmental and social impacts of JI projects might be. In order to look at this aspect, we have carried out site visits for selected case study projects in each of the two host countries of Estonia and the Czech Republic. The aim of these visits was not to carry out a complete environmental and social impact assessment. Rather, the intention was to accumulate as much data as possible concerning the impact of the case study projects.

In our view, an appropriate assessment methodology is unlikely to be able to account for all these impacts in a purely mechanistic fashion. Rather it will be necessary to pay attention to questions of public perception and local priorities when gauging the relative importance of different kinds of impact.

Except in very particular circumstances, any JI project is likely to have environmental and social impacts which extend beyond the very local area in which the project is implemented. For example, the area from which the fuel is mined, collected or harvested represents a minimum area in which impacts might be expected to arise. In addition, impacts might be expected to arise from the treatment, storage and transportation of the fuel. Assessing these kinds of impact is common in the fuel-cycle approach to environmental assessment (Chapter 6). In addition, there may be impacts related to fuel prices, employment, infrastructure and so on. These kinds of impact may occur very far from the actual location of the project. Even though they may remain small for individual projects, they could easily magnify with replication of specific project types. The question of the system boundary, therefore, becomes critical in assessing the environmental and social impacts of JI projects. In fact, this question has a broad relevance to the evaluation of JI projects, in particular when tackling the question of emissions leakage. Consequently, we address the system boundary issue in detail in Chapter 4. In Chapter 6 we discuss the development of appropriate environmental and social assessments procedures for JI.

Equity

Equity is an important consideration in international conventions such as the FCCC. Article 3.1 of the FCCC states that parties to the convention should 'protect the climate system for the benefit of present and future generations of humankind, on the basis of equity and in accordance with their common but differentiated responsibilities and respective capabilities'.

Chapter 3 of the IPCC 1995 working group III report (Banuri et al, 1996) approaches the issue of equity in international climate-change policy from what could be broadly described as philosophical, legal and (welfare) economic perspectives. The chapter usefully defines equity in terms of two conventional concepts: *procedural equity*, which is associated with participation and process, and *consequentialist equity*, which relates to outcomes of decisions. Procedural equity concerns equality in relation to stakeholders during a given process (the means), whereas consequentialist equity involves equality in bearing the impacts of a given course of action (the ends).

Since JI is both a process in which different interest groups participate and also a means towards a specific end, it is important to consider to what extent it embraces both procedural and consequentialist equity. It has been argued by developing countries (during the FCCC negotiations), by environmental/developmental non-governmental organizations (NGOs; see, for example, CNE, 1994) and by others (reviewed, for example, by Banuri et al, 1996) that JI may not be equitable. Here we list some of the arguments:

- JI may 'limit the host country's freedom to influence its own development path', whilst giving 'the donor country more flexibility in its development path' (CNE, 1994).
- JI may replace some of the assistance (financial, technological, etc) currently given to developing and transition countries, under current convention commitments and as part of overseas aid programmes (CNE, 1994).
- JI could skim off the cheapest projects (cherry-picking) so that, if and when developing countries are required to adopt emission constraints in the future, they will be faced by higher marginal abatement costs (Parikh, 1994).
- JI may allow a continued increase in GHG emissions from industrialized countries which will perpetuate the global inequalities in per capita emissions (Parikh and Gokarn, 1993).

However, since transition economies and developing countries are likely to be most at risk from the effects of climate change, it is argued by some (for instance, Pearce, 1995) that JI will benefit them because it will reduce costs and hence speed up mitigative or adaptive action. Furthermore, it is argued that the financial and technological transfers that are encouraged by JI will benefit the host country. These issues will be discussed under the specific procedural and consequentialist equity sections.

Procedural Equity

Arguments have been raised that the operationalization of JI will favour industrialized countries. For one thing, industrialized countries have greater research and analysis capabilities and, as a result, will have an upper hand in negotiations (Pachauri, 1994). Furthermore, internal pressures in developing countries may induce those countries to undertake projects which are disadvantageous to them in the long term (Maya, 1994).

It is important, therefore, that proper safeguards are put in place to prevent abuse of the system. Yamin (1993) suggests that a clear, legally binding framework is necessary. An illustration of a possible procedure for assessing the suitability or otherwise of a project is given by the European Bank for Reconstruction and Development (EBRD) in its environmental procedures (EBRD, 1996). This document details the process necessary for a private firm to gain approval for an EBRD development loan in Eastern Europe and emphasizes the need to identify and consult all those groups who may be affected by a given project – for example, local trade unions, local community groups and environmental and social NGOs.

Consultation and participation of stakeholder groups is thus seen as critical to the successful implementation of procedural equity. A recent study by the US Environmental Law Institute (ELI, 1997) examined procedural equity within the AIJ pilot phase. It found that consultation and participation occurred on an ad-hoc basis and advocated a systematic approach to incorporating transparency and participation within JI. Procedural equity involves clear and transparent processes and access to information. The institute proposed that ensuring national JI programmes operate transparently with provision for participation by interested organizations, businesses and members of the public assists with the goals of being compatible and supportive of host country development and of producing real, measurable long-term reductions. The host will have confidence that project commitments will be met and that local environmental and social effects have been taken into account, and the donor will be assured of a stable basis for its investment.

The benefits noted by the US Environmental Law Institute are that projects are more likely to succeed and to continue in the long term and that they are, therefore, more likely to meet the environmental goals of the convention. Additionally, the increased confidence with open procedures builds confidence in moving forward in climate change policy.

Some actions to promote procedural equity could include the following:

- assistance to hosts so that there is a level playing field in negotiations between donors and hosts;
- assistance to hosts to develop long-term strategies for sustainable development to avoid unsuitable measures;
- a legal framework to prevent exploitation of vulnerable hosts;
- a requirement for an environmental and social assessment of the impacts of the measure at pre-commissioning stage and audit during operation.

It is interesting to note that such *capacity-building* measures have been called for explicitly by developing countries during the FCCC negotiations (UN FCCC, 1999a).

Consequentialist Equity

Equity is important in considering the possible consequences of a JI project. If a project decreases emissions of GHGs, but has other negative effects such as an increase in unemployment or in poverty, then there is a trade-off to be made explicitly to decide if this is equitable. Hence, the decision on whether to implement a JI project should be based, in part at least, on an assessment of these secondary effects. One example of a method for doing so is an environmental impact assessment (EIA). Currently, development banks such as the World Bank and the EBRD require that such an assessment is carried out in order for a project loan to be granted. The EBRD currently requires that an EIA includes assessments of the project's effect on such things as: air quality, water quality, landscape, socioeconomic indicators, and land-use and settlement patterns (EBRD, 1996).

Of course, EIAs or other forms of assessment may significantly increase project costs. The EBRD deals with this problem by classifying projects A, B or C according to an initial assessment procedure and only requires detailed EIAs to be performed for A-type projects. It does not bode well for concerns about equity that the non-greenhouse related environmental and social impacts of a project have been marginalized in discussions on flexibility mechanisms – even in relation to the CDM, which explicitly refers to assisting sustainable development.

Possible benefits for the host from JI are significant nonetheless. These include:

- transfer of modern environmentally sound technologies without the expense of research and development (R&D);
- inward investment where capital is scarce;
- local environmental and social benefits from the measure, such as air quality improvements, or comfort and reliability improvements;
- capacity-building, such as training or provision of infrastructure;
- for developing countries, funding from the levy set up under article 12.8 of the protocol to assist in meeting the costs of adaptation to climate change.

These benefits have to be weighed up against any disbenefits at the approval stage before final agreement is reached. Though we would suggest that the provision of consequentialist equity is project and country specific, there could be some general conditions to ensure that these aspects are considered at the early stage, for example as a part of the host-country approval process or in the uniform reporting format. As part of a monitoring and verification scheme for project performance, there could also be some audit of expected benefits or avoidance of disbenefits. This is discussed further in Chapter 6.

Amongst the difficult aspects of consequentialist equity to address are those which relate to the consequences for future generations – that is, to *inter-generational equity*. One of the more contentious assessment issues is the conventional economic practice of discounting (the revaluing of future costs in terms of current costs by means of a discount rate), and this is discussed in more detail towards the end of the next subsection.

Economic Efficiency

The argument from economic efficiency is critical to justifying JI. Were it not for the possibility of achieving cost minimization through flexibility mechanisms, there would be no real reason not to require parties to meet their QELRCs through domestic measures. It is important, therefore, to be clear what this argument is, what it means in terms of choosing appropriate JI projects, and what it means for the assessment of actual JI projects.

To start with, it is worth remarking on two slightly different strands to the argument from cost efficiency. In the first strand, the argument recognizes that each country has different marginal abatement costs. For example, in Sweden, where standards of energy efficiency are already relatively high and carbon emissions per capita are rather low, the marginal cost of carbon abatement is higher than it is in a country such as Estonia, where standards of energy efficiency are lower and carbon emissions per capita are higher. Since this is the case – proponents of JI argue – it would make sense to reduce emissions first in Estonia, where abatement will be cheaper. Furthermore, it would be more attractive, economically, for Sweden to pay Estonia to make some of these reductions, rather than to carry out expensive abatement options in Sweden. The same level of emissions reduction could be achieved, but the overall costs would be lower. This is essentially the theoretical economic argument set out, for example, by Barrett (1994) and by Bohm (1997).

The second variant argues that JI is essentially a way of activating the efficiency of the market mechanism in pursuit of environmental goals. By encouraging a wide variety of private actors to invest in emissions reduction or sequestration projects, JI takes advantage of existing market structures, and reduces both the bureaucratic burden and the associated transaction costs of heavy international regulation. Since private investors automatically seek out the least-cost options, the market mechanism provides an inherent means of achieving cost effectiveness in climate change mitigation. This argument was raised frequently by early proponents of JI and is still explicitly or implicitly assumed in the literature (Jepma, 1995, 1998a)

On face value, both of these arguments seem to make sense. The undeniable differences in energy efficiency standards and carbon emissions per capita between countries certainly seem to vindicate the formal economic arguments. The existence of an institutional mechanism founded on the principle of economic efficiency would appear to provide a ready-made vehicle for stimulating investment in global GHG emissions reductions. On further investigation, however, both versions of the argument fall foul of some potentially serious problems.

In the former case, we need at least to have a recognized and robust methodology for assessing both the emissions reductions and the costs associated with GHG mitigation options. In order to be able to assess whether or not cost effectiveness was achieved, we would need to know whether a particular investment is the next least-cost option, not only in terms of the host country, but also in terms of the donor country. Later in this subsection we set out the established methodology for assessing the cost effectiveness of GHG emission-reduction projects, using the concept of specific incremental costs.

The theoretical and practical difficulties associated with this concept are daunting. Each JI investment should, ideally, be the least-cost option at the global margin. But figuring out which investment lies at the least-cost margin, at any one point in space and time, is no easy task, as subsequent analysis reveals.

In some sense, the variant position side-steps this problem by assuming that market investors automatically seek out the least-cost options. But the assumption of near-perfect market efficiency is demonstrably suspect in international energy markets which are dominated by hidden subsidies, a range of hidden external environmental and social costs, and a wide variety of institutional obstacles to the uptake of cleaner, more efficient technologies (see, for example, Jackson, 1997). Private investors may well seek out least-cost investments. But, generally speaking, they will compute what they mean by least-cost according to existing market conditions and private investment criteria. Choices which are optimal for a private investor in a distorted market are not necessarily optimal for the host country, for the donor country or for the global objectives of the FCCC. If we are to assess JI as a mechanism for achieving economic efficiency at this level, we must at least be able to show that choices taken by private actors in the JI market do not compromise the environmental and social objectives of the convention.

The starting point in achieving this must be clarity in the analytic framework. In particular, we need to establish appropriate concepts of cost and cost effectiveness with which to judge the arguments from economic efficiency. Even this task, as we shall see, is not straightforward.

A formal definition of the concept of cost effectiveness in GHG emission reduction flows from the concept of the *incremental cost* which has been coined to denote the difference in costs between two investments, each with different emission profiles (for example, King, 1993; Ahuja, 1993). In particular, the concept of incremental cost is used to denote the additional costs associated with making an investment with lower emissions (the *abatement option*) in place of an investment in conventional technology according to current projections (the *baseline option*).[2] We calculate the emissions reduction achieved by the investment by subtracting the emissions associated with the abatement project from the emissions associated with the baseline. The specific incremental cost (in US$ per tonne of CO_2 equivalent) can then be calculated by dividing the costs of the investment by the emissions reduction achieved. Formal definitions of all these factors are given in Chapter 7.

Using the concept of specific incremental costs, it is possible to build up a picture of the available emission abatement in a particular country against the cost of achieving that abatement. The graph of specific incremental cost against abatement is generally referred to as a cost curve (see Figure 3.1). The x-axis of the graph represents the total quantity of emission abatement and the y-axis displays the specific incremental cost of achieving abatement at the margin.

It is worth noting that a part of the cost curve lies below the x-axis, indicating that some of the abatement options incur a *negative* incremental cost. In this case, the abatement technology is considered to be less expensive than the baseline technology. A number of important issues flow from this observation, and we shall return to them later. The existence of negative-cost abatement options is, however, well documented and is one of the features of most country

Specific incremental cost

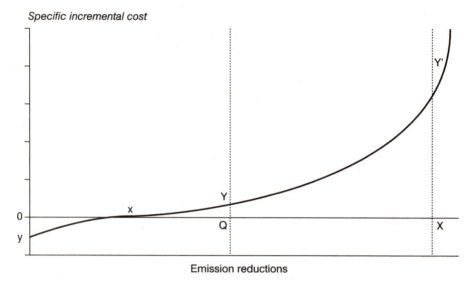

Emission reductions

Figure 3.1 *Illustrative Cost Curve for GHG Emissions Reduction*

cost curves that have so far been generated (see, for example, Jackson, 1991, 1995; Ardone et al, 1997; Morthorst, 1993; UNEP, 1994; Coherence, 1991).

The lowest (incremental) cost of achieving a given level of emission abatement, say X, can be deduced from the cost curve by calculating the area under the curve from the y-axis up to the given emission abatement level X, taking the area under the x-axis as negative. The curve illustrates what might be called the least-cost path for achieving emissions abatement, with rising marginal costs for increasing levels of emission abatement. A large part of what is meant by cost effectiveness in the context of emission reduction is that abatement investments should follow such a least-cost path. In other words, the cheaper options are implemented first, before the more expensive ones.

The total costs of abatement are provided by the (arithmetic) area under the curve (where areas below the x-axis are counted as negative). Thus, the total cost of achieving a target reduction of Q tonnes (along the least-cost path) is given by the area xYQ minus the area Oxy. It is easily observed that the overall costs of achieving the same reduction could be much higher, if the least-cost path were not followed. As an example, suppose that the same reduction target of Q tonnes was met by implementing measures between Q and X on the graph, where $X=2Q$. The overall costs are then determined by the area $QYY'X$, which is substantially larger than the area representing the least-cost path.

For a variety of reasons, two different countries may have rather different cost curves, and it is this fact which informs the theoretical argument for the cost effectiveness of joint implementation. To illustrate the argument in more detail, consider the following hypothetical example. Suppose that two countries A and B have exhausted the negative cost options for abatement, and the least-cost paths for further abatement are illustrated by the cost curves shown in Figure 3.2. It is evident that country A can meet a further target

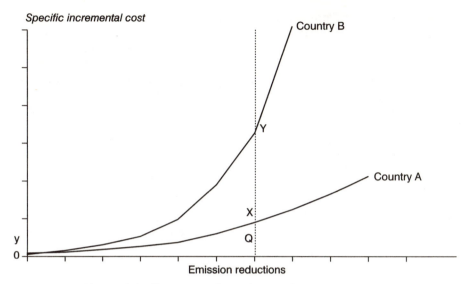

Figure 3.2 *Illustrative Cost Curves for Two Countries*

reduction Q at a considerably cheaper cost (given by the area OXQ) than the cost to country B (given by the area OYQ) of achieving the same reduction level. As a result, it is argued, there is an economic incentive for country B to invest in reduction options in country A.

Another way of presenting this argument proceeds via the use of *joint* cost curves for the respective countries (Jackson, 1995), in which the least-cost options are ranked on the same curve irrespective of geographical location. The general form of the argument for joint implementation from cost effectiveness follows from the result that the joint cost (the area under the joint cost curve) for achieving a reduction of 2Q tonnes is less than the sum of the costs for achieving reductions of Q tonnes in each country separately.

In practice, as we have already noted, a number of contentious issues are raised by the theoretical framework elucidated here. We explore some of these issues below.

No-Regrets Options

Firstly, in most countries, there are some abatement options which appear to offer negative incremental costs: that is, they lead to positive economic benefits as well as to reductions in emission levels. For instance, many demand-side management (or energy efficiency) options fall into this category.

There is considerable controversy over the extent of the financial benefits of these so-called *no-regrets* options. Some have argued that since they are economically attractive in their own right, no-regrets options should be taken up within the baseline (see, for example, Barrett, 1992). Others suggest that the apparent economic benefits – as assessed from a bottom-up technological analysis – are, in reality, eroded by a number of additional *transaction costs* associated with implementing the options, and might also incur costs at the system level which are not picked up by conventional calculations. Joskow and Marron (1993), for example, argue that monitoring, evaluation, marketing and administration costs can increase the costs of demand-side measures by up to 30 per cent. Barrett (1994) has identified transaction costs of around 10 per cent of the project costs in the AIJ pilot projects between Norway (as donor) and Poland and Mexico (as hosts). Others have pointed to the institutional, financial, fiscal and regulatory barriers which currently inhibit the uptake of cost-effective energy-efficiency measures (see Jackson, 1997). Michaelowa (1998) argues that pure microeconomic no-regrets options are scarce, while macroeconomic no-regrets options abound as the gain in these options is an externality accruing to others and not to the investor.

Whatever the upshot of these arguments, the potential for negative cost measures is robust enough to expect that at least some of it will survive a rigorous analysis. In fact, a recent analysis of the AIJ projects reported to the FCCC under the uniform reporting format suggests that pilot-phase projects are 'overwhelmingly no-regret measures with zero or negative cost' (Schwarze, 2000). In this case, a number of difficult questions arise. Are such measures appropriate for JI investment? If they are, then to whom should the economic benefits of the investment accrue? If they are not, and JI is restricted to those options which are not, in fact, the most cost effective, can this mechanism still be said to serve the goal of economic efficiency? These questions remain far from resolved.

Discounting

A further critical issue in this analysis is the question of economic discounting. Generally speaking, as we shall see in Chapter 7, economic costs are calculated on a net present value (NPV) basis by discounting future revenue and cost streams at a given discount rate. But the level of discount rate implicitly affects the level of importance given to intergenerational equity. A relatively high discount rate implies that costs borne much more than a decade into the future are negligible, whereas a discount rate of 0 per cent ensures that costs borne at any time in the future are as important as those of today.

The justification for the use of a positive discount rate is that resources invested today can be transformed, on average, into more resources later. This is considered to hold for investments in both physical capital (such as machines) and human capital (such as education). GHG-control programmes can be viewed in a similar way: investment in abatement and adaptation measures is made today to reduce the costs of climate change tomorrow.

According to Arrow et al (1996), there are two approaches to setting the appropriate discount rate to use in such situations: the *prescriptive* approach, which sets the discount rate according to an ethical assessment of how much we should value impacts on future generations; and the *descriptive* approach, which sets the discount rate according to current economic growth rates. The prescriptive approach gives low discount rates (around 2 to 4 per cent), while the descriptive approach gives higher discount rates which can be in the region of 8 to 10 per cent or higher. In this study, we have assessed JI projects using both approaches.

A further controversy surrounding discounting is the question of whether non-monetary measures – for example, GHG emissions – should be discounted. Currently, (see Munasinghe et al, 1996) costs of abating GHGs are calculated by implicitly discounting emissions. The assumption here is that the damage due to a tonne of CO_2 (or equivalent) remains constant over the period of assessment. Clearly this is a major assumption and needs further investigation. Further examination of this issue is carried out in Chapter 8.

The Baseline Issue

Finally, this whole theoretical assessment framework relies heavily on the elucidation of a baseline against which to calculate emissions reductions achieved by the abatement project and the incremental costs associated with it. As we have already remarked, the baseline is inherently counterfactual; it represents neither what has happened nor what will happen, but what (it is supposed) would have happened if the abatement project had not been implemented. This inherent counterfactuality turns out to be so critical to JI that we explore it in some detail in Chapter 4.

Conclusions

We have been concerned in this chapter to point out that flexibility mechanisms operate under multiple objectives, including, in particular, environmental effectiveness, equity and economic effectiveness. Typically, it is unlikely that there will be any single operational form of JI which maximizes performance with respect to all of these underlying objectives.

As is common in multi-attribute decision-making contexts, the operationalization of flexibility is characterized by the need to make trade-offs between objectives which are, to some extent, conflicting. For example, there is a critical trade-off between procedures which are more attractive to investors, but offer less environmental security, and procedures which are more watertight in environmental terms, but may pose greater investor risk and reduce participation levels. The presence of these conflicts and trade-offs goes some way towards explaining the contentious nature of flexibility mechanisms within global climate policy.

We contend that the appropriate way to proceed in this situation is to engage in a structured approach to the design of flexibility mechanisms which recognizes the existence of multiple objectives, and explicitly identifies the trade-offs which occur between them. This assertion provides the basis for the evaluation framework developed in later chapters of this book.

The Baseline Question: Dealing with the Problem of Counterfactuality

K Begg, T Jackson, P-E Morthorst and S Parkinson

Introduction

At first sight, joint implementation (JI) appears to offer a simple institutional mechanism for increasing the flexibility with which parties to the Framework Convention on Climate Change (FCCC) might meet their commitments under the convention. In practice, as we have already seen, JI is haunted by a multiplicity of underlying objectives and operational forms. The institutional complexity associated with such a situation goes some way towards explaining why the operationalization of JI has proved difficult. In addition to this complexity, JI labours under another, perhaps more intractable, problem – namely, the counterfactuality of the baseline.

The term baseline refers to the situation which would have existed if the JI project had not been implemented. It is essential to consider the baseline in order to assess both the emission reductions and the incremental costs associated with an abatement project. Since it must set out what would have happened if the abatement project had not been implemented, the baseline describes what is known as a counterfactual situation – a situation which by definition does not exist. The problematic nature of the concept arises because it is inherently impossible either to verify or to disprove conjectures about what 'would have happened'.

It may be possible to defend, *ex ante*, a number of possible future scenarios for a given project situation.[1] For example, when a heavy-fuel oil-fired boiler is converted for use with biomass, the most obvious choice of baseline is the old oil-fired boiler itself. However, this choice of baseline is by no means unique. We might also have supposed that a general move away from oil-fired district heating towards gas-fired individual heating was inevitable given concerns about other environmental impacts from heavy-fuel oil, and the opening up of natural gas networks. Under these assumptions, the most appropriate baseline would appear to be the provision of heat through gas-fired central heating systems. Choosing between such different scenarios is demonstrably difficult. Furthermore, it is clear that, from a philosophical point of view, the situation admits no unique, *a priori* correct choice. We simply cannot be sure, ex ante, what would happen in the future if the JI project were not implemented.

Some attempt can be made, as we shall show in subsequent chapters of this book, to undertake an *ex-post* revision of the baseline in order to reflect events which were not envisaged at the time the *ex-ante* baseline was constructed, but which have clearly influenced the environmental effectiveness of the abatement project.[2] Thus, if it becomes apparent that the shift away from heavy-fuel oil and towards gas has indeed been an influential feature in the heat sector with which we are concerned, then it is clear, *ex post*, that the gas-fired central-heating scenario would have been a better baseline than the oil-fired district-heating scenario. Even at this point in time, however, it is not necessarily true that gas-fired central heating is the most appropriate baseline for the rest of the project. A massive national programme of energy efficiency could alter the demand for heat and require a further recalculation of the emission reductions and costs of the JI project at some later date.

As a result, it should be clear that the existence of counterfactuality in baseline construction introduces an element of uncertainty into the analysis of JI projects which is largely irreducible, in particular when considered *ex ante*. Later chapters of this book look in detail at the magnitude of this uncertainty (see Chapters 7 and 8). We will also undertake an interest group analysis to identify the impacts of this uncertainty on the relevant stakeholders in JI, and investigate the possibility of managing the impacts of the uncertainty through various institutional safeguards (see Chapter 9). Generally speaking, it can be argued that the shorter the time over which predictions about the future have to be made, the more reliable they are likely to be. This recognition informs our suggestion for the use of baseline revision and limited crediting life as a means of reducing counterfactual uncertainty in JI.

In this chapter, however, it is our intention to set out the main parameters of the baseline problem. We start by examining the question of the appropriate system boundary for an assessment of JI projects. In particular, we make a distinction between separable projects – for which it may be possible to define the baseline at a project level, ignoring second-order, system-level or macroeconomic effects – and non-separable projects for which we are likely to require at least the construction of a system-level baseline. Next, we set out some of the specific elements which need to be taken into consideration when constructing credible baselines at different levels of complexity. We then review the approaches to baseline construction that have appeared in the literature. Finally, we discuss the institutional implications of this analysis and identify a specific approach to the baseline question, which motivates subsequent analysis in this book.

The System Boundary

Any effective methodology for assessing the technological, environmental, economic and social impacts of technology must begin by defining an appropriate system boundary. Nowhere is this truer than in the energy sector, where technologies can have impacts at a variety of different levels.

Defining the Level of System Boundary

We define three levels at which the system boundaries could be set: the country level, system level or project level. These are illustrated in Figure 4.1 and described in detail below.

The project (or independence) level

A necessary prerequisite for this level is that the projects under consideration are independent of other parts of the energy system. Following this approach, a JI project directly substitutes an existing plant or a well-defined planned project (for example, a planned development of a coal-fired district-heating plant is changed to a natural gas-fired plant). Typically, these kinds of JI projects are related to the supply side of the energy system.

The system (or interdependence) level

This level of analysis is necessary when the JI project under consideration is not independent of other parts of the energy system, and introducing it into the energy system will cause systems interactions. An example is a conservation programme which substitutes a well-defined part of the energy demand system (for example, an efficient lighting programme where compact fluorescent lamps substitute ordinary incandescent light bulbs). Typically, these kinds of JI projects are related to the demand side of the energy system, although supply-side projects – such as electricity supply – can also have system impacts.

The country (or macro) level

Typically, analysis at the overall country level will take place when the JI undertaking includes large energy programmes that have a significant impact on the overall economic and social development of the country. It is clear from Figure 4.1 that the project level is a subset of the system level, which again is a subset of the overall country level, and interactions are possible between these three levels.

Appropriate levels of analysis

Figure 4.1 also gives an indication of which kinds of projects are related to which level of analysis. If the JI proposal is a large hydro-power plant development programme, this might have considerable effect on society and economy; but if a smaller hydro programme is carried out to substitute an existing or planned development of conventional power plants, this might be treated at the energy-system level, independent of the macro level.

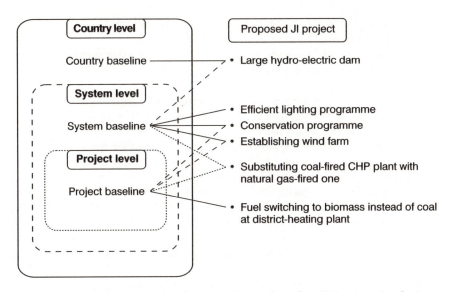

Figure 4.1 *Three Levels of System Boundary for JI Project Analysis*

Obviously, the details of each project will determine exactly which level of analysis is necessary. As an example, unless a heating conservation programme is restricted to buildings with individual supply, this would be expected to have system-level interactions as well. Whether the analysis of establishing a wind farm, or substituting a coal-fired cogeneration plant with a natural gas-fired one, would have to be carried out at the system level or at the project level depends upon technical characteristics. The lack of regulating capabilities for wind power might necessitate the use of a system model. Unless the coal-fired and the natural gas-fired cogeneration plants are fairly identical, the mixed production of electricity and heat may demand analysis at the systems level as well. However, the importance of these interactions for the estimation of emission reductions has still to be explored.

Defining Separability

In principle, the restrictions on the use of the project-level approach are given by the substitutional boundaries both for the JI project under consideration and for the substituted project in relation to the total system. In other words, the question which needs to be asked is: can both projects be assumed either to be independent of other parts of the energy system or to have approximately identical interactions with this system? If this is the case, the substitution of a JI project for an existing or planned project can be assumed to be *separable* from the overall system.

Defining the conditions for separability is a complex matter and normally is related to inputs to the plant and outputs from the plant. From this, two extreme cases can be identified:

1   the *single-input, single-output case*, which typically might be represented by a district heating plant;
2   the *multi-input, multi-output case*, which might be represented by a coal- or oil-fired cogeneration plant.

We will restrict our attention to the single-input, single-output case 1. However, many concerns related to the multi-input and/or multi-output cases are also covered by this analysis.

Most energy technologies will in some way or another interact with part of the total energy system. As an example, we will look at a planned natural gas-fired district-heating plant. The single output from the plant is the quantity of heat demanded by consumers connected to a limited district-heating network. The performance of the plant will be directly influenced by the following variables, which determine interactions with the total energy system:

- the consumers' demand for heat, which will determine the operating hours of the plant;
- the availability of the required fuel – in this case, natural gas.

These direct variables will again be influenced by a number of indirect variables. The consumers' demand for heat will depend upon the cost of district heating which, among others, will be given by the cost of the input fuel (the price of natural gas) and the district heating tariff policy. Finally, the consumers' demand for heat will depend upon the possibilities for energy conservation, which again might be a part of the government's energy and environmental policy.

The availability of the required natural gas quantities will, of course, depend upon the supply situation for natural gas. Is natural gas a domestic energy source or is it imported, making it vulnerable to policy changes abroad? Is there a shortage in the supply of natural gas? Is there strong competition in the demand for natural gas, making it probable that even a small project can increase the price of natural gas? These are amongst the questions that need to be addressed when assessing the relationship between the project and the rest of the energy system.

Taken together, these considerations determine the system boundary for the project in mind. In fact, the planned district-heating project based on natural gas has only a limited number of interactions with other parts of the energy system, as indicated by the small area *A* in Figure 4.2.

When looking at fairly simple energy-producing plants, the interactions with the total system will normally be represented by certain exogenously defined data. For the case in question – the natural gas-fired district-heating plant – these exogenous data will include:

- the annual utilization time for the plant, specifying the total energy production and the needed fuel input;
- the development of the price of natural gas and other fuels.

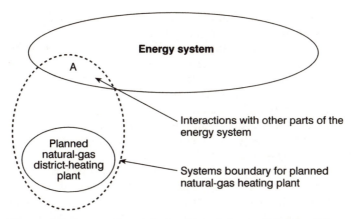

Figure 4.2 *System Boundaries for a District-Heating Plant*

For an *ex-ante* baseline, these data may need to be specified for the total lifetime of the project. Typical projections of data may be specified as a time series incorporating such influences as conservation policies, which affect the demand for heat (and thus the utilization time of the plant), and international projections on fuel prices. Some of these data might be calculated by an energy-economic model, taking into account the interplay with the rest of the energy system.

If, as a JI undertaking, it is proposed that this planned natural gas-fired district-heating plant is converted to a biomass-fired district-heating plant, which assumptions are then necessary to allow the project to be analysed separately from the rest of the energy system? In other words, what conditions are necessary to allow the substitution of a natural gas-fired district-heating plant with a biomass-fired one to be assessed at a project level?

The question of separability can be divided into two parts: separability in inputs and separability in outputs. To assess the above case at a project level, the following assumptions need to be fulfilled in relation to the separability of inputs:

- the necessary quantities of biomass for fuelling the plant must be available;
- the increased use of biomass must have a low impact, both upon the existing market price for biomass and on the expected future price development for biomass;
- the decreased use of natural gas must have insignificant influence on the existing and the expected future price of natural gas.

Separability with respect to output requires the following assumptions to be fulfilled:

- the quantity of energy output produced must be identical for the natural gas and the biomass plant;[3]
- the cost of heat to consumers must be identical for the two plants, implying that there will be no price-induced changes in the demand for district heating in the network area.

If both input and output separability assumptions are fulfilled, it will be possible to assess the JI project at a project level.

In practice, it is very difficult to completely assure the separability of a JI project. For example, in the Estonian biomass district-heating projects, a large variation in biomass prices has been observed both over time and across different regions of the country. It is very difficult, therefore, to tell if a given JI project has significantly influenced these prices. As a result, when carrying out a project-level assessment, several simplifying assumptions have been made for each JI project. Details of these assumptions are given in Chapter 7, along with the results of the assessment,.

Furthermore, where it was believed that a JI project was not separable from the energy system, both system-level and project-level analyses were carried out so that the size of the differences in estimates of emissions reduction and incremental costs could be seen (Chapter 8). Since all of the JI projects investigated in this study were small – approximately a few megawatts (MW) – a country-level assessment was not considered necessary for any of them.

It is important to realize that expanding the system boundaries up to the next level (for example, from project to system level) will inevitably increase the amount of data and the number of variables needed to estimate the emissions reduction and incremental cost. This may actually lead to an *increase* in uncertainty in the estimates rather than the desired decrease, and therefore needs careful consideration. A number of other researchers have considered the issue of system boundaries, specifically in the context of constructing the baseline; we review these later in this chapter.

The detailed methodology for both the project-level assessment and the system-level assessment carried out in this study is given in Chapters 7 and 8, where a brief description of the energy–economic models used at the system level may also be found.

The Problems of Leakage and Spreading

Despite taking care in setting system boundaries, it is very difficult, in practice, to include all the important effects relating to a JI project. For example, in the above discussion on converting a natural gas boiler to a biomass boiler, we did not go into any detail on fuel-cycle effects (environmental impacts associated with extraction and transportation of the fuel). However, such issues are critical in determining whether a JI project really reduces GHG emissions or merely shifts them to another geographical location. If a JI project increases emissions outside of its system boundaries, it is said to cause *leakage*. If it reduces emissions outside of its boundaries, it is said to cause *spreading* or *spillover*.

The question of where the natural gas supply comes from applies to this example. If the gas supply derives from Siberia, for instance, environmental damage in the gas fields and associated methane leakage from the pipes would reduce the benefit of the project from a global perspective.

Of particular concern in the biomass energy projects that we introduce in Chapter 5 is whether the CO_2 emitted in burning the fuel is offset by regrowth of – and therefore CO_2 uptake by – *standing* biomass. This problem of CO_2-*neutrality* cannot be ignored. One solution is to assume that the biomass fuel produces no emissions, and then to subtract the corresponding area of standing biomass from the national inventory of sinks to prevent double counting. However, this does not determine whether the project leads to a loss of standing biomass in a particular area through, for example, deforestation.

In this study, we have attempted to locate the source of the biomass fuel used by the JI projects, and hence to ascertain whether it is a CO_2 neutral source, such as a well-managed forest. However, a detailed assessment of the CO_2 uptake of a particular area of biomass is outside the terms of reference of this study.

Critical Elements in the Construction of Baselines

In this section we set out the critical parameters which need to be addressed in the construction of credible baselines. In line with the discussion in the previous section, we distinguish three separate situations: the construction of project-level baselines, the construction of system-level baselines and the construction of macro or country-level baselines.

Project-Level Baselines

Constructing a baseline at the project level requires consideration of the following factors.

Choice of technology/fuel and timing

The choice of technology or technologies for the baseline plant (sometimes known as the *reference* plant) and the timing of its introduction are critical when calculating emissions reductions and costs. It is often the case (NUTEK, 1995, 1996; USIJI, 1998) that the baseline is considered simply to be the continuation of the existing pre-JI situation. However, it is possible that a replacement plant would have come into operation had the JI project not been undertaken. Country-level scenario information (see subsection below) may shed light on possible replacement plants. Obviously, if any plans relating to such a plant exist, these must be used in constructing the baseline.

Time-frame

The time-frame of the JI project may be the technical lifetime of the technology, or it may be adjusted by consideration of what might have happened in the baseline. For example, if the host country has GHG emissions targets, it has an incentive to introduce low-emission technology. As a result, it is possible that the JI project simply represents an acceleration of developments likely to happen (the baseline might be the JI project itself delayed by, for example, ten years). Consequently, the accounting time-frame may be the length of this delay: significantly shorter than the technical lifetime.

Equivalence of energy service

As discussed earlier, the incremental cost concept requires a comparison between the JI project and the baseline for providing the same energy service.

Essentially, the demand or output from the project should also be met by the reference plant. In practice, assuring that this is true may not be straightforward. For example, if the JI project plant has a different capacity than the baseline, then it is necessary to assess whether peak demand can be met by the lower capacity plant. If not, would this peak demand be met from another source? Differences in efficiency, reliability or fuel price between the JI project and the baseline may all cause plants to respond differently to demand. How important this is may well be project dependent.

Country-level 'background' scenario

As discussed above, it is, in practice, very difficult to ensure the complete separability of a JI project. It is therefore important to place the JI project in the country context and to consider possible economic, environmental and social policy developments within that country which may help define credible baseline options. Projections of exogenous variables such as fuel prices (which may be national or international) may also be defined by this scenario.

Technical parameters

For each type of plant and fuel, the technical operating parameters such as efficiency, utilization factor and emission factor need to be specified over the time-frame of the assessment. Of course, these will be defined by the choice of the baseline technology.

Financial parameters

For each type of plant and fuel, financial data such as investment costs and operation and maintenance (O&M) costs are needed for the time-frame of the assessment. Again, these will be defined by the choice of the baseline technology.

Leakage

It is important to consider whether the JI project is likely to lead to GHG emissions being increased outside the system boundaries, as discussed in the previous section. If such an effect is likely, then an estimate of this is needed.

It should be noted that even where JI projects are treated as separable, and the baseline is therefore constructed at the project level, some consideration still has to be given to country-level conditions. For example, in constructing the baseline for the Estonian heat supply projects in this study, we have taken into account issues of national fossil-fuel availability and national legislation on air pollution. Consideration of such national economic, environmental and social factors plays a significant role in the baseline construction.

System-Level Baselines

As discussed above, a system-level analysis requires the use of an energy–economic model. Hence, the baseline at this level is constructed using such a model. In general, a system-level baseline can be developed using many of the elements of a project-level approach but with a considerably greater data need. The details are as follows.

Present energy sector

An energy–economic model requires a detailed description of the current technologies, fuels and the networks that link it together.

New technology

The system model also requires details of new technologies which may become financially viable within the time-frame of the analysis.

Policy factors

Details of national policies which affect the energy use need to be incorporated explicitly within the model. This includes emissions targets (for instance, GHG targets agreed at Kyoto), planned power/heat plants, etc.

Exogenous variables

Future projections are needed of variables such as national energy demand (disaggregated by sector) and international fuel prices. These are produced by macroeconomic models.

Time-frame

The time-frame of the system baseline should equal or exceed the technical lifetime of the JI project so that all relevant system interactions are included.

Technical parameters

Technical parameters, such as emission factors, efficiencies and plant merit order, need to be specified for every technology and fuel combination in the model.

Financial parameters

Financial parameters – for example, investment and O&M costs – also have to be specified for every technology and fuel combination.

Leakage

Leakage that occurs within the energy system can be accounted for using a system model. However, effects in other sectors of the economy, or indeed outside the country (such as upstream impacts in the fuel cycle), would have to be considered separately.

A system-level assessment has the added advantage that it can be used to assess the interaction between a number of different JI projects which are being executed at the same time. Hence, the job of calculating the emissions reduction due to each project is made more rigorous.

Country-Level Baselines

Constructing a baseline at the country level will require the use of a macro-economic model, including a well-developed module for the energy sector.

While such models have been built recently for examining climate change policy in industrialized countries, to our knowledge, none exist for countries which are likely to be JI host countries (transition economies or developing countries). Therefore, we do not consider this option further in this study. However, given that large-scale JI projects which have a significant macroeconomic effect are possible, this is an area for further work.

A Review of Approaches to Baseline Construction

A number of other researchers have investigated the baseline issue in the context of JI. Much of this discussion has revolved around the issue of whether to construct the baseline at the project level or the system level.[4]

Several researchers (for example, Jackson, 1995; Ardone et al, 1997; Rentz et al, 1998) have argued that, in principle, an energy–economic model is needed to model the feedbacks and interdependencies between a project and the wider energy system. Rentz et al (1998) have developed a detailed generic system model (PERSEUS) which can be adapted for different countries, and proposed its use for baseline construction.

Fritsche (1994) believes that, since the relevant actors (in terms of quantified emission limitation and reduction commitments – QELRCs – under the protocol) are countries, only baselines for the whole country are acceptable. Country baselines could make use of the national reporting projections established under the FCCC and the national emissions targets. Stepping down from a national to a regional or project scale would require very specific plant information on fuels, which – it is claimed – may increase uncertainties.

Michaelowa (1998), on the other hand, argues that the uncertainties are so high in macroeconomic models that construction of such baselines 'amounts to pure guesswork'. He suggests that practicality demands a project-level approach. The GEF incremental cost study (Ahuja, 1993) also uses a project-level approach.

The FCCC's Subsidiary Body for Scientific and Technical Advice (SBSTA) takes a central line, suggesting that baselines should be constructed at a level appropriate to the complexity and scale of the project, but should also incorporate considerations of leakage (SBSTA/1997/INF.3). Furthermore, it argues that such decisions should be determined by project participants and then approved by the relevant governments to minimize bureaucracy. It could be argued, however, that this is open to exploitation by parties aiming to maximize their credits.

These arguments are reflected in the different approaches to be found in the literature on baseline construction. In the following sections we summarize the approaches taken according to the type of baseline and then consider some overarching baseline issues.

Project-Specific Approach

The project-specific approach constructs a baseline specifically appropriate to a particular project. The approach adopted so far within the AIJ pilot phase has been to construct a relatively simple project-specific baseline, usually based on an assumption that, in the absence of the JI project, the situation prevailing before the project should continue. There is generally no attempt to incorporate future environmental policy changes for the country within the baseline or to consider effects on the continuing additionality of the project over time. Once formulated, these baselines have then been subject to negotiations with the host country, and this has sometimes led to a protracted process in which there is some potential for gaming (see Chapter 9).

Baseline construction within the pilot phase has largely remained experimental and ad hoc in nature. To improve on this situation, we suggest that a full project-specific baseline, at the project level, should take account of all the relevant elements outlined above. To recap, these include:

- choice and timing of reference technology/fuel;
- equivalence of energy service;
- crediting lifetime; and
- country-level background scenario.

Thus, a considerable amount of information is required to construct the emissions-path scenario for project-specific baselines. This effort is justified if this is the only way of carrying out the estimation, but means that transaction costs are high for all projects. Even with this effort, the uncertainties can still be high, particularly because of the counterfactual nature of the baseline. The existence of these uncertainties informs the approach to baseline construction pursued in this book, in which a range of counterfactual baselines is constructed and a range of values is calculated for the emission reduction and costs associated with a project (see Chapter 7).

In the following discussion of other baseline approaches, most try to move away from the time-consuming project-specific approach towards various kinds of simplification based on project type – as in the default-matrix and the benchmarking approaches. In other cases, as in the system and macroeconomic models, the level of analysis is the main consideration; these models automatically leave behind project-specific factors.

Default-Matrix Approach

The default-matrix method was suggested by Luhmann et al (1997). The starting point is that JI projects are 'standardized'. The standardized project has the general characteristics of the project under consideration, but situation-specific factors are not taken into account. These standardized projects are then assigned default baseline or reference technologies. The default technologies are determined by a 'filter model' which selects appropriate baseline matches to each standardized project type. Once selected, these are set up in a matrix for the country, sector and type so that baseline emissions are calculated using this default technology (and fuel). The default baseline technology has a characteristic *specific emissions* value, measured in tonnes of carbon dioxide equivalent of output from the plant (tCO_2e/MWh). Provided there is equivalence of the energy service supplied in the project and baseline, the specific emissions of the project can be subtracted from the baseline and multiplied by the output from the plant.

Such a standardized methodology offers two benefits:

1   simplification of baseline construction for investors; and
2   removal of arbitrary baseline setting which may be exploited to maximize credits.

The lifetime over which crediting is recommended on the basis of these baselines is not more than 15 years for long-term projects. One limitation of this methodology is its inability accurately to represent fluctuating or intermittent energy sources, such as wind energy and photovoltaics.

Benchmarks

The Center for Clean Air Policy (CCAP) (1998) has introduced the idea of benchmarks which are defined as the future emissions paths either at the project, system or the country level. These again are expressed as specific emissions for the technology and fuel in the energy sector in tCO2e/MWh. Benchmarks differ from all other baseline types because they include the assumption that any project which produces reductions relative to the benchmark is automatically additional, and there is no separate check on the actual project situation.

Benchmarks tend to be sectoral, regional or country level for application to project types. They have the advantage of reduced costs but also the possible disadvantage of reduced environmental integrity depending upon how they are implemented and monitored. The time-scale for crediting is subject to the same constraints as other baseline types.

Investment-Analysis Approach

This approach, which is advocated by the World Bank (Heister, 1999), has been briefly discussed under the question of financial additionality in Chapter 3. It depends upon the existence of an economically efficient market in the host country for the determination of investment additionality. The baseline is specified as the most profitable use of the finance in an equivalent project (in a similar sector or country) in the absence of GHG emissions-reduction benefits. No-regrets projects would, by definition, be excluded. It models investment behaviour and would require confidential financial information from the project investor. It is a project-level approach.

System Model

A system model baseline could be sector specific or cover a range of sectors. In this method there tends to be an assumption of continuing growth of gross domestic product (GDP), and an estimate of the growth rate is made. Based on this, an estimate of annual demand is made which is the input to the model. The model itself is a *bottom-up* or energy–economic model and is based on existing or likely technologies in the sectors. It minimizes costs to meet the demand subject to emission constraints. There are two main ways to use these models. For small projects, the baseline generated by the model is a series of annual specific emissions (tCO_2e/MWh) for the sector. This is, therefore, a benchmark sector baseline which is the result of a complex modelling process based on uncertain assumptions, such as that for GDP growth. For a very large electricity supply plant, the whole model could be run with and without the project since these models deal with the possible interactions in the system between the project and what would be substituted. An example of this approach is given by Rentz et al (1998).

Top-Down Model

Top-down models produce highly aggregated sector- and country-level baselines and are macroeconomic in nature. They examine carbon emissions per unit of GDP. They have no direct relationship with the project technologies under consideration and are usually based on a series of assumptions about economic growth. An example of this approach is given by Puhl et al (1999).

Summary of the State of the Art

The latest studies in this field have been assembled in the proceedings of a recent meeting in Tokyo on CDM baselines, summarized by Matsuo (1999), while Ellis and Bosi (1999) have reviewed options for project-emission baselines. A summary of the various approaches and their origins is given in Table 4.1.

Further Issues

Besides the system boundary issue illustrated in the different approaches outlined above, there are discussions on the form of a constructed baseline. For example, they can be *historic* or *forward looking*. This means that they are either based on past historic emissions or planned future development. These historic or forward-looking baselines may also be static in that they are not altered over the lifetime of the project, or they may be *dynamic*, which means that some baseline revision or updating will occur during the project-crediting life.[5] There can, of course, be all the combinations of these – for example, one could define an historic, static baseline.

In all cases it will be important to examine the equivalence of service between the project and the baseline, as we have pointed out in earlier sections of this chapter.

It is clear from this brief review of the literature that the question of baseline construction is far from resolved. In fact, we would argue, there are elements of the baseline problem which cannot be resolved in any mechanistic or deterministic sense. The implications of this conclusion are discussed below and form the basis for the rather different approach to the evaluation of JI which we develop in this study. In Chapters 7 and 9, we offer some guidelines towards establishing credible sets of baselines for different levels of assessment. It should be re-emphasized, however, that none of these precautions will lead to the formulation of a unique *ex-ante* baseline for any given situation.

Table 4.1 *Summary of Approaches to Baseline Construction*

Authors	Type	Level	Method
Various: performed by individual investors where necessary	Project specific	Project	Individual project characteristics and all relevant information included to construct specific project and baseline emissions path.
Luhmann et al (1997)	Default-matrix approach Technology based, standardized projects and associated default-baseline technologies	Project (specific to technology/ sector/host country)	Standard projects with associated pre-selected standard baseline projects (identified from a 'filter model'). Periodically updated.
CCAP (1998)	Benchmarks	Project type or sector or country type	Assumes additionality for all emission reductions. Generalized for application to a range of project categories.
Heister (1999)	Investment-analysis approach	Project	Based on financial additionality of investment. Simulates financial/ behaviour aspects.
Rentz et al (1998)	System model	Sector	Projects future emissions of sector based on assumptions regarding demand. No-regrets measures are part of the baseline.
Puhl et al (1999)	Top-down baseline	Country or sector	Aggregated approach either using absolute emissions or tonnes C/GDP. National or sectoral planning models.

Conclusions

The discussion in Chapters 2 and 3 should have dispelled any illusion that JI represents a simple mechanism offering a straightforward institutional fix to the problem of GHG emission reduction. In fact, each JI mechanism operates under multiple objectives and each JI-type situation is defined differently, according to a number of operational parameters.

It is our contention that the appropriate way to proceed in this situation is to engage in a structured approach to the design of flexibility mechanisms which recognizes the existence of multiple objectives, and explicitly identifies the trade-offs which occur between them. This task is, however, rather complex. Firstly, it requires us to assign specific values to each of the operational variables which define any individual JI arrangement. Secondly, we need to evaluate certain critical performance variables, such as the emissions reduction achieved by the project and the incremental costs involved. In addition, we need to identify and design specific institutional measures capable of addressing the complexities under which flexibility mechanisms operate. Furthermore, it is clear from the discussion in this chapter that JI-type mechanisms are haunted by an almost intractable epistemological problem – namely, the counterfactuality of the baseline. As we have seen, this problem introduces an element of irreducible uncertainty into the assessment of JI projects, and seriously undermines our ability to determine accurately the extent to which a particular investment is reinforcing or compromising the underlying objectives of the convention.

The remainder of this book sets out a quite specific, structured approach which attempts to negotiate the complexities and uncertainties associated with this situation. This approach comprises the following three steps.

1   We specify a range of baselines against which the selected JI projects can be assessed. These baselines are constructed according to the guidelines set out above for project-level baselines, and the results of our analysis of case study projects are presented as a *range of values* for emissions reductions and costs (Chapter 7) and are calibrated, as far as is possible, against the associated uncertainties (Chapter 8).
2   We examine (Chapter 9) a variety of institutional measures which are designed to manage both the operational complexity and the epistemological uncertainty associated with JI, and show how these measures can be combined into operational packages which provide both a degree of standardization and the implementation of certain institutional safeguards.
3   Finally, we show (in Chapter 10) how the use of a multi-attribute decision-making context allows us to evaluate each such package of measures against the underlying objectives discussed in Chapter 3.

5

Case Study Projects

K Begg, T Kallaste and K Leutgöb

Introduction

Most of the projects described in this chapter and studied in depth in the subsequent sections were implemented under the activities implemented jointly (AIJ) pilot phase, which was instigated in order to gain experience with real projects designed to test the concept of joint implementation (JI) as a mechanism for achieving greenhouse gas (GHG) emission reductions. Since its inception, the AIJ pilot phase has led to the implementation of 143 projects over a range of fields, from reafforestation projects to lighting demand-side management (DSM) projects (Schwarze, 2000). Each official pilot-phase AIJ project must be registered and documented according to an established uniform reporting format (UN FCCC, 2000).

Several donor countries have started to implement funding programmes under the AIJ pilot phase. These include Australia, the US, the Netherlands, Sweden, Germany, Canada, Belgium, France, Japan, Norway and Switzerland (Michaelowa et al, 1999). Many potential host countries have established an AIJ office to deal with project proposals, and this has been stimulated by the United Nations Environment Programme (UNEP) and the World Bank, who have initiated workshops and information channels to enable host countries to learn about JI and the opportunities presented by it. Despite the range of sectors covered, some concern has been expressed that so far most AIJ pilot-phase projects have been limited to small-scale projects in the energy sector.

In this chapter, we summarize the JI projects selected for detailed analysis in this study. The first section sets out the selection process, describing the original large project set and the criteria under which this set was subsequently narrowed down. The following two sections provide brief country contexts for each of the chosen host countries and the main donor countries (respectively). Next, we detail the data collection process and reflect on some of the difficulties involved. Finally, we discuss the insights generated as a result of the data collection process.

Project Selection

In order to investigate a range of energy system projects in terms of system interactions, baseline construction and the costs and emission reductions, it was decided to explore both supply- and demand-side options and within those categories to study both heat and electricity sectors. Cogeneration was also included. An initial list of projects with available data was therefore requested from collaborators at EVA (Austria) and NUTEK (Sweden). This list was derived from information available through the respective country programmes which are described below. From this preliminary list of projects a further selection of projects was made on a number of criteria. Firstly, a decision was made to limit the number of host countries to two – Estonia and the Czech Republic – reflecting the primary interests and experience of the collaborators in this study. This was beneficial in that it also limited the amount of background data on the host countries that needed to be collected. As discussed in more detail in Chapters 4 and 7, such data are necessary in order to carry out a thorough investigation of baseline construction. While this initial selection of projects covered heat supply and demand, electricity supply and cogeneration, it did not cover electricity demand. Attempts were made to locate a suitable project in this area, but none were found. All the projects are relatively small scale as no large-scale projects were available.

On the basis of this selection of JI projects, attempts were made by project collaborators to collect detailed project data on as many of those projects located in the chosen host countries as possible. However, some projects had insufficient data or were not as initially described, and subsequent site visits also revealed that others were inappropriate. Consequently, a number of the initial projects were rejected from further consideration.

Two additional projects which were not on the original list were identified in order to maintain the range required in the study. The first was a German-funded programme to install wind power at Lettland in Latvia. Although this project lies outside our chosen host countries, it was included in the study in order to expand the project-versus-system level comparison using the PERSEUS system model developed at Karlsruhe (Rentz et al, 1998). Subsequent analysis (see Chapter 8) treats the Lettland plant as though it were located in the Czech Republic.

The other project was a multilateral cogeneration investment at Děčín in Northern Bohemia. At the time of the site visits, this project – involving three US utilities, Denmark and the Czech Environment Fund – was, in fact, the only AIJ project formally accredited to the Czech Republic. Data were obtained from the plant after arrangements had been made through the Czech Ministry of Environment.

Not all of the projects are considered successful. For example, a number of technical and economic problems have been experienced with the wind farm at Jeseník in the Czech Republic. It is, nevertheless, instructive to consider the project in this study, partly because it offers an example of an electricity-generation JI project, and partly because failure can, in itself, offer some guidance about the appropriate design of institutional instruments such as JI.

A total of 13 projects were investigated in detail (see Table 5.1). The projects fall into several main categories:

- nine heat-supply projects, mainly conversion of district-heating boilers to biomass;
- one heat-demand project, based on building energy-efficiency improvements;
- one cogeneration project, based on natural gas;
- two electricity-supply projects, based on wind energy.

Host Country Contexts

One of the contentions of this study is that JI projects need to consider the local and national context in which the projects are to be implemented. This context is necessary for a number of reasons:

- to determine the extent to which the project is appropriate in terms of local needs and national policy plans;
- to inform the construction of appropriate baselines;
- to establish the likely environmental and social impacts of such an intervention.

In this section, therefore, we provide brief summaries of the national context for each of the chosen host countries: the Czech Republic and Estonia.[1]

The Czech Republic

The Czech Republic is an inland country lying in the central part of Europe. It has an area of 78,864km^2 and a population of 10 million (1995), with a population density of 131 inhabitants per km^2. The Czech Republic began its transition to a market economy in 1990. With a stable currency, low national debt, rapidly rising exports and a privatization programme, the economic outlook for the Czech Republic is promising. Since 1989, trade with Western countries has increased from 40 per cent to 80 per cent as a proportion of total trade. After an initial fall of 22 per cent, gross domestic product (GDP) has been growing, spurred by the separation of the Czech Republic from Slovakia on 1 January 1993. The growth rate for 1996 was 4.4 per cent. The private sector share of GDP rose in that time from 12.3 per cent to 66.5 per cent. The per capita GDP in the mid 1990s was approximately US$3500.

Energy demand per unit of GDP in the Czech Republic increased in the period from 1991 to 1993, and then declined from 4.12 petajoules (PJ) per billion Czech crowns (CZK) GDP to 3.97 in 1995. This energy demand is much higher than in other Western European countries, despite this decrease. Over 90 per cent of this energy is provided by lignite, which is a low-grade,

Table 5.1 *Summary of JI Projects Examined in This Study*

Project	Type	Fuel	Donor	Capacity (MW)
Estonia				
Aardla-Tartu	Heat supply	Biomass	Swedish government	6
Haabneeme	Heat supply	Biomass	Swedish government	6
Mustamäe #				
(two stages)	Heat demand	n/a	Swedish government	
Türi	Heat supply	Biomass	Danish government	4
Valga	Heat supply	Biomass	Swedish government	5
Võru	Heat supply	Biomass	Swedish government	7
Czech Republic				
Děčín	Cogeneration	Natural gas	Danish government/	7.2 (engines)
			US industry	11 (boilers)
Jeseník	Electricity supply	Wind	Danish government	3
Kardašova				
Řečice	Heat supply	Biomass	Austrian government	2.5
Lettland*#	Electricity supply	Wind	German government	1.2
Mrakotin #	Heat supply	Biomass	Austrian government	2.8
Staré Město	Heat supply	Biomass	Austrian government	2.8
Velesin #	Heat supply	Natural gas	Austrian government	5.8

Note: * This project was actually undertaken in Latvia, but the assessment was carried out as though it had been situated in the Czech Republic in order to carry out a comparison between a project-level assessment and a system-level assessment using the Czech EFOM model (see Chapter 8). # There were no site visits to these projects and therefore no new data.

high-sulphur, high-ash coal, which consequently gives rise to high emissions of CO_2 per capita (11.9 tonnes for 1995). Lignite is now gradually being replaced by mainly liquid and gaseous fuels. Energy production is responsible for 51 per cent of 1995 CO_2 emissions, followed by 23 per cent from industry, 10 per cent from residential homes, 7 per cent from transportation and the rest from commercial and other sources.

The decline in the economy during the early part of the 1990s resulted in a decline in CO_2 emissions of about 20 per cent . The policy of the Czech government is to try to stabilize at this reduced level, despite expected economic growth of about 3 per cent. This means that compared to the base year of 1990, GHG emissions should be reduced by 5 per cent between 2000 and 2005. The new nuclear power plant at Temelin, when operational, is expected to contribute to achieving this goal, along with more efficient technologies and a switch to gas.

Estonia

Estonia is in the north-western part of Europe on the Baltic Sea. It has a land area of $45,216km^2$ of which 9.2 per cent is made up of small islands. The population in 1990 was 1.575 million. It has been undergoing economic restructuring since 1990 and the cumulative decline in GDP from 1990–1994 has been 36 per cent. From the middle of 1994, some stabilization of the economy has occurred, with an increase in GDP in 1995 of 2.9 per cent. Manufacturing and agriculture, which accounted for 35 per cent and 21 per cent of GDP in 1989, have declined to a 15 per cent and 7 per cent share respectively in 1995. At the same time trade, transport and the service sectors have all increased significantly. This growth is thought to result from the privatization programme, new investment and access to new markets.

Estonia is relatively rich in natural resources, both mineral and biological. The most important is oil shale (63 per cent), and both the energy and chemical industries are based on this resource. Oil shale has a high-ash, high-sulphur and low-calorific value. CO_2 from the combustion of oil shale is produced from the carbon in the fuel and carbonate decomposition in the mineral component. Other domestic fuels are peat and wood. Energy production based on oil shale is a key part of the Estonian economy and only two large power plants fired by oil shale produce over 95 per cent of the electricity requirements. The electricity industry is ranked among the ten biggest sources of pollution in Europe. Total CO_2 emissions, mainly from the consumption of fossil fuels, have fallen from 37.2 million tonnes in 1990 to 21.2 million tonnes in 1996.

Hydro-power potential is less than 1 per cent of current generation capacity and there is no nuclear power in Estonia. Wind potential is substantial, particularly on the islands, but there are still barriers to its development. Forests are an important sink for Estonia and represent 47 per cent of the total land area. Biomass currently contributes 8 per cent to Estonia's primary fuel supply. However, the current potential for biomass is estimated to be 15 per cent of total primary-energy supply and will be steadily developed. In the future, it is also expected that new oil-shale oil plants will be very expensive.

The motivation for the conversion of boilers in Estonia is both economic and environmental. Economic pressure arises because Estonia now has to pay world prices for oil. Before Estonian independence in 1990, *mazout* (heavy-fuel oil) was available cheaply direct from Russia to fuel boilers. The environmental pressure not to use *mazout* arises because of its high sulphur content. Combustion of the oil produces sulphur dioxide (SO_2), which damages forests and buildings through acid precipitation and leads to low air quality locally.

As a result, Estonia has a significant incentive to use woodchips, which are available locally and have a very low sulphur content. Harvesting of wood uses the conventional forest management practice of thinning, in which young trees and the branches of larger trees are selectively felled. This is currently done at a rate which allows regeneration of the forest biomass. This wood, therefore, can be considered CO_2-neutral (the CO_2 released during combustion is fixed by the biomass regeneration).

According to the Estonian Ministry for Environment, interest in the AIJ pilot phase was purely as a legal agent to enable the projects to take place. The ministry supports the future use of biofuels but foresees a continuing dependence on oil-shale oil, hence its reluctance to set targets under the Long-Range Transboundary Air Pollution (LRTAP) Convention. So far, there is little interest in renewables since the state electricity company has a virtual monopoly.

Host Country Comparisons

In this subsection we discuss the main aspects of interest in the host country contexts, and show that there are similarities but also surprising differences between the hosts.

Joint Implementation Participation

The government of the Czech Republic is much more active in AIJ than that of Estonia. This seems paradoxical since Estonia currently has more AIJ projects in place than does the Czech Republic. However, the Estonian government is much more removed from environmental issues in Estonia and there is no indication that this will change.

Fuel

The basic fuel in Estonia is oil-shale oil; in the Czech Republic it is lignite (brown coal). Both fuels are responsible for large-scale pollution, particularly atmospheric. In Estonia, woodchips are plentiful: about 70 per cent of the land area is forested. However, market prices for woodchips have risen dramatically (as they did with the heavy-fuel oil) since independence. This has meant that district heating with biomass has been expensive and householders have begun to turn to individual electric boilers. This trend has subsequently been reversed, to some extent, with the privatization of the Estonian electricity-supply industry. With the development of the Russian gas supply there has subsequently been a move to individual gas heating. The Czech Republic also has large biomass resources, but seems to be turning more to gas supplied from Russia for individual heating and district heating.

Electricity Supply

Both countries have large, powerful electricity-generating companies who are tending to bias the market against renewables. However, there are hopeful signs in both countries that renewables will gain some ground. For example, in Děčín a new geothermal plant is planned.

Donor Country Contexts

In addition to an assessment of the host country context, it is also useful to assess the national context of the donor country. In particular, this may indicate the extent to which JI activities are indeed a cost-effective alternative to domestic emission reductions. In this section, we summarize briefly the national context for the two main donor countries – Austria and Sweden – involved in the bilateral projects studied.

Austria

Austria has a population growth of 0.3–0.4 per cent annually, which is low, and an economic growth rate estimated at 2.5–3 per cent. It borders on eight countries and has considerable transit traffic across the country. Forests cover 46 per cent of the land area and have a significant sequestration effect in the order of 15Mt CO_2 per year. There is a (voluntary) national target to reduce CO_2 emissions by 20 per cent compared to 1988, while the Kyoto Protocol target under the EU burden-sharing scheme is a 13 per cent reduction from 1990 levels.

Biomass use has increased and represents 12 per cent of the total energy balance in 1995, an amount matched by the share of hydro-power. Hydro-power is the main (65–70 per cent) electricity supply source, but this has almost reached the limits of its development. The remainder of the energy supply is covered by fossil fuels, with coal usage on the decline as subsidies to domestic brown-coal production are phased out. Cheap coal imports from neighbouring countries are still possible to obtain. Natural gas supplies are increasing. Around 30 per cent of the heat demand is supplied by biomass and there are district-heating facilities in 10 per cent of the housing stock. Electricity imports and exports are significant, amounting to 15–20 per cent of production, but with exports and imports evenly balanced. CO_2 emissions were estimated at 59.2Mt in 1990. The main sources are energy conversion (27.8 per cent), transport (27.3 per cent) and industry (24.3 per cent).

Structural change has made the Austrian economy much less energy inten-sive in the last two decades. It has also enjoyed strong growth and less unemployment than the Organization for Economic Cooperation and Development (OECD) average. More deregulation of the energy sector is envis-aged, with competition introduced to the predominantly monopolistic structure of the present system.

Austria has a national environmental plan and is integrating climate change policies within all sectors. There are changes in taxation due to be introduced. An increase in mineral oil tax is in place and an energy tax on natural gas was introduced in 1996. There is a large programme to improve energy efficiency in private dwellings and to promote renewables. Biomass is consistently promoted and is competing in some areas with natural gas. Cogeneration plants are encouraged for heat supply with a subsidy scheme. The transport sector is expected to grow, especially heavy lorry traffic.

The Austrian-funded JI projects investigated in this study have been financed by the East-Ecology Fund set up by the Austrian government in 1992. It has supported approximately 100 projects through the Austrian Kommunalkredit bank in Slovenia, Slovakia and the Czech Republic. These projects are mainly SO_2 reduction measures, energy efficiency projects and water-treatment plants, located near the Austrian border. Once projects receive approval and funding for a feasibility study by the Austrian fund, project initia-tors must find investors to finance the actual implementation of each project. Successfully implemented projects are not monitored in any way and there is no official procedure for their evaluation. Data provided by the Austrian Energy Agency (EVA) was based on feasibility analyses. Actual performance data used in this study were obtained from site visits by the project team.

Sweden

Sweden has a moderate population growth of 0.4 per cent per year; the 1995 population figure was about 8.87 million. In 1995 the GDP was US$234.4 billion with an average long-term growth rate of about 2 per cent. GDP per capita shows a relatively high income level at US$26,500 in 1995.

In Sweden, CO_2 emissions were reduced by 30 per cent during the 1980s due to a large-scale nuclear programme, making electricity the most cost-effective option for heating houses and replacing individual oil heating. An increase in biomass burning as a substitute for oil and an increase in energy conservation due to rising oil prices also contributed to the reduction of CO_2 emissions. Emissions from the electricity sector are therefore small and from the industrial and residential sectors are far less than in 1982. Only the transport sector shows an increasing trend. Sweden currently has a low value for CO_2 released per unit of GDP despite a large share of energy intensive industries.

Electricity supply is currently dominated by nuclear and hydro-power which provide 95 per cent of the total production. Renewables are expected to rise only modestly, while nuclear expansion in the future is limited due to the referendum to phase out all nuclear capacity by 2010. Additional renewable electricity capacity is increasingly expensive and no major CO_2 reduction can be expected from a larger share of electricity in final energy use. The major change is to move from fossil fuels to renewables, mainly biomass for process heat. Sweden has a relatively high proportion of biofuels and district heating in the energy system and high taxes on fossil fuels. The CO_2 tax introduced in 1991 covers 75 per cent of these emissions. It is seen as the major policy measure for the reduction of CO_2 emissions in Sweden and forms the basis for the targeted reduction to 1990 levels by 2000. Measures in place to incorporate climate change concerns within decisions on all sectors of the economy are expected to produce an emission reduction of 14 per cent compared with the level projected in 1990. Projections of CO_2 emissions growth predict a sharp rise if nuclear capacity is phased out along with a significant contribution from the transport sector. The alternative to nuclear plant for electricity is oil-fired power plant. Sweden is in the process of an electricity reform which will allow further integration within the Nordic and later the European electricity market.

Swedish forests absorb the equivalent of half of the annual CO_2 emissions, but are predicted to level off in terms of net sequestration and will need a sustainable forestry policy in a few decades.

During late autumn 1992 and spring 1993, the Swedish government initiated a programme aimed at mitigating climate change through improving energy systems in the form of energy efficiency measures and increased use of renewable energy sources in the Baltic states and in Eastern European countries.

Sweden's environmentally adapted energy system (EAES) programme in the Baltic region and Eastern Europe is designed to be in line with the criteria for the AIJ pilot phase as agreed at COP 1 in Berlin in April 1995. The main activities are directed towards a reduction of emissions that are hazardous to the climate and the environment from oil- or coal-fired energy production plants. The programme is financed through special allowances from the government budget. Up to 1997, a sum of 293.5 million Swedish kronor (SEK) – equivalent to around US$40 million – has been allocated to the programme. Following the Swedish energy bill (1997), SEK40 million of this sum were allocated to the EAES programme for 1998 for investment projects. NUTEK, the Swedish National Board for Industrial and Technical Development, was assigned by the government to implement the programme up to the end of 1997. From 1 January, 1998, the new Swedish National Energy Administration (STEM) took over the responsibility for the EAES.

Donor Country Comparisons

A major difference between the donors has been the type of financing given. Denmark and Austria have preferred to give grants, while Sweden gives preferential loans. The Danish and Austrian grants tend to cover around 10 per cent of the investment costs, whilst the Swedish loan tends to cover around 100 per cent. In this latter approach, NUTEK has set aside a fund for AIJ projects; its interest rate for loans is approximately half the market level. As loans are paid back into the fund, money is made available for financing future AIJ projects.

Another difference has been the level of involvement in setting up AIJ projects. NUTEK in Sweden has been very involved in Estonia, giving consultancy advice and some training using Swedish technology. Both the Austrian and Danish governments appear to have a more hands-off attitude, but have supplied training for new technology. At all the sites visited, the impression was given that irrespective of who the donor was, more training and access to expertise over a longer time period would have been very helpful.

Data Collection

There were two rounds of data collection within the project. The first round involved the formulation of a questionnaire with the data requirements; the second involved follow-up site visits to selected projects.

Initial Data Collection

Data requirement sheets for the different types of plant, such as boiler conversion projects, were sent to NUTEKand EVA for data input to the study.[2]

The main categories of data requested were for the baseline and JI project in terms of technical data, economic and financial data, environmental and socioeconomic data, as well as information on risk and on equity. In this initial phase, it was difficult to obtain sufficient quantitative data for the construction of the baseline scenario. This meant that, in some cases, the analysis required assumptions which are made explicit in the text and which are explored in Chapter 7.

The seriousness of the problem in acquiring sound data may be endemic, or it may be that the data have not been requested by other workers in the field. As a result, it may be necessary to make a particular effort to collect the information needed.

Site Visits and Further Data Collection

The second round of data collection occurred in conjunction with the need to conduct site visits in order to obtain and assess the environmental and social impacts of the projects under study. A supplementary data collection form was devised for both Estonian and Czech projects to elaborate on some of the technical information.

The external costs and benefits of AIJ projects are an important aspect of this study, but there is very little data available generally and only a small amount of data was returned as part of the original questionnaire. Site visits were therefore arranged to all the boiler conversion sites in Estonia. On the basis of this experience, site visits to two boiler conversions – the cogeneration plant and a wind farm – were undertaken in the Czech Republic. The environmental and social results of these trips are discussed in Chapter 6. The trips also provided an opportunity to obtain further operating data from plant managers, which has been invaluable.

Problems of Data Acquisition and Insights

A number of problems arose during the data-collection phase of this project. Some of these problems are detailed below:

- Reliable data were sparse, inconsistent and in some cases non-existent.
- For the projects in the Czech Republic, no operating data were readily available. Some operating data were collected as a result of site visits carried out by the project team.
- Some projects from the initial list were incorrectly detailed or simply did not exist. During one site visit in particular, it became clear that the description in the data sheet of a 60MW gas-fired plant was not the correct description for the conversion of domestic heating to gas.
- Extraction of boiler-specific information was a problem in some cases; companies tended to be the heat suppliers for whole towns, and the converted boiler was only one of several boilers operated.
- One of the most difficult discussions with plant managers concerned the situation before conversion. At almost all boiler houses, new managers were employed since conversion took place. Therefore, it was not possible to find out what the major arguments were for changing from the existing fossil-fuel based heating to biomass.

Project Descriptions

Table 5.1 details all the projects that were evaluated within this study. In this section we provide short summaries of each project. The sites are grouped in the following sections into project types; it can be seen that even within a grouping, there are significant differences in the way a plant is operated and how it treats the fuel supply. Further details of each project may be found in Appendix 4 of Jackson et al (1999).

Heat Supply-Side Conversions

In assessing the conversion of conventionally fired plant to biomass, it is important to describe the fuel supply in order to estimate whether the biomass can be considered CO_2 neutral. This issue is discussed further below. In the JI projects assessed in this study, woodchips were either from managed forests (thinnings) or from waste wood. Thus, for the purposes of our assessment they were considered CO_2 neutral.

Some of the biomass projects also burn waste from sawmills. Whether this still qualifies as a CO_2-neutral source is problematic. However, in Estonia, waste wood which has to be disposed of must be taken to a landfill site, and a charge applies. Much of this material is therefore made available free of charge if used as biomass. Unfortunately, there is no information about the sustainability of the original source from which the wood comes. However, if this waste would have been burned anyway, possibly with no energy gain, or if it would have been left to rot, then it is reasonable to assume CO_2 neutrality. In the former case, this would be because of the gain in energy from the fuel, and in the second case because the methane released from rotting has a greater global warming potential than CO_2.

As mentioned earlier, the data originally available for projects in the Czech Republic were for boiler conversions only, and then only feasibility data could be obtained. In order to obtain more operational, environmental and social data and to form a picture of these operations in the Czech Republic, a visit was arranged to two of the boiler conversions, the cogeneration plant and the wind farm. In general, the operators of the boiler conversion sites had less information available than did their counterparts in Estonia. A third boiler conversion visit to Veseli, which was a coal-to-gas conversion, yielded no information since it turned out to be purely conversion of individual flat and family house boilers to gas from coal. This involved building a gas main network in the town; the district-heating plants were to be converted later. As a result, no useful data were available. The cogeneration site at Děčín and the wind farm at Jeseník had more automated systems which generated more data.

Aardla, Tartu

Tartu is a large university town situated in the southern part of Estonia about 200km south of the capital of Tallinn. It has a population of about 110,000 inhabitants to whom heat is supplied by six boiler plants. Heat is supplied from several sites in Tartu, burning mainly gas. The plant studied in this project is owned by the municipality and has three identical boilers, two of which were already converted from steam to hot water production. One of these boilers was then converted by NUTEK to burn woodchips by connecting to a pre-furnace. Flue-gas cleaning was also installed, along with a fuel silo and fuel handling equipment. In this plant there is also an economizer which was not installed at Türi (see below). Operators at the plant had found a way of using unburned gases from the pre-furnace in the main furnace, thus increasing the rated output from the plant from 6 to 10MW. In the summer, the fuel is mainly sawmill waste, while in the winter it is a mixture that includes woodchips. The fuel is delivered as required on the basis of the heat output of the fuel rather than by volume. The advantage of this arrangement is that there are no large storage requirements on site and the supplier gets to know what constitutes an acceptable mix. As a result, the station manager only pays for the energy delivered rather than just the quantity of biomass. The distribution network had also been upgraded at Tartu, but with overground pipes due to the cost of underground pipes, and network losses were running at 18 per cent.

Haabneeme

Haabneeme is located on the outskirts of Tallinn in Estonia and close to a small town called Viimsi of about 6000 people. Tallinn is on the northern coast of Estonia and is a large conurbation of about 110,000 people. The boiler house that was studied has three boilers. One has been converted to burn woodchips and peat (6MW of output). The other two boilers burn natural gas and heavy-fuel oil. About 70 per cent of the heat output is produced from biofuels. The gas is used mainly for peak demand in the winter, but oil is also used periodically since its lifetime is five years in reserve. NUTEK (Sweden) was the donor in this case.

The boiler house is owned by a company (A S Tamult). The woodchip/sawdust mix that is primarily used was not specified, but a high proportion is sawdust. Woodchips are priced on a volume basis. Since 1997 this has been augmented by Tetrapak waste on a trial basis (1 per cent). Tamult receives about 700 Estonian kroons (EEK) per tonne for burning the waste. The additional pollution charge which Tamult pays is small compared to the economic returns of burning the new fuel. The fact that air pollution regulations allow emissions of polychlorinated biphenyls (PCBs) from burning this type of fuel needs to be rectified within the country. It is a worrying development that the environmental impacts of the fuel are not properly recognized and could more than offset any environmental gains from abatement of greenhouse gases.

Demand has decreased as industrial customers have built their own boilers and domestic customers have switched to electric heaters. Output from the plant in the first years of operation was below expectation as a result of probably too high a percentage of sawdust in the fuel, coupled with technical problems and insufficient training.

Türi

Türi is a small town in the middle of Estonia with a population of about 7000 people. It is served by two district-heating plants. The plant which was visited has three boilers which consist of old 2.5MW and 7MW oil-fired boilers and the new biomass woodchip/peat boiler (4MW) sponsored by Denmark. The other plant is at a different site which has just been converted by NUTEK to a woodchip boiler supplying 4.5MW. Both sites are owned by the same company; when the new NUTEK boiler came on line this year, the 7MW oil-fired boiler at the main site was closed. The Danish conversion is the one studied in this analysis. However, the overall network has been important in distinguishing data as a whole from specific boiler data.

The fuel is mainly woodchips for the biomass boiler, though 20 per cent of this can be sawmill waste provided only in October, March and April. At Türi, the fuel wood is bought as forest thinnings and is stored on site for about six months before use. Local farmers and a local enterprise provide the wood, which is priced in terms of EEK/solid m^3. Since forest thinnings are used which would have been burned or left to rot, it is assumed that the wood is sustainably managed and is effectively CO_2 neutral. When the site was visited in November 1997, the network had not been renewed and losses were in the region of 30 per cent.

Valga

Valga is in the south of Estonia near the border with Latvia. It has a population of 18,000 people. It has one major district-heating plant which has three oil-fired boilers dating from 1981. With the help of NUTEK (Sweden), these boilers were converted from steam to water, and one of these was further converted in 1993 to biomass with the construction of a pre-furnace and associated equipment such as flue-gas cleaning. The converted boiler is rated at 5MW and burns mainly woodchips with some bark (4 per cent) and sawdust (1 per cent). The use of woodchips at the plant has been variable. Initially, the share of production due to woodchips was 46 per cent, but this fell in 1995–1996 to 24 per cent, rising again in 1996–1997 to 46 per cent. This seems to have been mainly due to the original policy on fuel supply, though there were also technical problems. It appears that the fixed grate design used requires more sophisticated operation and a tendency to more frequent cleaning outages, and is not, in fact, recommended as a future plant type. Since 1997, it has been cheaper to run the biomass than the fuel-oil boilers. Peak loads are still supplied by the heavy-fuel oil. There are plans to convert another boiler and to integrate the network and close a coal-fired plant. Demand is expected to rise, but due to the relative high cost of district heating there has been, as in the rest of Estonia, a tendency to shift to individual electric heating.

In the beginning, the company also owned and operated the firewood collection, transport and chipping operation. However, this proved both inefficient and costly, and woodchips are now provided by three suppliers on a solid-volume basis. Environmental considerations of noise and dust produced in the chipping process have also led to the change to off-site operation.

The forest boundary is hard to define under these circumstances since the suppliers to the sawmill and wood manufacturing company have not been identified, though local farmers are involved. The sustainability of the fuel cannot be fully guaranteed; however, from the point of view of the alternatives of landfill disposal or burning without energy production, the fuel has been assumed to be CO_2 neutral.

Võru

Võru is a small town of 18,000 people in the south-eastern part of Estonia near the border with Russia. There are two main plants in the town with separate networks which are planned to merge in the future. The boiler plant which NUTEK has funded has three oil-fired boilers dating from 1988. One boiler has been converted to woodchips by fitting a pre-furnace (7MW) and associated equipment. It has also a new 4.5MW oil burner for peak or low-load operation. The addition of this small boiler has not been successful due to a number of factors. The boiler, for example, was not designed for heavy-fuel oil and burner damage has occurred. Communication problems and design mistakes have compounded the problem. As a result, one of the two original boilers is normally used to meet peak load, though this is inefficient. Generally, there has been a drastic fall in demand due to industrial customers switching to their own boilers or to electric heating.

Woodchips are supplied under contract with a limit of 25 per cent for bark and sawdust and a moisture content of 35–50 per cent. Sawdust is supplied free in the summer. Eight firms supply the plant and the price is fixed at 50 EEK/m^3 on a volume basis. The woodchip suppliers appear to have formed a cartel. Only one company uses forest thinnings, which represent about 20 per cent of the fuel. The rest use waste wood from sawmills. During the summer, it is still necessary to take fuel supplies, which are stored on asphalt ground when the silos are full.

Kardašova Řečice

This town is in southern Bohemia (the Czech Republic) close to the border with Austria. An unused 2.5MW boiler in a pencil-making factory was converted to supply heat to local apartment blocks. Until this time, heat was produced by inefficient individual boilers supplied by brown coal and some wood. Hence, the project also involved the construction of a new district-heating network. The Austrian government provided a grant for the cost of the project, which was constructed by an Austrian company. The supply of waste wood for the boiler came from the manufacture of pencils. The network belongs to the municipality while the factory owns the boiler.

Mrakotin

This project is also based in the Czech Republic. A new district-heating boiler house with two boilers (1.8MW and 1.0MW) fuelled by biomass, together with a new district-heating distribution network, has been built to substitute single boilers in apartment blocks chiefly based on brown coal. The project has not been visited either by the Austrian funders or as part of this study, and hence there is little further detail.

Staré Město

Staré Město is a small town of about 1000 people in southern Bohemia near the Austrian border and is surrounded by forest. The project is a district-heating boiler with fuel storage at the edge of the town. Previously, the flats and houses were heated individually with coal. However, a new network has been installed for 600 homes and public buildings and there are plans to extend this. The district-heating plant has two biomass boilers of 1.0MW and 1.8MW. It is owned by the municipality, which also owns the surrounding 60ha of forest from which the woodchips come. These wood thinnings used to be left to rot or were burned in the forest. Now they are chipped and delivered to the site, and therefore we consider this to be a CO_2-neutral practice. The woodchip costs are in the labour to chip and to transport to site. Sawdust is also delivered to the plant and mixed with the chippings to a maximum burn of 50 per cent, but the proportion is normally less. There are also sawmills and another large boiler conversion in the area; however, this is not expected to affect the local supply. The project was funded by the Austrian government.

Velesin

Some of the heat from a central boiler house (Jihostrij AG) based on brown coal has been substituted by two new decentralized boiler houses with natural gas boilers (1.2MW and 4.6MW). The main motivations for this project have been to reduce local pollution from brown coal, and to improve the efficiency of the heat supply, which was suffering from large network losses. Again, the project has not been visited either by the Austrian funders or as part of this study, and hence there is little further detail.

Demand-Side Management Projects

This study examined one demand-side management project in Estonia, in which energy efficiency measures were carried out in apartment blocks near Tallinn.

Mustamäe

This is an apartment block insulation project in Tallinn in Estonia and was carried out in three separate phases. We have only carried out analysis of the second two phases. The project was implemented through a loan from NUTEK to the city council.

In the first phase, a demonstration pilot project was implemented in one building during 1994/95. Based on this study, a second phase of four apartment blocks was undertaken as a demonstration of energy savings on a larger scale. There were significant problems with windows and doors and leaking roofs and piping. The entrance doors were left open even on extremely cold days. The project replaced roof insulation, entrance doors and weather stripping, and installed new substations in the building and improved heat balancing. The measures carried out have been tailored to the specific requirements of the building. A study was carried out to compare the operation of the newly insulated house with a similar block nearby. Before the project was implemented there was a large (4°C) temperature difference between the roof flats and the rest of the building. The new measures equalized the temperatures through the block, but there are signs that people still open windows to allow for the flow of air to which they have become accustomed.

In the third phase, four cooperatives and seven buildings were involved, again financed through a NUTEK loan. The results of the energy saving estimations seemed to imply that the cooperatively owned buildings manage their energy consumption better than do the municipally owned blocks.

The data used in the calculations are taken from the official data provided by NUTEK. No site visit was undertaken.

Electricity-Supply Projects

Two electricity-supply substitution projects were examined. Both of these consisted of the substitution of grid-supplied electricity with wind power.

Jeseník

Jeseník is a small town of about 8000 people at the far eastern part of the Czech Republic in the mountains. The wind farm, which is privately owned but which received a nominal grant from the Danish government, is at the edge of a national park and encountered opposition from the park management for the area. It consists of six 0.5MW wind turbines 40m high on the crest of a hill and these are visible for at least 8km, creating a visual impact. The farm does not operate efficiently as the wind measurements for the feasibility study were taken at 10m while the towers at 40m have a different wind regime. There have been problems in operating the turbines due to icing problems in winter and a fire caused by flooding in the transformer section from heavy rains during the summer of 1997. The cost of the electricity to run the turbines, while there are low wind speeds, is much higher than the price paid for any electricity generated, which is subject to very stringent tariff structures by the newly privatized but monopolistic Czech electricity-supply company.

Lettland

The data for the Lettland wind farm, in Latvia, were provided by the Institute for Industrial Production at the University of Karlsruhe. For the purposes of this study, the Lettland project has been assessed as though it were based in the Czech Republic.

Cogeneration Projects

The study investigated one combined heat and power project, namely the gas-fired cogeneration plant at Děčín in the Czech Republic.

Děčín

There are now two gas-fired cogeneration plants at Děčín. The newer one, at Zelenice, received a grant from the Danish government and is otherwise funded by the Termo company. The older plant at Bynov is the only approved Czech AIJ project assessed in this study. The project succeeded in gaining funding through the mediation of the Centre for Clean Air Policy in Prague and involved three US utilities, Denmark and the Czech Environment Fund.

Both plants are connected to a central heating network and supply heat to municipal buildings and flats in the area. They use telemetry to control the buildings and find faults. They also supply electricity to the grid and, as with Jeseník, the price paid depends on the time of day, the day of the week and the season. For example, high tariff times are between 0700–0900 am and 1800–2000 pm; 1200–1400 pm is a medium tariff time and 2100–0000 pm is a low tariff time. During the summer, the plants only supply to the grid at peak times and are switched off otherwise.

Both plants replace old brown-coal (lignite) fired boilers and supply the same set of apartment buildings as before. The AIJ plant at Bynov serves 50 buildings with 60 flats in each and has an exchange station at each building; however, unlike Zelenice, it does not have full central control. The system also allows electricity production without heat supply. The network is new (4km) with the longest pipe being 2.1km and sustaining a loss in temperature from 100°C to 96°C. Monitoring is carried out once a year by a certified laboratory.

Training given for operating the plant involved one week on the plant and one week on the engines. The engines receive a two-year guarantee and every ten years they need a major service. Bynov uses only 60 per cent of the capacity of the plant.

One further point to note about the AIJ cogeneration plant at Děčín is that demand is expected to decrease over the next five years due to further investment in network efficiency over this time. This will partly be offset by increasing demand, but the overall effect is a net drop of 13 per cent over five years.

Conclusions

This chapter has set the scene in terms of the projects which have been analysed in detail within this study. Using real projects has provided an insight into the realities of data availability and collection, the performance of these projects and the country contexts in which they operate. It has also allowed full exploration of possible baselines, sources of uncertainty and the implications of different approaches. The divergence between available information and the data requirements for assessment, as well as the diversity of conditions at each site and the specific conditions that are inherent within each country, are used in the study to ground our view of JI according to what really happens with JI projects.

In summary, we set out the following conclusions from the data-collection phase of this study. In order to construct baselines for credible emission-reduction unit (ERU) calculations under article 6 of the Kyoto Protocol, reliable project data are necessary. In order for the data to be of the correct standard, we suggest that there should be guidelines for acquiring key data during the design, approval and reporting stage of projects. Data for technical as well as environmental and social aspects need to be actively collected. For example, some projects did not have output monitoring and this should be included at the design stage. There is a real need to verify that the project actually exists in the form represented by the data: in one case we found that the project description was totally misleading. In all cases there appeared to be minimal training of operators in the new technology, and it was generally agreed from the interviews that more training would have been beneficial. In one case, the lack of appropriate training has led to a decrease in the life of the plant. For the biomass plant, it was obvious that the CO_2 neutrality of the wood source is a major factor which needs to be included in the project system boundary for monitoring and verification. Where a country also has forest sinks, some safeguard is required to prevent double counting of the forest as a sink and as a CO_2-neutral source.

The country contexts illustrate the need to take specific country conditions into account during the construction of baselines. Significant differences in the structure of energy sectors and environmental legislation can exist even for countries which appear to be broadly similar.

6

Environmental and Social Aspects of Joint Implementation: Methodologies and Case Study Results

M Chadwick, K Begg, G Haq and T Jackson

Introduction

This chapter explores the issue of the need for joint implementation (JI) actions to address environmental and social impacts. These impacts are not the ones arising from JI projects specifically in terms of the desired reduction in greenhouse gas (GHG) emissions that the action is intended to achieve. They are the other potential environmental and social impacts that follow from the changes wrought in the course of the JI action – in fact, a much broader set of impacts.

The chapter will briefly give the background to activities implemented jointly (AIJ) to reduce GHG emissions. It then discusses the non-climate change related context of environmental impacts of JI. There follows a review of the procedures available for assessing these and other social impacts. Each assessment process is presented first in terms of the framework and general procedures that form its basis; examples are then given, where relevant, of the use of the assessment methodology and its procedures. Results are presented from JI projects in Estonia and the Czech Republic and are assessed by using one of these approaches: the environmental impact assessment (EIA) approach. Finally, this chapter suggests ways of encouraging progress in implementing environmental and social assessments of JI projects under the Kyoto Protocol and discusses what form such impact assessments ideally might take.

The Environmental Context of Joint Implementation

All fuel use, for whatever purpose, has environmental impacts. Fossil fuels, hydro-power, nuclear energy, biomass use, wind or wave power all result in impacts on the environment when utilized as sources of heat, or generate electricity to provide power for industry, transport, commerce, agriculture or domestic use. One impact is the emission of carbon dioxide (CO_2) and other GHGs; but there are also many other impacts resulting from other gaseous emissions, from liquid effluent flows and from solid waste generation. Just as a change from one fuel and generating facility may result in a change in the level of GHG emission, so it also may result in a shift in other environmental impacts.

Very little attention has so far been paid to the full range of potential environmental impacts that may ensue from JI projects. The potential environmental impacts embrace a range of agents that can cause environmental harm. These include gases, water vapour, aerosols and particulates dispersed to the atmosphere, effluent with chemical loads and suspended solids disposed of in water courses and on land, and the disposal of solid waste to surface areas or subsurface cavities. These impacts may variously result from the exploration of fuel sources, from mining and other methods of fuel gaining, from its processing, storage and transport, and from conversion and utilization processes. As well as any disbenefits from these activities, benefits may also accrue. The scale and balance of the benefits and disbenefits may be altered and this needs assessing: the impacts may be mainly on the local environment but may also have more widespread regional or national consequences.

The impacts of JI projects may also be of social and economic significance. Potential social impacts need to be evaluated when JI projects are proposed. This is particularly important since the whole issue of the equity of the arrangements is central to JI (see Chapter 3). It would be paradoxical if the emphasis on fairness in the JI process was found to be offset in terms of unequal social disbenefits in the wider social sphere, through its implementation.

As originally envisaged in the UN Framework Convention on Climate Change (FCCC) process, JI did not imply any necessity for an evaluation of the environmental and social impacts of the proposed projects. However, the language both in the FCCC and the Kyoto Protocol seems to indicate that these aspects are important to the aims of the convention. Moreover, some countries have required such impacts to be evaluated as a condition of their participation and approval during the AIJ pilot phase (Michaelowa et al, 1999). The Netherlands requires that the project is beneficial locally, both socially and environmentally, and in line with the host country's development priorities. The German programme calls for a scientific analysis of the positive and negative consequences of projects, but this is in order that the results of such an analysis might be utilized to guide future practice, not to form the basis of current approval procedures.

Furthermore, the uniform reporting format (URF) established under the AIJ pilot phase provides no real guidance concerning environmental and social assessment of AIJ projects. There is a section under which the environmental and social benefits of the projects can be reported. But negative environmental and social impacts are relegated to a section at the end on 'additional comments (if any)'! Neither section imposes any requirement or provides any guidance towards appropriate environmental and social assessment procedures for JI projects. Article 12.2 of the Kyoto Protocol declares that assisting developing countries in achieving sustainable development is one of the principal aims of the clean development mechanism (CDM). However, there is no guidance on how this is to be achieved.

There are two main reasons why JI projects have not had mandatory environmental or social impacts included as part of their approval procedures. Firstly, there is a tacit assumption that the host country, which must approve projects before they can proceed, has a regulatory framework in place in respect of environmental and social issues. If the host country raises no objections to the project, it is assumed that it complies with such regulations which, in turn, will be enforced. Such assumptions are not necessarily justified. The qualifications surrounding some transition economy countries being brought into the European Union (EU), because the environmental standards and regulations in place in these countries do not meet the minimum framework for EU law, bear witness to the shortcomings in the prevailing regulations for environmental protection.

There is by no means agreement on the framework and processes that could form the basis of environmental and social assessment. There are many procedures that can be, and have been, used for EIA and, to a lesser extent, for social impact assessment (SIA). Other options exist that could be adapted for such a purpose. So far, however, it is rather early in the process for agreed procedures to have been evolved, and none has been identified as the most suitable for JI actions. This chapter will present and explore the approaches that might be suitable for adoption and give examples where environmental and social impact assessments have been applied.

It is important to address the 'non-climate change related' environmental and social impacts of JI projects, at a local, regional and national scale, for the following reasons:

- It is unlikely to make sense to institute actions that help to solve climate change related impacts if these are 'exchanged' for a set of other significant environmental and social impacts, unless a clear and rational analysis of the balance of impacts, in relation to environmental and social priorities, has been explored. This requires that appropriate assessments have been undertaken and evaluated.
- If negative environmental and social impacts ensue from JI actions, it is important that these are recognized and solutions sought in order that they are not repeated if further JI actions are taken.
- Environmental and social impacts may act as precursors of further impacts that will follow with time, and this possibility should be investigated.
- If impacts can be minimized, subsequent JI actions will find more willing acceptance.
- If impacts are assessed in advance, in a transparent manner, local participation in the acceptance of such impacts, or in collaboration to avoid the disbenefits, will be easier to obtain and decrease the chance of the JI actions becoming failures.

- JI projects require investment and it is prudent to take steps to ensure that the benefits of such investment are maximized and the disbenefits are minimal. This can only be achieved if impacts are recognized, assessed and evaluated and the environmental and social costs internalized in the activity.

Methods of Environmental and Social Impact Assessment

Environmental impact assessment (EIA), often with an accompanying environmental impact statement (EIS), is a well-established method of investigating the potential impacts that development projects are likely to have. Although social impacts are sometimes included in an EIA, social impact assessment (SIA) has been developed to avoid the tendency to ignore social impacts or regard them as secondary. Furthermore, the process of strategic environmental assessment (SEA) has also evolved as a means of assessing the impacts that result from actions that go beyond an individual project – the impacts of a policy, plan or programme.

Along with the development of EIA, other environmental impact assessment frameworks and procedures have been devised. Eurostat, together with the European Environmental Agency (EEA), has developed a DPSIR framework of assessment (EEA, 1999) that links driving forces (D) to an environmental pressure (P) giving rise to a state (S) in which an impact (I) is exerted, requiring some response (R).

Impact assessment procedures usually require some method of quantification and of tracking environmental trends over time. This also enables valid comparisons to be made from one location or sector to another. *Indicators* have been developed and employed for these purposes.

There has also been much activity in using the concept of the fuel cycle to delimit energy system boundaries and to trace the pathways of impact and damage. Finally, estimates of the monetary cost of those *external costs*, or externalities, not included, or only partially included, in the cost of the service or product can be attempted.

Environmental Impact Assessment (EIA)

The EIA tool, and the accompanying EIS, came into being in the late 1960s and early 1970s (Catlow and Thirwell, 1976; O'Riordan and Hey, 1978; Wathern, 1988; Morris and Therivel, 1995; Glasson et al, 1994) for actions 'significantly affecting the quality of the human environment'. By today, a large number of international organizations, national governments, bilateral and multilateral development agencies and banks (such as the World Bank, 1991; EBRD, 1996) have established environmental guidelines to ensure consideration is given to the environment in the implementation of development projects.

The EIA Framework

From the many guidelines that exist for EIA, a set of procedures emerges that usually includes:

- screening, consisting of a review of the environmental components likely to be affected;
- a scoping exercise to identify what the key impacts are likely to be and what constitutes the main impact area;
- identification of which environmental parameters, of those components that are likely to suffer impacts, will be measured;
- collection of data, both primary and derived, on these parameters to give baseline data, which are then evaluated;
- documentation of the project to be undertaken (and possible alternatives);
- prediction and evaluation of the impacts of the project (impact prediction);
- proposal of mitigation measures;
- development of a monitoring schedule for implementation during construction work;
- assignation of relative importance to the impact components;
- preparation of an EIS.

Figure 6.1 summarizes this process. Table 6.1 gives, as an example, the kind of matrices that result from a more general and typical EIA process.

The Application of EIA

EIA represents an existing and practiced set of procedures that can be applied to JI projects. In the study on which this book is based, ten projects were assessed for non-climate change environmental and social impacts. Full details of these projects are given in Chapter 5, and the results from the application of a retrospective EIA approach to the ten JI projects are summarized later in this chapter.

Strategic Environmental Assessment (SEA)

Usually the actions evaluated by EIA are one-off projects. These may be projects with large potential environmental impacts, such as the construction of a large combustion plant, extending a major road system, an industrial installation or developing an area for housing or leisure activities. However, over the last 10 to 15 years, there has also developed an interest in the environmental impacts of policies, plans and programmes (PPPs) – actions that go beyond an individual project and may bring about far-reaching and long-term impacts on society. To assess this represents a form of policy appraisal and shifts the focus of assessment of environmental impacts from the project to the strategic level (see Figure 6.2). The process is known as strategic environmental assessment (SEA). An SEA may be linked to budget proposals or national development plans. Thus, it may accompany policies for implementation at the local, regional or national or international level. SEA may also be

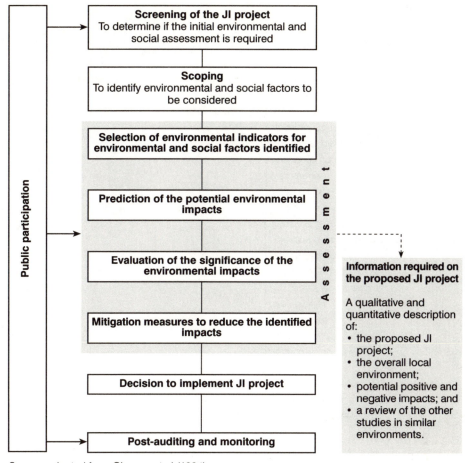

Source: adapted from Glasson et al (1994)

Figure 6.1 *EIA Procedures as Applied to JI Projects*

combined with more exploratory procedures, such as the development of scenarios, and is now seen as particularly relevant in terms of promoting sustainable development.

It is not difficult to appreciate the potential of SEA for JI. Where there is a concerted attempt to promote actions implemented jointly within a region or country, the combined actions are likely to constitute a policy initiative, an overall plan of action or a specific action programme. The relevance of an SEA approach will then be evident and may also be used to evaluate the impacts compared to the prevailing conditions in the absence of such a programme.

The SEA Framework

SEA is a 'formalized, systematic and comprehensive process for evaluating the environmental impacts of a policy, plan or programme and its alternatives'

Table 6.1 Example of an Impact Assessment Matrix

Characteristics of the existing situation	Construction																	Operation																		
	Land requirements	Site situation	Labour requirements	Company expenditure patterns	Raw material inputs	Transport of raw materials	Transport of employees	Water demand	Electricity demand	Gas demand	Population changes	Noise and vibration	Particulate emissions	Dust	Aqueous discharges	Solid waste disposal	Emergencies	Site utilization	Permanent labour requirements	Company expenditure patterns	Raw material inputs	Transport of raw materials	Transport of employees	Transport of products	Water supply	Gas supply	Population changes	Noise from plant	Vibrations from plant	Gaseous emissions	Particulate emissions	Odours from plant	Dust	Aqueous discharges	Solid wastes	Emergencies
Land																																					
Water																																					
Climate																																					
Land use																																					
Landscape quality																																					
Ecological characteristics																																					
Resident population																																					
Employment structure																																					
Traffic movement																																					
Electricity supply																																					
Gas supply																																					
Water supply																																					
Sewerage																																					
Solid waste disposal																																					
Transportation																																					
Finance																																					
Education																																					
Housing																																					
Health service facilities																																					
Emergency services																																					
Air pollution																																					
Water pollution																																					
Noise and vibration																																					

Source: O'Riordan and Hey (1976)

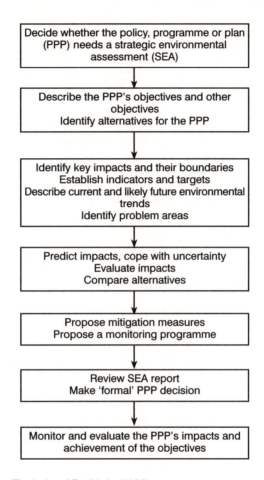

Source: adapted from Therivel and Partidario (1996)

Figure 6.2 *Strategic Environmental Assessment Relationships*

(Therivel et al, 1992). A framework for the preparation of a SEA is given in Table 6.2.

The Application of SEA

SEAs have played a role in the investigation of alternative energy strategies. Some of the alternatives explored are those which are employed when a JI project involves the replacement of, for example, a fossil-fuel electricity generating plant by a plant that produces reduced GHG emissions, as is claimed for wind farms. The other environmental benefits (and disbenefits) also require assessment. Kleinschmidt et al (1994) attempted such a strategic assessment in the Northern Rhine region of Germany and the result is shown in Table 6.3.

Table 6.2 *Stages in a Strategic Environmental Assessment*

Stage	Action
1	Decide whether the programme warrants a SEA.
2	Describe the programme's objectives; identify the alternatives; describe the programme.
3	Establish the system boundaries and identify the key impacts; establish indicators and targets; describe the current and likely future environmental baseline; identify problem areas.
4	Predict impacts making uncertainties transparent; evaluate impacts; compare alternatives.
5	Propose mitigation measures; prepare monitoring programme outline.
6	Prepare the SEA report.
7	Monitor and evaluate the impacts.

Source: adapted from Therivel and Partidario (1996)

Social Impact Assessment (SIA)

SIA developed in the 1970s and 1980s in recognition of the wider range of impacts that were becoming evident during EIA studies. It seemed as if economic and social issues ran the risk of being treated only superficially or being marginalized if confined to sections within an EIA. Indeed, SIA has sometimes been characterized as a 'Heineken' approach – an attempt to include all those vitally important but often intangible impacts that other assessments cannot reach! However, it is a way of estimating and appraising the conditions of a society organized and changed by the application of technology (Wolf, 1974). Bowles (1981) describes the process as a way of assessing 'impacts on the day-to-day quality of life of people and communities when the environment is affected by development or change'.

SIA Framework

In SIA, interest focuses on demographic issues, such as population increase, immigration or change in structure; housing and accommodation; services, such as education, health and social care; and also the incidence of crime and deviancy. Employment patterns, income levels and the pattern of household expenditure are also of interest. Life styles and community features such as integration, cultural traits and gender issues are also addressed, particularly to identify trends and changes that can be linked to external actions. Table 6.4 gives an outline of the variables attempted in an SIA (Burdge, 1989; Glasson, 1995).

There are a number of decisions to be made in addressing the variables shown in Table 6.4. These include the time period over which they should be considered, the geographical area of interest, variations in the impacts (rather than just the average effects – the winners as well as the losers in the community) and the question of real versus perceived impacts. Details related to certain energy-sector developments will be presented in the next section.

Table 6.3 *The Possible Impacts of Wind Farms*

Criteria for:	Land use	Noise	Landscape impact	Bird strike	Disturbance of fauna	Electro-magnetic disturbance
Exclusion and restricted areas						
Electrical transmission corridor						✔
Nature conservation areas	✔	✔	✔		✔	
Area for the protection of the natural environment						
Scarcity of birds in Soest district	✔			✔	✔	
Existence of Red List bird species	✔			✔	✔	
Structural diversity	✔		✔		✔	
National/regional/local importance	✔		✔	✔	✔	
Biotype in accordance with National Nature Conservation regulations[1]	✔		✔		✔	
Area for nature protection	✔	✔	✔		✔	
Bird migration route				✔	✔	
Area for the protection of landscape						
Landscape conservation area	✔				✔	
Landscape protection area	✔		✔		✔	
Protected parts of the landscape	✔	✔	✔		✔	
Floodplains	✔	✔	✔		✔	
Area for the protection of recreational suitability						
Recreation area	✔					
Relaxation/convalesence area	✔	✔	✔			
Health resort/spa	✔	✔				

Source: Kleinschmidt et al (1994)

Table 6.4 *Social Impact Assessment Variables*

Variable
Demography
population structure and size
population growth rate
family size and changes with time
settlement patterns
Economy
employment levels
employment characteristics (skill groups, gender)
labour supply and training
Households
household size and variation
residence size and domestic facilities
household income and expenditure
housing tenure
homelessness
Community infrastructure
governance and participation
cultural, religious and other groupings
social networks
planning processes
Local services
education
health and social support
other services (leisure, transport, police, fire, commerce)
Sociocultural
lifestyle and quality of life
illness and social deviancy
community stress and conflict; group integration

Application of SIA

It is unlikely that the adaptation of relatively small facilities – from coal combustion to gas burning, or from lignite combustion to the use of biomass as a fuel, would have large impacts on, say, population features, employment structure or income levels. However, the institution of full-scale change in a region could have a significant impact on certain social components, and social assessments are necessary to display – in a transparent manner – that JI projects are not disadvantaging host country communities in the cause of cost-effective GHG emission reductions.

The scale of the socioeconomic impacts regarding a 'new' development in the energy sector can be gauged by the cause-and-effect relationships illustrated in Figure 6.3. Socioeconomic impacts of JI programmes need a full treatment of the kind indicated by this diagram.

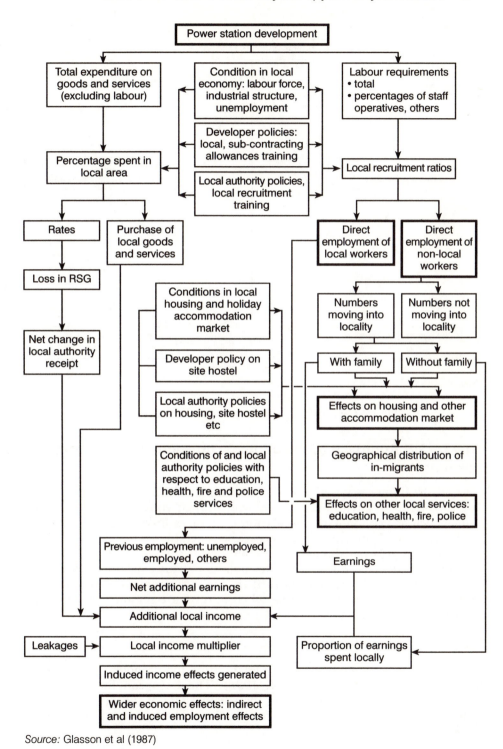

Source: Glasson et al (1987)

Figure 6.3 *A Cause-and-Effect Diagram for the Local Socioeconomic Impacts of a Power Station Development*

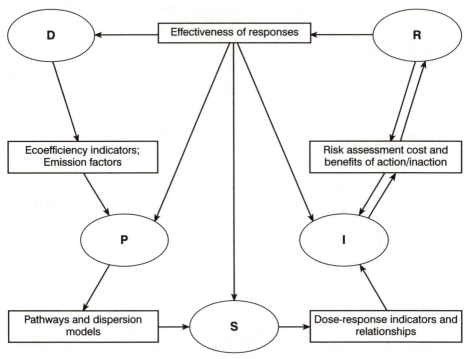

Source: EEA (1999)

Figure 6.4 *Concepts Linking the DPSIR Elements*

The DPSIR Approach (driving forces, pressure, state, impact, response)

The DPSIR framework is a way of representing a chain of causal links relating the origins of environmental problems to their consequences. A *driving force*, such as economic or population growth, is linked with a *pressure*, such as increased emissions and other waste generation, which leads, in turn, to a particular physical, chemical or biological *state*, such as reduced air quality or an increased level of water pollution. This constitutes an *impact* on the ecosystem (or human health) that is measurable and should lead eventually to a political *response*, where targets are set and priorities for action are established.

DPSIR Framework

This approach was initiated by the Organization for Economic Cooperation and Development (OECD) (1994, 1996). The European Environmental Agency's studies of the current and foreseeable state of the environment in Europe (EEA, 1999) have used this methodology. The framework is shown in diagrammatic form in Figure 6.4.

Application of DPSIR

The DPSIR approach has also been applied, in part, to Central and Eastern Europe. Denisov et al (1997) attempt to assess the 'state of the environment' country by country by this method.

A method of analysis such as DPSIR, that links causes of environmental impacts to consequences, could be applied in the field of JI actions. In developing the DPSIR approach, OECD (1994) placed emphasis on the identification of 'indicators' necessary to give 'reliable, readable, measurable and policy-relevant' environmental signposts of changes and trends.

Indicators

In any complex system there is a need for some indication of the existing condition and, through quantification, the direction and scale of change and the way in which this change may be linked to the stresses and changes that occur within the system. Such indications are sought in the establishment of *indicators* for environmental and social conditions. They have been developed implicitly and explicitly over many decades (Inhaber, 1976; Moldan and Bilharz, 1997).

The concept of an indicator is not a simple one (Gallopin, 1997). An indicator is a system variable that represents an attribute of the system, of which a description is obtained in terms of its quality, characteristic or property. The description is defined in terms of a specific measure. Emissions to the atmosphere are indicators of an environmental pressure; the outcome of these emissions, such as the pH of precipitation, is an indicator of the environmental state.

If appropriate indicators were set up and used simultaneously for JI projects or groups of projects, it would be possible to obtain a picture of the environmental conditions that formed an environmental quality profile. Such a profile is a generalization of conditions and can be compared to a profile where actions were not undertaken, as part of joint implementation.

Fuel-Cycle Approach

The use of a fuel-cycle approach allows system boundaries to be clearly established and a systematic treatment applied within these boundaries. For example, the generation of electricity may occur from the use of coal, gas, oil, biomass and nuclear fuel, as well as other fuels, or through the use of hydropower, wind energy, wave energy or solar power. Using a fuel-cycle approach, it is possible to distinguish phases of the overall process that are relevant to a total environmental impact assessment. These phases include:

- production and construction of materials;
- transport of construction material;
- plant construction;
- fuel exploration;
- fuel extraction;

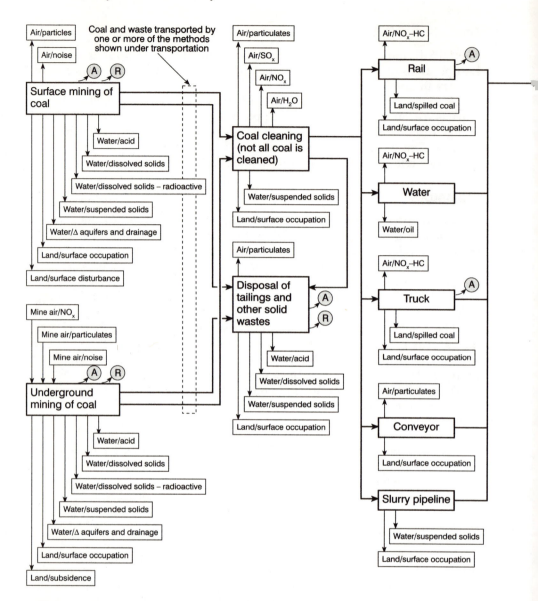

Source: Chadwick (1990)

Figure 6.5 *An Effects Diagram for Coal to Electricity Generation*

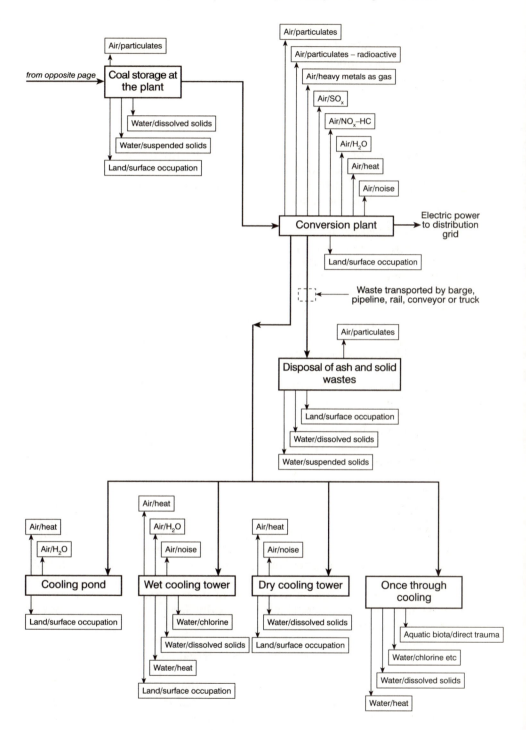

- fuel processing;
- transportation of fuel;
- transport of personnel;
- storage of fuel;
- waste production from fuel conversion;
- waste treatment;
- removal of plant at the end of its service lifetime.

The consequences of these stages may include aquatic and atmospheric impacts, as well as impacts to the land surface itself (occupation, disturbance, disposal facilities and subsidence), However, it is important to define the technological details of the system in order to predict the nature of the impacts accurately.

The well-defined nature of the fuel-cycle approach allows a comparison of impacts to be made in a manner that is more structured, since the impacts are confined to similar facets of the process. As well as environmental aspects, this approach has been well developed for the comparison of human health risks (Hamilton, 1982; 1984).

The fuel-cycle concept has contributed greatly to the definition of system boundaries in assessing environmental impacts associated with the energy sector. It is equally important to designate system boundaries for JI projects. Careful consideration of the potential impacts resulting from the construction and operation of an electricity-generating plant or district-heating plant, for example, will suggest the range of activities that may contribute to the overall environmental impacts.

One of the virtues of adopting rigorous system boundaries is that the validity of comparisons between systems is significantly strengthened. Figures 6.5 and 6.6 give a schematic representation of potential impacts from the use of two different fuels.

Externalities

In the context of environmental impacts, an external cost, or externality, arises when the social or economic activities of one group, through environmental modification, are not fully accounted for by the first group. The full cost of the operation has not been taken into account. Thus, by adopting an externalities approach, it is possible to move the analysis from the pressure, through the state, to the impacts and on to the *cost* of these impacts. Monetary valuation of environmental impacts is not universally acceptable. There are moral and practical objections; nevertheless, in society there is an allocation of resources and services according to a willingness and ability to pay.

One approach that seeks to fully assess external costs of energy systems is the ExternE project of the EU (see Holland et al, 1999). This study has sought to make explicit the costs imposed on society, and the environment, that are not accounted for by the producers and consumers of energy and thus are not included in the market price. Traditional economic assessment has tended to ignore such impacts. It has addressed issues such as discounting and how to deal with irreversible damage. The methodology has been applied now to a wide

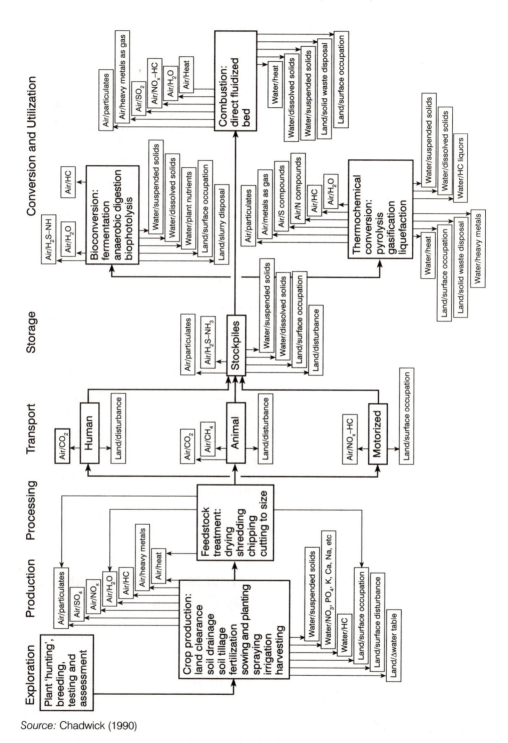

Source: Chadwick (1990)

Figure 6.6 *An Effects Diagram for Biomass Combustion and Conversion*

Table 6.5 *The Function, Fuel Conversion, Location and Host Country*
of the JI Projects

	Conversion from	to	Site and Host Country
Heat supply	HFO	Biomass	Türi, Estonia
	HFO	Biomass	Haabneeme, Estonia
	HFO	Biomass	Valga, Estonia
	HFO	Biomass	Võru, Estonia
	HFO/Gas	Biomass	Aardla, Tartu, Estonia
	Brown Coal	Biomass	Staré Město, Czech Republic.
	Brown Coal	Biomass	Kardašova, Czech Republic.
	Brown Coal	Biomass	Mrakotin, Czech Republic
Cogeneration	Brown Coal	Natural Gas	Děčín, Czech Republic
Electricity generation	Brown Coal	Wind	Jeseník, Czech Republic

range of different fossil fuel, nuclear and renewable fuel cycles (so far 12) for power generation and energy conservation options. The impacts are quantified and the evaluation made in monetary terms in a transparent and consistent way.

Significant problems still haunt the monetarization of external costs of energy-sector projects. Nevertheless, it is clear that real, economic costs are associated with energy supply and distribution. Decision-making processes which ignore these costs are consequently flawed and liable to lead to the implementation of inappropriate technologies. External costing establishes an accounting framework for comparative assessments that can be applied to a range of different fuel-use systems (Holland et al, 1999), and represents an approach that could potentially be used in evaluating the environmental actions undertaken jointly within the Kyoto Protocol.

A further approach to evaluating external environmental and social impacts is provided by decision analysis. This approach does not attempt to monetarize the costs of these impacts. But it can deal with criteria which are difficult to monetarize by integrating them in a systematic way within the decision-making process. This approach is discussed in some detail in Chapter 10.

A Retrospective Environmental Impact Assessment for Case Study Projects

Recognizing the need to make some kind of assessment of the environmental and social impacts of JI projects, this study has applied a limited, retrospective EIA (see Table 6.1) to ten JI projects in Estonia and the Czech Republic (Jackson et al, 1999). A listing of these projects with the plant function, the fuel conversion and the location and host country of each is given in Table 6.5.

Many JI projects are relatively minor adaptations of existing facilities, and the filing of a complicated and detailed EIA would be inappropriate. However, a set of guidelines for preparing the main environmental and social impacts that

Table 6.6 *Environmental and Social Factors Addressed in the JI Projects*

Factor	
Air	Emissions of SO_2, NO_x, CO, particulates and heavy metals
Visual impacts	Qualitative assessment
Transport	Number of journeys, distance travelled
Socioeconomic	Employment, income levels, cost of services
Water	Discharge of polluting effluent
Land use	Type and occupation density
Human health (occupational and public)	Accidents, noise and disturbance
Waste	Production rate and disposal
Forestry	Source of feedstock

can be foreseen would help considerably in an overall assessment of the non-climate change aspects of JI actions. The environmental and social aspects that were addressed are shown in Table 6.6. This is a considerably truncated group of factors, but they represent what was feasible in terms of the available data.

A detailed example of the EIA carried out for one site – Türi (Estonia) where a district-heating system was converted from heavy-fuel oil (HFO) to biomass combustion – is provided in Table 6.7. An overall integrated assessment of the results of this EIA appears in Box 6.1. A summary of the changes detected for all ten sites is given in Table 6.8 and a more detailed comparison for one factor, emissions to the atmosphere, before and after adaptation of the plants is shown in Table 6.9.

It is worth recording that, for the ten JI projects, non-climate change environmental and social impacts resulting from the adaptation of the plants showed only minimal alteration in terms of land-use features, water quality, soil contamination, visual effects, accident rate, forestry, noise energy consumption, or any of the socioeconomic variables (see Table 6.8). An overall improvement in emissions to the atmosphere, normalized on a MWh basis, was detected, mainly in terms of SO_2 and NO_x (see Table 6.9). Particulate emissions were reduced at some plants but increased at others. On the other hand, plants converted to biomass combustion from HFO and gas showed a higher solid waste output but a lower one for those converted from the use of brown coal. For one conversion, the price of heat delivered to the consumer showed a significant price increase following conversion to biomass fuel.

Amongst the contributions to atmospheric emissions (and to other kinds of environmental impact such as noise and disturbance) is fuel transport. Particularly, the oil to biomass conversion projects tended to have higher numbers of lorry movements (and consequently higher transport-related emissions) associated with the JI project than with the baseline – a fact not altogether surprising since biomass is a low-density fuel. There may be some potential for reducing these impacts through more efficient collection and distribution systems, but this possibility would require further investigation on a site-by-site basis.

Table 6.7 Environmental and Social Assessment of the District-Heating Plant at Türi, Estonia

Factor	Impact	Indicator	Unit	Reference: HFO boiler (output equivalent to biomass plant)	Project: biomass boiler woodchips (1997)	Project: biomass boiler oil-shale oil (1997)	Change
Air	Emissions of SO_x, NO_x, CO, particulates and heavy metals	Quantity of SO_2 emitted from the plant	tonne/year	64 estimated	1 estimated	0.09 as SO_2	++
		Quantity of NO_x emitted from the plant	tonne/year	9 estimated	2 estimated	0.03	+
		Quantity of CO emitted from the plant	tonne/year	1 estimated	31 estimated	0.09	—
		Quantity of particulate matter emitted from the plant	tonne/year		soot and dust 6	0.02	+
		Type and quantity of heavy metals emitted from the plant	tonne/year			V, Zn, etc; not measured but considered to be an insignificant amount	0

Factor	Impact	Indicator	Unit	Reference: HFO boiler (output equivalent to biomass plant)	Project: biomass boiler	Change
Water		Amount of discharge from the plant	m³/year	sewage – 720	sewage – 720	0
		Concentration and type of pollutant discharge	mg/m³	sewage, bathing water and toilets	sewage water, phosphorous, biological oxygen demand (BOD)	0

Factor	Impact	Indicator	Unit	Reference: HFO boiler (output equivalent to biomass plant)	Project: biomass boiler	Change
	Discharge of pollution	Destination of discharge	sewer/ river	Via Türi sewerage to Pärmu River	Via Türi sewerage to Pärmu River	0
	Emissions into water	Existing quality of watercourse affected by the discharge		new sewage treatment plant (phosphorus removal) at Türi which has been in operation since 1995	new sewage treatment plant (phosphorous removal) at Türi which has been in operation since 1995	0
		Quality of groundwater in the area			good	0
		Rate of groundwater extraction for the operation of the plant	m^3/year	720	720	0
				In total, drinking, bathing and technological water intake is 1440 m^3/year		
		Number of leakage/spillage events to watercourse	Number/ year	No accidents, storage tanks are well equipped	No accidents, storage tanks are well equipped	
Land use		Number of people in a 10km radius of the plant	number	6970	6980	0
		Distance of the nearest population from the plant	km	0.3–0.5	0.3–0.5	0
		Land use in a 10km radius of the plant		industrial, residential, agricultural	industrial, residential, agricultural	0

Factor	Impact	Indicator	Unit	Reference: HFO boiler (output equivalent to biomass plant)	Project: biomass boiler	Change
		Contamination of soil from the leakage/spillage of oil	State of soil quality on site	area affected and depth	storage 50x80m, soil unaffected.	Oil storage is still in operation as a back-up and peak power support provision, therefore tanks are well maintained. Woodchip and timber storage areas in four locations, altogether around 1 hectare partially affected by solid organic waste
Visual	Effect on	Change in infrastructure of the plant		landscape, visual intrusion from chimney	no change	0
Human health	Occupational health effects	Accident rate and type per year (fatal, serious injuries, injuries)	number/ year	No significant accidents	During a five-year period, two small injuries occurred during the preparation of woodchips	–

Factor	Impact	Indicator	Unit	Reference: HFO boiler (output equivalent to biomass plant)	Project: biomass boiler	Change
Noise	Noise from the operation of the boiler	Noise levels within the plant	decibels (dB)	–	highest noise level inside the building at the control pump 80dB(A)	0
	Disturbance of local residents	Distance of residential area from the plant	km	0.3–0.5	0.3–0.5	
		Noise level at the nearest residential area to the plant	decibels (dB)	not measured	gates and entrance to site 40dB(A)	+
Transport	Air polluting emissions from lorries delivering oil/woodchips	Number of lorry movements	Number/year	230 trips to fill 5000-tonne storage tanks	2–3 times a day, 150 days, 400 trips on average	
		Distance travelled	km	46,000 Tallinn and Kohtla-Järve, both 100km one way	one way 25km, two–three round trips up to 150km daily 22,500	+
		Type of vehicle	petrol/diesel	Zil/MAZ/KMAZ consumption 50l/100km	40l/100km MAZ diesel plus four tractors in use. Total diesel fuel consumption per year = 12,000 tonnes	

Factor	Impact	Indicator	Unit	Reference: HFO boiler (output equivalent to biomass plant)	Project: biomass boiler	Change
Waste	Generation of waste	Type of waste generated		soot	bottom and fly ash	
		Amount of waste generated for each type of waste	tonnes/year	1.2	31	
Forestry	Use of forest resources	Final disposal of waste	landfill/fertilizer	landfill	fertilizers to local farmers.	
		Source of forest fuel		-	1. forest management companies 50% 2. timber exporters 30% 3. Sawmills 15% 4. Farmers 5%.	
Socio-economic	Employment	Number of employees	number	15–16	20	+
		Unemployment rate in the area	%	2%	2%	0
		Population of the town	number	6980 (1996)	6980 (1996)	0
		Level of average wages	EEK	500 monthly gross wage	3200 (1996)	
		Are the wages of the plant higher than average?	%	0.62 (compared to 1992 IV quarter average)	0.97 (1996 IV quarter)	+
		Price of heat	EEK/kWh	0.224	0.3399	–
		Demand for heat	kWh/year	8,500,000 (low demand year)	9,500,000	
		Effect of the project on local businesses	number	positive	good; supports local business	
		Present condition of the local economy		good	good	0

Box 6.1 Statement of the Results of the EIA for the District-Heating Plant at Türi, Estonia

Air and Land Use

In Türi, the biomass plant meets most of the current demand. There has, therefore, been a significant decrease in SO_2 and some decrease in NO_x emitted from the plant due to the replacement of HFO with biomass. The estimated figures calculated for the same demand show the effect on SO_2 clearly. There is some uncertainty in the NO_x emission factor, which makes the decrease in NO_x unclear, while the CO emissions appear to have increased. All the boiler conversions studied in Estonia had multicyclone flue-gas cleaning, which means that though the total solid waste burden is higher, the dust emissions are limited. In the case of Türi, different demand in the different years quoted could mean that there is no change in dust emissions. The decrease in the emissions of SO_2 and NO_x has positive effects on the health of the local population. The plant is situated in an area with a mix of industrial, agricultural and residential land. The number of people in a 10km radius of the plant has increased slightly.

Water

The amount of water discharged from the plant has remained the same at 720m³ per year, which is mainly in the form of sewage and bathing water. The destination of the discharge has also remained the same: the Pämru River via the Türi sewerage system. There has been no change in the existing water quality. This has been helped by a new sewage treatment plant, which came into operation in 1995. The rate of groundwater extraction for the operation of the plant has not changed. There have been no spillage or leakage incidents to watercourses due to the fact that the storage tanks are well equipped. No data were available on the concentration of pollutants in groundwater and freshwater.

Soil

The plant continues to store oil on site to ensure that there is provision to support a peak power demand. Due to the oil being stored in well-maintained tanks, soil quality on site has not been affected by the spillage or leakage of oil. There are four woodchip storage sites, and in total about 1ha is partially affected by solid organic waste.

Visual

There has been no change in the visual impact of the plant due to additional infrastructure. The main visual impact caused by the plant is due to its chimney.

Human health

During a five-year period, two small injuries have occurred at the plant. These injuries were sustained during the preparation of woodchips. The decrease in SO_2 and NO_x emissions has been beneficial for the health of the local population while the increase in CO will have had a negative effect, although this has not been quantified.

Noise

No data were available on noise levels within the plant when the heavy-fuel boiler was in operation. With the biomass boiler, the highest noise level is 80dB (A), which is reached at the control pump. The nearest residential area to the plant is 0.3–0.5km distant. No data were available on noise levels at the residential area and on the number of people affected. However, the noise level at the entrance to the plant is 40dB (A) and there was no noticeable problem during the site visit.

Transport

The transportation of heavy-fuel oil for use in the boiler resulted in 230 trips to fill 5000-tonne storage tanks. The oil was transported from Tallinn and Kohtla-Järve, which are 100km distant from the plant. In total 46,000km were travelled within Estonia to transport oil to the plant. The number of lorry movements due to the boiler conversion has increased, but the total kilometres have decreased. This has been due to the need to transport woodchips to the plant up two to three times a day. On average 400 trips of 50km were undertaken over 150 days. Therefore, the overall kilometres travelled to transport fuel have decreased from 46,000km to 22,500km. The decrease in total kilometres will reduce vehicle-related CO_2 and air pollution, which can contribute to the improvement of local air quality levels. However, the increased frequency of movement will increase traffic-related noise and nuisance.

Waste

The main type of waste generated from the biomass boiler is bottom and fly ash (31 tonnes/year), which is used by local farmers as fertilizer. This is much more than the soot from the heavy-fuel boilers for the whole plant, which was sent to landfill (1.2 tonnes per year).

Forestry

The source of biomass fuel is forest management companies (50 per cent), timber exporters (30 per cent), sawmills (15 per cent) and farmers (5 per cent). Data on the rate of forest felling and plantation, and on whether the initial forest source was managed sustainably, were not available.

Socioeconomic

The number of employees at the plant has increased from 16 to 20. The level of wages has also increased; wages are higher than the average. The price for heat has increased significantly and this is discussed elsewhere. Demand has decreased from the 1990s level of about 50,000kWh to about 8500kWh, which appears to be a fairly stable level in line with the condition of the local economy and is considered to be good. Overall, the impact seems to be positive for employment, but the price of heat has caused problems.

Discussion

The main impact of the plant has been in local air quality. Compared to the high sulphur fuel burned in the reference plant, there is a significant reduction in the emissions of SO_2 with the biomass conversion. There is some possible reduction in NO_x, while CO has increased and the change in particulates is uncertain. The effect of the increase in CO is unknown. The decrease in the total kilometres travelled for fuel deliveries will also contribute to the improvement of local air pollution. There is an increase in the burden of solid waste, though most seems to go as a gift to farmers as fertilizer. This waste will contain heavy metals and is known to be unacceptable as a fertilizer in Austria. The woodchips used come from wood thinnings which, according to the local staff, used to be burned in the forest. As a result, this is a positive improvement in CO_2 reductions. Sawmill waste is also in this category. Most other impact areas given appear to have either improved or remain unaffected by the JI project.

It should also be noted that the exercise described in this section was a fairly limited attempt to account for the non-climate related environmental and social impacts of the projects. Since these projects were already operating, the assessment could only be carried out retrospectively. This in itself gave rise to problems in accessing the appropriate data on which such an assessment should be based. Nevertheless, the exercise provides an illustration not only of what could be achieved, but also of the potential difficulties involved in assessing the environmental and social impacts of JI.

Environmental and Social Impact Assessment: Routine Methods for Joint Implementation Actions

From the language used in the Kyoto Protocol, it is clear that the non-climate change environmental and social impacts of JI projects are regarded as important. This is hardly surprising in view of the emphasis that has been put on the equity principle within the FCCC. Nevertheless, there has been little concerted activity to agree methods generally for evaluating the environmental and social implication of individual JI projects or more far-reaching JI programmes and plans. The Netherlands and Germany have indicated that certain requirements are necessary or desirable in a host country, but there is no overall agreement on objectives, criteria or procedures.

Current Approaches

EIA is a well-accepted procedure for evaluating the potential outcome of development actions. It is an open-ended, flexible and transparent procedure that can be adapted to a whole range of plans, programmes and projects, including those instituted under JI agreements. However, this very flexibility gives rise to problems of data acquisition. Data sources are varied and so are the methods

Table.6.8 An Overview of the Main EIA Factors for the JI Projects

Environmental factor	Czech Republic					Estonia				
	Coal/gas	Coal biomass	Coal biomass	Coal biomass	Coal wind	Gas/biomass	Oil biomass	Oil biomass	Oil biomass	Oil biomass
	Děčín	Kardašova	Staré Město	Mrakotín	Jeseník	Aardla, Tartu	Haabneeme	Türi	Valga	Võru Soojus
Air										
SO$_x$	○	○	○	○	○	○	○	○	○	○
NO$_x$	○	○	○	○	○	○	○	○	○	○
CO$_x$	○	□	●	●	○	●	●	●	●	●
Particulate matter	○	○	○		○		●?	○?	●?	□?
Land use	□	□	□		●	□	□	□	□	□
Water										
Discharge						□	○	□	□	□
Extraction						□	○	□?	●	□
Soil										
Visual	○	□	□		●	□	□	□	○	□
Human health										
Local air quality	○	○	○			○	○	○	○	○
Accidents						●	●	●		
Noise					●	□	□	□	□	
Transport										
Lorry movements	○	○	□?			□	●	●	●	●
Vehicle kilometres travelled	○	○	□?				●		●	●
Energy consumption	○	○	○		○	○	○	●	●	●
Waste			○			●	●	○		
Employment										
Number of employees	□	□						○		□
Local economy										
Employment	□	□				□	□	○	□	□

Key:
○ Positive change;   ○? Positive change suspected;   ● Negative change;   ●? Negative change suspected;   □ No change;   □? No change suspected

Table 6.9 Emissions to the Atmosphere for the JI Projects – Before and After Plant Conversion

Kg/MWh Project	SO$_2$ Ref	SO$_2$ Project	NO$_x$ Ref	NO$_x$ Project	CO × 10^{-3} Ref	CO × 10^{-3} Project	Dust Ref	Dust Project	Waste Ref	Waste Project
Oil to biomass:										
Türi	5.3	0.091	0.74	0.16	0.08	2.6	.92-.56	0.49	0.048	2.55
Haabneeme	5.1	0.086	0.66	0.13	0.03	2.7	0.11–0.14	0.42	0.011	5.75
Valga	2.6	0.1	0.69	0.15	0.05	2.7		0.126	0.002	no data
Võru	2.6	0.1	0.7	0.15	0.05	3.0	0.174		0	3.0
Gas/oil to biomass:										
Aardla 85% gas 15% oil	0.7[a]	0.04	0.33[b]	0.13	0.03	2.6	0[c]	0.08	0	3.15
Coal to biomass:										
Staré Město	4.2	0.08	0.95	0.057	2.0	1.0	1.13	0.35	2.56	0.17??
Kardašova	4.7	0.09	3	0.16	3.0	3.0	7.8	0.11	38.4?	0.36
Mrakotín	3.8	0.06	2.16	0.17	2.0	3.0	1.17	0.56	12.3	no data
Coal to gas:										
Děčín	7.6[d]	0.004	3.8	0.27	1.0	0.04	0.6	0	5.3	0
Coal-fired electricity to wind:										
Jeseník	11	0	5.6	0.08	1.0	0	No data	0	no data	0

Key:
a due to oil burn 0 for gas only; b gas only; c no data for the oil but gas = 0; d assuming heat and electricity from off-site old brown-coal power station

of collection and the reliability of the data. It is often difficult to quantify the data. There are many attempts at assessments that are thus forced to designate elements in the data matrix as 'unavailable' or as 'unquantified'. This is a particular problem in comparative work where even if data for one facility have been recorded they may not be available for others. The outcome of these deficiencies is that evaluation of EIA results has to be qualitative and objective comparisons are difficult. These difficulties are evident in the data that hav been presented here for the plant at Türi, Estonia, and in some of the data for all ten JI projects.

At present, where attempts have been made to assess the wider impacts on the environment and society of the implementation of JI projects, there has been little in the way of an alternative to the retrospective EIA approach (Jackson et al, 1999). The use of EIA allows qualitative and quantitative data to be employed and is an open-ended process. A procedure that begins with a *screening* of the projects to determine if an initial environmental and social assessment is required, based on evidence of adverse impacts, can be followed by a systematic *assessment*, where necessary. A programme of *post-auditing* and *monitoring* can also be put in place. At all of these stages, but particularly during screening, selection of indicators and the evaluation of the significance of the impacts, as well as public participation (see Figure 6.1), should be encouraged. Since it is the local citizenry who will have to live with the consequences of the project, they should be involved in the decision regarding project implementation. This can be achieved by citizen advisory committees, panels or juries, initiatives from the public, focus groups, negotiated rule-making, mediation, and benefit-sharing or compensation.

Any shortcomings in EIA are also to be found in other environmental assessment methods such as SEA, SIA or externality costing and concern data availability, reliability and quantification. In SIA and externality costing, these problems may be further complicated by the need for public participation in the process of data gathering. Public involvement is a way of collecting data on certain variables; where data on 'impact perception' are required, then public participation is not only advisable for the reasons given above but also an essential aspect of data acquisition.

Use of the DPSIR approach will also have to confront the need to improve data collection. In addition, because of the 'pathway' element in this procedure, there will be not only parametric challenges inherent in its use but also structural ones.

New Directions for Joint Implementation Assessment Procedures

As with so many environmental issues, the goal of achieving an acceptable impact assessment procedure has certain implications that appear to be conflicting. On the one hand, there is an urgency to the matter of agreeing effective GHG emission reductions. On the other hand, it does appear that participatory and representative environmental assessments, leading to fair decisions on implementation, might become cumbersome, time-consuming and difficult to agree, thus delaying progress. For this reason, it would seem prudent to examine what might constitute acceptable alternative procedures.

If a concerted effort was made to identify and agree a limited number of indicators for use in conjunction with JI actions, these indicators could provide the basis for a streamlined assessment of all but the largest project types. Such a set of indicators, which would need to mirror sustainability concerns (particularly in the context of the CDM) would represent a significant step forward in consistent and comparative assessment of JI actions. These indicators, probably no more than 12, could be divided between environmental indicators, socioeconomic indicators and a group that was project, programme or plan specific.[2] The indicators would have to be agreed through a dialogue with experts and would form the basis for assessing all projects as part of the implementation and reporting procedure for projects. Additional environmental and social concerns specific to the project would need to be addressed through local public participation; this should occur as part of the project implementation procedures. All of these procedures (including those for collecting and auditing indicator data) would, of course, need to be integrated within the Kyoto flexibility mechanisms through the appropriate operating entities. This task is beyond the scope of this analysis. However, there is a clear case for arguing that the uniform reporting format of the AIJ pilot-phase should be properly upgraded to reflect these concerns.

The incorporation of external impacts within the decision-making process could proceed either through externality costing (such as the ExternE work) or through a decision analysis method. Either of these methods would enable comparisons between very different kinds of JI projects to be made – for example, a forest planting, restoration or conservation project and the conversion of a coal-burning plant to biomass or natural gas combustion. The ExternE work has already been applied and extended to the marginal external costs of climate change damages of GHG emissions (Eyre et al, 1999), while decision analysis methods are routinely applied in the comparative evaluation of different technology options.

How these techniques could be applied and used in practice would need to be carefully considered, and this is beyond the scope of this book. However, in Chapter 10 we discuss an illustrative application of decision analysis to evaluating JI.

Conclusions

The flexibility mechanisms established under the Kyoto Protocol are designed to facilitate the environmental goal of reducing GHG emissions. However, climate-related environmental concerns represent only one aspect of a broader concern over the impact of anthropogenic activities on the environment. It would be inappropriate for interventions designed to mitigate climate change to lead routinely to increases in other kinds of environmental pollution. Equally, it would be inappropriate for such actions to lead to environmental and social disbenefits to host communities. Both the broader environmental aim and the concern for social equity are clearly established in the language of the FCCC (see Chapter 3).

Determining whether or not JI actions incur non-climate related environmental or social benefits or disbenefits is, however, no easy task. All interventions in the energy sector are likely to have some kind of environmental and social impact. A number of methodologies have been developed to try and assess these impacts. In this chapter we have outlined the basic principles of several of these methodologies, including: environmental impact assessment, strategic environmental assessment, social impact assessment, and approaches based on various models, system boundaries and evaluation procedures. It is worth reiterating that each of these methodologies has been the subject of a considerable literature, and many of them have been routinely applied to energy-sector projects.

In this study we have applied a limited retrospective EIA approach to ten case-study JI projects in the Czech Republic and Estonia. These assessments have illustrated both the application of the methodology in the context of JI, and the difficulties under which such an exercise labours. In the light of these difficulties, this chapter has highlighted the need to develop a consistent methodology for the environmental and social assessment of JI projects; and has called for a set of agreed procedures for implementing this methodology within the Kyoto flexibility mechanisms.

Accounting for Emission Reductions and Costs: Methodology and Case Study Results

S Parkinson, P Bailey, K Begg and T Jackson

Introduction

The basis of this project has been to carry out detailed assessments of real-life pilot joint-implementation (JI) projects. The aims of these assessments have been rather wide ranging – a consequence of the varying objectives which motivate JI. Amongst those objectives lie two which are clearly critical to the success of JI as a mechanism for promoting the aims of the Framework Convention on Climate Change (FCCC). These are environmental effectiveness and economic efficiency. Evaluating JI with respect to these objectives requires, amongst other things, the application of a robust accounting methodology with which to determine, firstly, the environmental benefits of a particular JI project and, secondly, the economic costs associated with the project.

In this chapter, we set out what we believe to be the best available methodology to account for the emission reductions achieved by JI projects and the associated economic costs. In fact, we define four *critical accounting variables* which are suitable for this task. These are:

1 total emissions reduction achieved by a JI project over its lifetime;
2 specific emissions reduction achieved by the project per unit of energy output;
3 incremental cost of the JI option over and above the cost of the baseline; and
4 specific incremental cost (per unit of emissions reduction).

Having defined the critical variables, we then evaluate each of these variables for each of the case study projects described in Chapter 5.

An integral aspect of this methodology lies in determining the baseline against which both emission reductions and costs should be assessed. It is our contention that the counterfactual nature of the baseline introduces an element of irreducible uncertainty within the accounting procedures for JI (Chapter 4). At a later stage of this report, we will set out some institutional procedures for dealing with this uncertainty. In the analysis that follows, however, we have decided against any arbitrary attempt to reduce this uncertainty by pre-selecting a single baseline. Rather, we have identified a number of baselines, each of which could be regarded as defensible, taking into account the local and national context. We have then evaluated the case study projects against the selected baselines. Accordingly, this chapter presents a range of results for each project and for each of the critical variables. Considerable care needs to be taken in interpreting these results for any policy purposes.

All the assessments in this chapter have been carried out at the project level. Comparison between project- and system-level assessments for non-separable projects is explored in Chapter 8.

Methodology

Project-level assessments of the case study projects have been carried out using a spreadsheet model of each JI project. The spreadsheets consist of a Microsoft Excel file with typically five layers: the first layer contains a summary of major input parameters and output results; the second has details of the JI project on a year-by-year basis; the third has details of the baseline case on a year-by-year basis; the fourth calculates emissions and costs for one discount rate and lifetime; and the fifth layer calculates another set of discount rate and lifetime assumptions.

Outputs from the spreadsheet models are values for each of the four critical accounting variables: emissions reduction over the lifetime of the project in tonnes of CO_2 equivalent (tCO_2e); the lifetime-averaged specific emissions reduction (tCO_2e/MWh); the incremental economic cost in US dollars (US$); and the specific incremental cost in US dollars per tonne of CO_2 equivalent (US$/$tCO_2e$). The detailed methodological calculations are described below.

Calculating Emission Reductions

In order to calculate the emissions reduction associated with a JI project, we must first find the total emissions of both the baseline and the JI options. To do this, we use the CORINAIR/EMEP (1996) methodology, which is compatible with the official guidelines for national greenhouse gas (GHG) inventories (IPCC, 1996). The basic equation is:

$$E_i = e_i Z \tag{7.1}$$

where E_i is the emissions of gas i (tonnes/y), e_i is the emissions factor of gas i (tonne/GJ), and Z is the activity of the plant, normally the fuel consumption (GJ/y). E_i and Z are normally given in annual figures since these are more practical to measure or calculate. Z is calculated using:

$$Z = H_u \, M_{in} \tag{7.2}$$

where H_u is the net calorific value[1] of fuel (GJ/t) and M_{in} is the mass of the fuel consumed annually (t/y). It should be noted here that H_u and M_{in} should either both be adjusted to 'moisture and ash free' (maf) values or both be unadjusted. Since many fuels – for example, biomass and brown coal – vary a great deal in their moisture content and the percentage of ash produced in the combustion process, CORINAIR/EMEP (1996) recommends the use of these maf values to produce consistent figures. Z can also be calculated using:

$$Z = \frac{P_{out}}{\rho_{plant}} \tag{7.3}$$

where P_{out} is the annual energy production of the plant (MWh/y), and ρ_{plant} is the plant efficiency (%). If there are no measurements of P_{out}, an approximate figure may be calculated thus:

$$P_{out} = Ct_u \tag{7.4}$$

where C is the capacity of the plant (MW), and t_u is the number of available hours (h/y) – that is, the number of hours each year that a plant is available to produce energy.

Research into the calculation of emission factors is ongoing. A relationship has been derived for CO_2 and is given in equation 7.5, while for CH_4 and N_2O, emission factors are derived directly from experimental data and standard values are given in tables (see, for example, CORINAIR/EMEP, 1996). For CO_2, the emission factor e_{CO_2} is calculated thus:

$$e_{CO_2} = \frac{44}{12} f_c \, \varepsilon_c \, \frac{1}{H_u} \cdot 10^6 \tag{7.5}$$

where fc is the fraction of fuel which is made up of carbon (%), and ε_c is the fraction of carbon oxidized (%). Again moisture and ash free values should be used. Standard values for $f_c \, \varepsilon_c$ and H_u are available for different fuels from CORINAIR/EMEP (1996).

A value of annual GHG emissions is obtained by converting tonnes of CH_4 and N_2O emissions to CO_2 *equivalent tonnes* (tCO$_2$e) by using global warming potentials (GWPs) (IPCC, 1996), as given in equation 7.6:

$$E = \sum_{all \; i} G_i \, E_i \tag{7.6}$$

where E is the annual GHG emissions, E_i is the emissions of gas i, G_i is the GWP of gas i and i = CO_2, CH_4 or N_2O. GWPs account for the differences in radiative forcing and atmospheric lifetime between the gases. GWPs are cumulative over time. As a result, they are calculated for a number of time periods: 20, 100 and 500 years. Here, we follow standard practice and use the 100-year GWPs.

Having calculated the annual GHG emissions for the baseline case, B, and the JI or abatement case, A, we use equation 7.7 to find the annual emissions reduction, E_{AB}:

$$E_{AB} = E_B - E_A \qquad (7.7)$$

The total emissions reduction $E_{AB,T}$ over the lifetime, L, of the JI project can be calculated by summing over this period:

$$E_{AB,T} = \sum_{t=1}^{t=L} E_{AB,t} \qquad (7.8)$$

Calculating Specific Emissions Reductions

A further variable we can calculate is the *specific* GHG emissions, s_i, of either the JI project or the baseline – that is, the emissions of GHG i (CO_2, CH_4 or N_2O) per unit energy output (for example, tCO_2e/MWh). This is useful for comparing across project size, technology and fuel. It is calculated thus:

$$s_i = \frac{E_i}{P_{out}} \qquad (7.9)$$

We can substitute for E_i using equations 7.1 and 7.3, such that equation 7.9 becomes:

$$s_i = 3.6 \frac{e_i}{P_{plant}} \qquad (7.10)$$

where 3.6 is the factor needed to convert GJ into MWh. In order to obtain a total value for all GHGs, s, we again have to take account of the GWPs of the gases as in equation 7.6:

$$s = \sum_{all\ i} G_i s_i \qquad (7.11)$$

As discussed in Chapter 4, some researchers have argued for the standardization of baselines by the use of standard values for the specific GHG emissions of given technologies in a particular country or region. Using data from both the JI projects and the pre-project plants, we can explore the implications of this procedure.

In Tables 7.1 and 7.2 we show values of s_{CO_2} calculated for different technology/fuel combinations using data from standard tables (CORINAIR/

Table 7.1 *Specific CO_2 Emissions for District-Heating Boilers by Fuel*

Fuel	e_{CO_2} *(t/GJ)*	p_{plant} *(%)*	s_{CO_2} *(tCO$_2$/MWh)*
Wood chips			
(CO$_2$ neutral)	0.0	85	0.00
Wood chips			
(not CO$_2$ neutral)	0.100	85	0.42
HFO	0.079	85	0.33
Natural gas	0.056	90	0.22
Hard coal (Czech Republic)	0.112	85	0.47
Brown coal (Czech Republic)	0.091	85	0.39
Peat	0.098	85	0.42

Source: adapted from CORINAIR/EMEP (1996); Grohnheit (1996)

EMEP, 1996; Grohnheit, 1996). In Table 7.3 we compare values derived using data from the case study projects, in particular, the pre-project heavy-fuel oil (HFO) boilers in Estonia. Obviously, since e_{CO_2} is a constant for this technology/fuel combination, the only difference between the specific GHG emissions is due to different values of efficiency. It can be seen that there is, in fact, little variation in this case (10 per cent difference between the highest and lowest values). In general, the GHG emission factor for a given technology/fuel is well defined (CORINAIR/EMEP, 1996). Therefore, if a given plant is operating to specification (its efficiency is known), then the specific emissions can be defined quite accurately.

However, there are exceptions to this. For example, if we were to compare the values for the biomass boilers, the situation may be different depending upon the extent to which the harvested biomass is replaced by biomass regrowth (how CO_2 neutral the fuel is). As far as we could ascertain, the biomass used in the JI projects analysed in this study are, at present, from approximately CO_2-neutral sources and look likely to remain so. Nevertheless, measurements of CO_2 neutrality are very difficult and we have not, in this study, attempted to make any. Consequently, the variation in the specific emissions for biomass boilers could be more significant than this analysis suggests.

Table 7.2 *Specific CO_2 Emissions for Electricity Supply by Fuel/Technology*

Fuel	e_{CO_2} *(t/GJ)*	p_{plant} *(%)*	s_{CO_2} *(tCO$_2$/MWh)*
Wind/turbine	0.0	not available	0.00
Natural gas/combined cycle	0.056	52	0.39
Hard coal (Czech Republic)/			
Condensing unit	0.093	36	0.93
Brown coal (Czech Republic)/			
Condensing unit	0.091	33	0.99

Source: adapted from CORINAIR/EMEP (1996); the Czech EFOM-ENV energy–economic model (see Chapter 7); and van Harmelen et al (1995)

Table 7.3 *Specific CO_2 Emissions for Estonian HFO Boilers*

HFO plant	e_{CO_2} (t/GJ)	ρ_{plant} (%)	s_{CO_2} (tCO₂/MWh)
Haabneeme	0.079	84	0.34
Türi	0.079	79	0.36
Valga	0.079	86	0.33
Võru	0.079	86	0.33

In Table 7.4 we give an example of how the other GHGs (CH_4 and N_2O), contribute to the specific emissions of an activity. Again, we use the case of HFO district-heating boilers. As can be seen, the contribution of the non-CO_2 gases to the total value for specific emissions is fairly small.

It is important to note that the above discussion does not consider the efficiency of the supply network. If the system boundaries of a project include this network, then the efficiency in equation 7.9 should be the *total* efficiency of both the plant and the network.

In order to calculate the annual specific emissions *reduction*, s_{AB}, for a given JI project, we take the difference between the specific emissions of the JI (abatement) project, A, and baseline, B, thus:

$$s_{AB} = s_B - s_A \qquad (7.12)$$

However, the fact that we have assumed equivalence of energy service (see Chapter 4) between the JI project and baseline is significant. If this is not so, as with a non-separable JI project, simple differencing is inappropriate and consideration of plant performance characteristics, such as utilization times, is necessary. We discuss this issue where relevant for each of the JI projects assessed.

Table 7.4 *Specific Emissions of Different GHGs for HFO and Wood-Fired District-Heating Boilers*

GHG	e_i (t/GJ)	G_i	ρ_{plant} (%)	s_i (tCO₂e/MWh)
HFO				
CO_2	0.079	1	85	0.33
CH_4	1.0×10^{-6}	21	85	0.001
N_2O	2.0×10^{-5}	310	85	0.03
Total				**0.36**
Woodchips (CO_2 neutral)				
CO_2	0.0	1	85	0.00
CH_4	2.0×10^{-5}	21	85	0.002
N_2O	4.0×10^{-6}	310	85	0.005
Total				**0.01**

Source: adapted from CORINAIR/EMEP (1996); Grohnheit (1996)

Again, the specific emissions reduction can also be calculated over the lifetime of the JI project. Formally, the latter case is defined by:

$$s_{AB,T} = \frac{E_{AB,T}}{P_{out,T}} \qquad (7.13)$$

where $P_{out,T}$ is the total energy produced by the JI project over the lifetime. The assumption of equivalence of energy service means that $P_{out,T}$ is also the total energy produced by the baseline. Where the baseline technology and fuel are assumed constant over the lifetime of the JI project, the lifetime-averaged specific emissions reduction reduces to the annual-specific emissions reduction. Where the baseline technology and fuel are construed as changing over the lifetime of the JI project, the lifetime-specific emissions reduction is a weighted average of the annual-specific emissions reduction over the lifetime of the plant. The values for specific emissions reduction that we present in the following sections are lifetime-averaged values.

Calculating Incremental Cost

As discussed briefly in Chapter 3, it is possible to take a number of different cost perspectives on JI projects, depending upon the different organizational actors involved. Thus, the JI investor may have a very different cost perspective from the host, and both may have different perspectives from the perspective implicitly assumed within the concept of economic efficiency. A thorough analysis of JI projects from each of these perspectives could considerably strengthen our understanding of the behaviour of different actors in JI situations. Due to time constraints, we have restricted the following analysis to the *economic* perspective. Thus, our concepts of both incremental cost and specific incremental cost follow standard economic practice, and are calculated using net present values at a given discount rate. Formally, we define the net present value, NPV $(x)_d$ of an investment x at discount rate d (%) by:

$$NPV(x)_d = \sum_{t=1}^{L} \frac{x_t}{(1 + d)^t} \qquad (7.14)$$

where x_t is the cash flow at year t, and L is the crediting lifetime or time-frame of the project in years.

The incremental costs – necessary for the economic assessment – will, of course, be calculated using a counterfactual baseline. The first step in this process is therefore to find the total economic costs of both the abatement and the baseline case. In each case, the following equation is used:

$$C_e = C_{inv} + C_{trans} + NPV \left(c_{om} + c_{mv} + P_{out} \left(\frac{c_{fuel}}{P_{plant}} + c_{va} \right) \right)_d \qquad (7.15)$$

where:
C_{inv} = investment costs (US$)
C_{trans} = transaction costs (US$)

c_{om} = annual operation and maintenance costs (US\$/y)
c_{mv} = annual monitoring and verification costs (US\$/y)
c_{fuel} = annual fuel costs (US\$/GJ/y)
c_{va} = annual variable costs (not including fuel costs) (US\$/MWh/y)
P_{out} = annual energy production (MWh/y)
e = A (abatement case, ie the JI project) or
              B (baseline case)

We define the incremental costs of the project, C_{AB}, by:

$$C_{AB} = C_A - C_B \tag{7.16}$$

Calculating Specific Incremental Cost

One of the objectives underlying the use of JI as an instrument in climate policy is to ensure economic efficiency in GHG abatement. As discussed in Chapter 3, this objective is generally evaluated by looking at the cost effectiveness of emissions reduction or abatement projects. Essentially, the aim of cost effectiveness is to ensure either that we achieve the highest level of reduction for a given economic cost or, alternatively, that we achieve the lowest cost for a given level of emission reduction. As the discussion in Chapter 3 illustrates, cost effectiveness (in this sense) is delivered by choosing investments at the margin which have the lowest incremental cost per tonne of emission reduction (the lowest *specific* incremental cost, c_s). We note here that there are various different formulations of specific incremental cost.

For example, the standard methodology for cost curves (see, for example, UNEP, 1994) calculates a level annual generation cost and divides this by the annual emissions reduction. It can be shown that under certain assumptions, this procedure is formally equivalent to taking the incremental cost (as defined above) and dividing by the *discounted* total emissions reduction over the lifetime, that is:

$$(c_s)_{AB} = \frac{C_{AB}}{\mathrm{NPV}(E_{AB,T})} \tag{7.17}$$

In some respects, this seems a rather odd way to calculate specific incremental costs. The implication that it is appropriate to discount future emissions (as well as future costs) is contentious, and the implications of doing so are unclear. Furthermore, it is possible to define specific incremental cost in a more straightforward way, by dividing the incremental cost (equation 7.14) by the difference in *undiscounted* total emissions reduction over the project lifetime (equation 7.7):

$$(c_s)_{AB} = \frac{C_{AB}}{E_{AB,T}} \tag{7.18}$$

In this book, we have elected to use the standard (UNEP, 1994) methodology on the grounds that this appears to be as close to accepted practice as it is possible to get in what remains a rather confused methodological field.

Nonetheless, equation 7.18 may ultimately turn out to be a more acceptable way of calculating specific incremental costs. At the very least, it should be made clear that significant policy issues can become imbedded in what appear to be purely technical or economic formulae. Furthermore, the variability in results to which different methodologies give rise makes hard and fast conclusions about economic efficiency extremely rare.

A further methodological possibility would be to define specific incremental cost in relation to the perspective of a JI investor. In this perspective, the relevant question is: how much reduction credit can be achieved for a given financial investment? As discussed earlier, this definition is likely to lead to different results than would be derived from the economic perspective, and will depend upon cost streams, revenues, rates of return and profitability, which are likely to be local and particular to each individual case. Although we have not attempted such an analysis in this study, we have looked in some detail at how different discount rates and the use of emissions discounting affect the incremental costs and specific incremental costs. The results of this analysis are presented in Chapter 8.

Assumptions for Project-Level Assessment

A series of general assumptions have been made in producing the results of the project-level assessment, and the main ones are listed below. Discussion then follows of some of the more specific assumptions – for example, simplifying system effects when electricity-supply or demand-side projects are concerned.

General Assumptions

The following assumptions apply to all the project-level analysis in this chapter.

- All projects are separable from the energy system (where projects are part of a system, the project-specific assumptions are discussed below).
- The baseline energy demand is equal to the project energy demand (there is *equivalence of service* as discussed in Chapter 4).
- Changes in energy demand, except where measured, are negligible during the lifetime of the projects.
- The network losses are the same in the project case as in the baseline case, except where explicitly stated.
- All baseline costs before the project start date are regarded as sunk costs.
- Investment in a given plant is levellized over its lifetime, but only the costs incurred during the project lifetime are compared. For example, if an investment is made in the baseline 15 years after the start of a 20-year project, then only the first (20–15) = 5 years of levellized costs of that plant are counted in the baseline.
- All fuel prices are known for the first year of the project operation, and are assumed not to vary thereafter for the lifetime of the project.[2]

- Changes in the fuel quality of both the project and the baseline are negligible during the lifetime.
- For all projects whose fuel is woodchips (Aardla-Tartu, Haabneeme, Türi, Valga, and Võru in Estonia; and Kardašova Řečice, Mrakotin and Staré Město in the Czech Republic), it is assumed that the fuel is from a CO_2-neutral source (CO_2 uptake in forest regrowth is equivalent to emissions from the plant).
- The technical lifetime of supply-side projects (Aardla-Tartu, Haabneeme, Türi, Valga, Võru, Děčín, Jeseník, Kardašova Řečice, Mrakotin, and Staré Město) is taken to be 25 years.
- The technical lifetime of demand-side projects (Mustamäe-Vilde tee and Mustamäe-Sütiste tee 58) is 15 years.
- Costs are calculated at 1994 values, using an exchange rate of US$1 = 29 CZK = 13 EEK (COWI, 1996).

Specific assumptions

Both projects that supply electricity (Děčín and Jeseník) feed directly into the Czech national grid. Hence, it is necessary to make assumptions about the technology/fuel mix of the supply that is substituted. Electricity generation in the Czech Republic is based mainly on brown coal (~75 per cent) and nuclear (~20 per cent), with small contributions from other sources (EVA, 1994). COWI (1996) has carried out an assessment of Jeseník which assumes that it will substitute 100 per cent of brown coal (ETSU/COWI, 1994), whilst a USIJI (1996) assessment of Děčín assumes a substitution of a constant average fuel mix. Technically, the electricity from the wind turbines at Jeseník could be stored by the small amount of pumped storage hydro-power available in the Czech Republic. Furthermore, the technical characteristics of Děčín allow for the electricity to be produced at a time when it can be sold at the highest price (peak). As a result, both projects are likely to replace peak supply. However, without detailed price information the exact technology/fuel is hard to define. In the assessment here, we begin with an assumption of 100 per cent brown-coal substitution (produced by a power station with a typical thermal conversion efficiency of 33 per cent) for both Jeseník and Děčín, and then look at the change in emissions reduction due to the use of the average fuel mix.

For the heat-demand projects (Mustamäe-Vilde tee and Mustamäe-Sütiste tee 58), we have made a number of extra assumptions. Due to the lack of measurements for the total annual energy savings, we have used estimates made by the Swedish National Board for Industrial and Technical Development (NUTEK) based on comparisons both with unmodified apartment blocks and other modified blocks (Stockholm Konsult, 1994; NUTEK, 1995; 1996). We have also assumed that the GHG savings come from the reduced heat demand at an oil-fired district-heating boiler, efficiency 85 per cent, delivered through a district-heating network with losses of 30 per cent (typical figures for Estonia).

A very large proportion of the total cost was associated with maintaining and upgrading the roofs. The roofing and some of the plumbing were in a poor condition and would have needed maintenance independently of any energy saving concerns. How these costs are allocated – all or part to the energy-conservation measure costs or not – has large implications for the cost effectiveness (measured by the specific incremental cost) of the improvements. A related issue is how much of the energy savings were associated with the roof and plumbing upgrades and making sure the assumed savings match up with the costs allocated to energy conservation. A preliminary project (Mustamäe-Sütiste tee 16: results not presented here) estimated that the roofing upgrades and reduction of heat losses in the plumbing accounted for approximately one third of the savings (Stockholm Konsult, 1994, p53, Table 6). This value has been used to adjust the baselines in the examples where it is assumed that the necessary building maintenance would have occurred anyway (baseline 2 in both projects).

For most of the projects, there were details of transaction costs (for example, cost of feasibility study, tender preparation, training). On average, this amounted to approximately 10 per cent of the investment costs. For some projects (Děčín, Jeseník, Türi), such data were hard to obtain. Hence, in these cases, a figure of 10 per cent was assumed. (Subsequently, Lile et al, 1998, have given an estimate of transaction costs for Děčín of 7 per cent: equal to the donor contribution from the US.)

Case Study Results: Emissions and Costs

In this section, we present, firstly, our initial assessments of the GHG emissions associated with each of the projects and their associated economic costs. Table 7.5 summarizes these assessments. We show the energy output (in the first year), total emissions over the project lifetime, specific emissions and the net present value (NPV) costs for each of the 13 projects.

From Table 7.5, we can see that projects of the same type have similar specific emissions (as discussed above). One notable exception is Haabneeme, where a significant percentage of the fuel was peat, which is not CO_2 neutral, unlike the woodchips used. As mentioned earlier, it is important to note that the values for both specific and total emissions are in CO_2 equivalent units (CO_2e) – in other words, they include emissions of CH_4 and N_2O. Hence, they are not directly comparable with values in Tables 7.1, 7.2 and 7.3.

Case Study Results: Baseline Construction

Our overall aim in this chapter is to evaluate critical accounting variables for each of our selected JI projects. Before we can achieve this aim, however, we must first define appropriate baselines for each of the selected projects. As discussed in detail in Chapter 4, baselines are counterfactual: they correspond to situations which, it is believed, would have occurred if the JI project had not taken place. In reality, of course, a number of different scenarios might have been possible had the JI project not taken place. But it is simply impossible to establish with certainty, even in hindsight, which of these scenarios would

Table 7.5 *Summary of the Main Characteristics of the JI Projects*

Project (sector: fuel)	Output (first year) GWh/y	Emissions ktCO$_2$e	Specific emissions tCO$_2$e/MWh	NPV costs US$million
Děčín*				
(cogeneration: natural gas)	45	267	0.25	23.8
Jeseník				
(electricity supply: wind)	3	1	0.02	4.3
Lettland				
(electricity supply: wind)	3	1	0.01	2.6
Aardla-Tartu				
(heat supply: biomass)	30	7	0.01	3.3
Haabneeme				
(heat supply: biomass)	22	50	0.08	4.9
Türi				
(heat supply: biomass)	10	2	0.01	2.9
Valga				
(heat supply: biomass)	25	4	0.01	1.6
Võru				
(heat supply: biomass)	29	6	0.01	3.1
Kardašova*				
(heat supply: biomass)	5	1	0.01	1.7
Mrakotin*				
(heat supply: biomass)	5	1	0.01	2.2
Staré Město*				
(heat supply: biomass)	3	1	0.01	3.4
Velesin				
(heat supply: natural gas)	10	69	0.27	3.6
Mustamäe*				
(heat demand: insulation)				
Vilde tee	1	5	0.46	0.2
Sütiste tee 58	1	2	0.46	0.2

Note: * These figures take account of the efficiency of the network.

actually have occurred. In consequence, we have argued that there is a largely irreducible uncertainty associated with the use of baselines in JI project assessment. This means, of course, that our evaluation of critical accounting variables also operates under a largely irreducible uncertainty. Consequently, we make no attempt to defend, *a priori*, one particular baseline over another. Rather, our approach in what follows is to set out a number of different baselines for each project, and to present the results of our evaluation against each of these baselines. The question of how to treat the variability in results which arises from this procedure is addressed later in this book (Chapters 8, 9 and 10).

In this section, therefore, we attempt to establish a set of defensible baselines for a selection of the case study projects. This selection includes the following projects:

- Děčín (cogeneration);
- Jeseník (electricity supply);
- Aardla-Tartu, Haabneeme, Türi, Valga, Võru (heat supply); and
- Mustamäe-Vilde tee and Mustamäe-Sütiste tee 58 (heat demand).

We did not carry out a baseline assessment of the other projects for a variety of reasons. In the case of Mrakotin and Velesin, only feasibility data were available. For Kardašova and Staré Město, the data on the pre-project situation were almost non-existent. Furthermore, reasonable alternative baselines are very similar in form to those used for the Estonian heat-supply projects. Therefore, we felt that no new insights would be gained from their analysis in this case. The Lettland wind farm was only used as a surrogate Czech project to explore interactions at a system level (see Chapter 8).

In general, the baseline options were derived from consideration of possible replacement technologies/fuels and the timing of such replacement. We took into account the plant that was being replaced by the JI project where applicable, current energy-sector developments and possible future ones, environmental regulation and other factors where appropriate.

The baselines for the Czech projects – Děčín and Jeseník – are given in Table 7.6. Those for the Estonian heat-supply projects – Haabneeme, Aardla-Tartu, Türi, Valga and Võru – are given in Table 7.7. Those for the Estonian heat-demand projects – Mustamäe-Vilde tee and Mustamäe-Sütiste tee 58 – are presented in Table 7.8. All three tables also give brief descriptions of each project and its pre-project situation.

Baseline 1 for all the projects assumes that the pre-project situation continues for the technical lifetime of the project (25 years for the supply projects, 15 years for the demand ones). One reason for this is that it has been common, during the AIJ pilot phase, for project baselines to make this assumption, although the technical lifetime has often been shorter than that taken here (UN FCCC, 2000). In practice, this situation is unlikely for most of the projects. For example, in the Estonian heat-supply projects, the boilers that have been replaced are already old and would be unlikely to last for a further 25 years. However, if we only consider emissions and not costs of the baseline over this period, this option becomes more feasible since refurbishment of the old boilers, or replacement with new ones using the same fuel, is a larger possibility.

We have considered four other baseline options for Děčín. There were a number of factors which particularly influenced the choices.

- 85 per cent of the investment costs for the project came from the host country (through the Czech Environment Fund, or CEF); without the project, these funds would be available for investment in environmental options elsewhere.
- The Czech Republic has agreed to a national GHG target under the Kyoto Protocol.
- Czech local air-pollution laws require cuts to be made in pollutants such as SO_2 and NO_x.

Table 7.6 *Summary of Děčín and Jeseník JI Projects and Baselines*

	Děčín (Cogeneration)	Jeseník (Electricity supply)
JI project	7.2MW engines; 11.0MW boilers (peak only); natural gas; plant efficiency 86%; network efficiency 91%	6 x 0.5MW wind turbines
Pre-project situation	Heat (60%): brown coal; plant efficiency 63%; network efficiency 76%; electricity (40%): grid (brown coal, efficiency 33%)	Electricity from grid (brown coal, efficiency 33%)
Baseline 1	Pre-project situation continues for lifetime	
Baseline 2	Pre-project situation for ten years, then heat from gas boiler, efficiency 90%	New brown-coal plant, efficiency 40%
Baseline 3	Pre-project situation for ten years, then heat from biomass boiler, efficiency 86%	Pre-project situation for ten years, then JI project
Baseline 4	Heat from pre-project brown- coal boiler, efficiency 63%; electricity from new brown- coal plant, efficiency 40%	not applicable
Baseline 5	Pre-project situation for ten years, then JI project	not applicable

Consequently, three of the four baselines assume that the brown-coal boiler, which had been previously used to supply heat to the city of Děčín, is replaced ten years after the start of the JI project (see Table 7.6). One of those baselines (number 5) assumes that the above conditions will lead to the JI project itself being commissioned after ten years. The other baseline (number 4) assumes that the CEF will have invested (on the JI project start date) in measures which will have increased the efficiency of the electricity supply.

For Jeseník, two other baseline options are considered. Again, only a small fraction of the investment costs (10 per cent) were supplied from a donor country. As a result, these baselines again assume that the rest of the finance could have been invested elsewhere. The above constraints on emissions also apply. Consequently, one of the baselines assumes that, in the absence of the JI project, the finance will have been used to improve the efficiency of the supply to the national grid, while the other assumes that the JI project will have been commercially viable in ten years.

The baselines chosen for the five Estonian heat-supply projects are very alike due to the large similarities between the projects. As stated above, baseline 1 is the continuation of the pre-project situation. Again, there are a number of reasons why this situation may not continue. For example, the price of heavy-fuel oil (HFO, also known as mazout) has remained high since

Table 7.7 *Summary of Estonian Heat-Supply JI Projects and Baselines*

	Haabneeme	Aardla-Tartu	Türi	Valga	Võru
JI project	6MW; 85% woodchips; 15% peat; efficiency 78%	6MW; woodchips; efficiency 87%	4MW; woodchips; efficiency 88%	5MW; woodchips; efficiency 83%	7MW; woodchips; efficiency 80%
Pre-project situation	HFO; efficiency 84%	14% HFO; 86% gas; efficiency 86%	HFO; efficiency 79%	HFO; efficiency 86%	HFO; efficiency 86%
Baseline 1	Pre-project situation continues for lifetime				
Baseline 2	Pre-project situation for ten years, then new natural gas-fired boiler, efficiency 90%				
Baseline 3	Existing natural gas boiler, efficiency 90%	Pre-project situation for ten years, then JI project initiated			
Baseline 4	Pre-project situation for ten years, then JI project	not applicable			

independence. Also, like the Czech Republic, Estonia is an Annex I country (it has a GHG emissions target under the Kyoto Protocol). Another influence is the tightening of local air-pollution regulations, particularly concerning SO_2 (such emissions are especially high from HFO boilers). A final factor is the low investment costs of the biomass boilers.

Hence, we have chosen two other baselines where the fuel is switched: one where a new natural gas boiler is built ten years after the start of the JI project; and the other where the biomass JI project itself is undertaken after ten years.

In the case of Haabneeme, a considerable amount of the heat supplied from other boilers in the same boiler house as the JI project is currently produced using natural gas. Consequently, a further baseline in this case is that the HFO would have been replaced by natural gas from one of the existing boilers immediately.

There is one further point to note about the Türi and Võru projects: the output of both these biomass boilers is assumed to remain constant, at the level observed during the first year of operation, for the lifetime of the project. This is despite increases in both their outputs being observed in later years. The reason is that the increases are due to expansions in the district-heating networks (both due to separate JI energy-efficiency projects started shortly afterwards); as a result, the emissions reduction caused by these expansions should accrue to those projects and not to the boiler conversions under study here.

For the heat-demand projects, we have considered two baselines which focus upon the condition of the buildings. As stated above, the first baseline for both projects is a continuation of the pre-project situation. However, due to the poor condition of the buildings, another reasonable baseline is that

Table 7.8 *Summary of Estonian Heat-Demand JI Projects and Baselines*

	Mustamäe Vilde tee	*Mustamäe Sütiste tee 58*
JI project	Building insulation (new substations, roof insulation, weather stripping, heat balancing and new entrance doors)	
Pre-project situation	Apartment block with low-quality insulation and in need of roof maintenance	
Baseline 1	Pre-project situation continues for lifetime	
Baseline 2	Roof maintenance is carried out	
Scenario 1	Heat supply is limited (demand cannot increase due to capacity of district-heating network)	No other action occurs within lifetime
Scenario 2	Heat supply is able to rise with demand[3]	JI project (all energy saving measures) introduced after ten years

some of the low cost repairs – for example, roof maintenance – would have been carried out by the project start date. For each project, two additional scenarios have been analysed. In the case of the Mustamäe Vilde tee, two scenarios which influence the overall reference situation for the project were examined. They concern the nature of the heat supply to the building. The first assumes that the capacity of the heat supply is limited and therefore demand cannot rise above the pre-project level due to, for example, higher comfort levels. The second scenario assumes that the heat supply to the building is not constraining, hence more GHG emissions will be saved in this case. In the case of the Mustamäe Sütiste tee 58 project, the first scenario analysed assumes that no additional work is done on the building, while the second assumes that the JI project can be implemented in the baseline after ten years. For both heat-demand projects, the combination of two baselines and two scenarios means that four reference situations are considered per project.

It is assumed for both these projects that the heat is supplied by an HFO boiler for the whole of the project lifetime. Clearly, if the oil were replaced by woodchips from a CO_2-neutral source, then the projects would give negligible GHG emission savings even though they would still provide energy savings. Thus, the choice of fuel used in the district-heating network is an important assumption in these particular JI project baselines.

Case Study Results: Evaluation of Critical Variables

We are now in a position to evaluate the four critical accounting variables – emissions reduction, specific emissions reduction, incremental costs and specific incremental cost – for each of our selected case study projects. We begin this section by discussing in depth an example project (the Děčín cogeneration plant), and then discuss in general terms the results of all the projects and the implications of these results.

Table 7.9 *Effect of Baseline Choice on Critical Variables of Děčín (discount rate 4 per cent, lifetime 25 years)*

	Emissions reduction ktCO$_2$e	Specific emissions reduction tCO$_2$e/MWh	Incremental costs US$ million	Specific incremental cost US$/tCO$_2$e
Baseline 1 heat: old brown coal; electricity: old brown coal	730	0.62	14.9	33
Baseline 2 heat: natural gas after ten years; electricity: old brown coal	560	0.47	7.2	19
Baseline 3 heat: biomass after ten years; electricity: old brown coal	440	0.37	12.0	39
Baseline 4 heat: old brown coal; electricity: new brown coal	640	0.54	10.1	25
Baseline 5 existing supply ten years; gas cogeneration 15 years	290	0.26	7.7	33

Example Case Study Project: Děčín

Table 7.9 shows the values of the critical variables for each baseline choice for Děčín, assuming a discount rate of 4 per cent and a project lifetime of 25 years. We can see that there is significant variation in all four of the critical variables: emissions reduction varies from 290 ktCO$_2$e to 730 ktCO$_2$e; incremental cost varies from US$7.2 million to US$14.9 million; specific incremental cost varies from US$19/tCO$_2$e to US$39/tCO$_2$e; and specific emissions reduction varies from 0.26tCO$_2$e/MWh to 0.62tCO$_2$e/MWh. In all cases, the higher estimate is at least twice the lower one. Hence, it is clear that the choice of baseline technology, fuel and timing are, in this case, critical in defining both the number of emissions reduction credits and the price of these credits.

We should note one particular point in relation to the values of specific emissions reduction calculated in this case (as in many of the cases which follow). While the specific emission for a given technology/fuel combination may not vary much, as discussed earlier, if this combination changes in the baseline (for example, from an HFO boiler to a natural gas boiler), then the average value *over the lifetime* of the plant will vary significantly.

In this example, it is interesting to compare baselines 1 and 5, which effectively contrast the results between the project having a crediting lifetime equal to the technical lifetime of 25 years (baseline 1) with one where the crediting

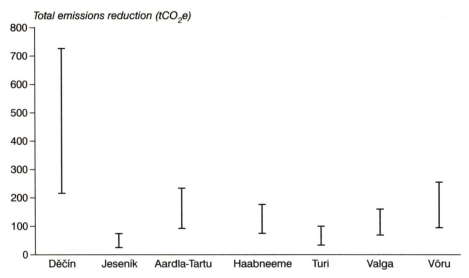

Figure 7.1 *GHG Emissions Reduction for Case Study JI Projects*

lifetime is only 10 years (baseline 5). Not surprisingly, the emissions reduction and specific emissions reduction both drop by 60 per cent (equal to the reduction in the crediting lifetime). The incremental cost, however, drops by only 50 per cent; the smaller drop is a result of unchanged up-front investment costs. The specific incremental cost, however, is unchanged between baselines 1 and 5 using the standard methodology. Thus, the cost of credits remains the same in both cases.[4]

As discussed earlier, it is not certain which particular technologies and fuels are being substituted by the electricity produced and fed into the grid by Děčín. If we assume this baseline to be an average Czech fuel/technology mix (held constant at present levels) instead of one based only on brown coal, then we find that for baseline 1 the emissions reduction falls by $130ktCO_2e$ (18 per cent). If we further use a projection of the specific emissions of the Czech electricity sector over the lifetime of the plant (using the energy–economic model EFOM-ENV; see Chapter 8), then the estimated emissions reduction falls by a further $60ktCO_2e$: a total drop of 26 per cent. A similar percentage fall is seen for baseline 5, the lowest baseline. Hence, our range of uncertainty in emissions reduction due to baseline choice is even higher: the lowest baseline ($215ktCO_2e$) is 70 per cent lower than the highest ($730ktCO_2e$).

Having looked at one project in detail, we now take a broader perspective for the remaining projects in order to identify any general patterns.

Emissions Reduction

Figure 7.1 summarizes the results for the total GHG emissions reduction over the lifetime of the case study projects.

The results for the two Mustamäe projects are not shown in Figure 7.1 because they are so small: 1.4 to $2.9ktCO_2e$ for Mustamäe Vilde tee, and 1.2

Table 7.10 *Uncertainty in GHG Emissions Reduction of Case Study JI Projects*

Project (sector: fuel)	Uncertainty (%)
Děčín (cogeneration: natural gas)	±54
Jeseník (electricity supply: wind)	±60
Aardla-Tartu (heat supply: biomass)	±43
Haabneeme (heat supply: biomass)	±43
Türi (heat supply: biomass)	±44
Valga (heat supply: biomass)	±44
Võru (heat supply: biomass)	±47
Mustamäe (heat-demand: insulation)	
Vilde tee	±35
Sütiste tee 58	±37

to 2.6ktCO$_2$e for Mustamäe Sütiste tee 58. In common with the Děčín results, it is clear that the uncertainty in total emissions reduction is high for all the projects. Table 7.10 summarizes the uncertainties for each of the projects.

In general, the highest emissions baseline for these projects has been the continuation of the pre-project situation for the JI project lifetime, whereas the lowest has been the early transition (normally after ten years) to the JI project itself. For the energy-supply projects, this is effectively a comparison between using a 10-year lifetime for calculating emissions reduction (and therefore issuing credits) and a 25-year lifetime. In the case of the heat-demand projects, only a 15-year lifetime is assumed; therefore, the range of uncertainty is lower. The higher uncertainty in the projects which supply electricity is due, as discussed in the case of Děčín, to the difficulty in knowing exactly what grid-connected sources are being replaced.

Specific Emissions Reduction

Figure 7.2 summarizes the results for the specific GHG emissions reduction over the lifetime of the projects.

The results of the two Mustamäe projects are again not shown in Figure 7.2. This is because of a lack of detailed data on the heat delivery system. Without such data, values for specific emissions reduction are not meaningful. Again, the range of uncertainty is very large due to the possibility that significantly different technology and fuel options will be available during the project lifetime. The relative range of uncertainty for each project is similar to that for the total emissions reduction (and given in Table 7.10), since energy demand, plant efficiency and fuel quality are assumed to remain constant in most cases.

Comparisons between project types lead to some interesting insights. The highest specific emissions reduction is, not surprisingly, the wind project, mainly because of the assumptions of replacing coal with electricity. Interestingly, however, the coal-to-gas cogeneration project has a higher (on average) specific emissions reduction than the HFO-to-biomass district-heating projects. While there are large savings from using CO$_2$-neutral biomass, the efficiency gains of the cogeneration project are more significant.

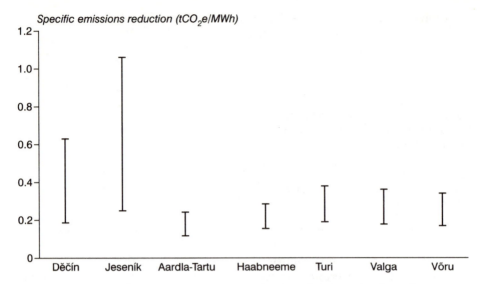

Figure 7.2 *Specific GHG Emissions Reduction for Case Study JI Projects*

It is also interesting to compare projects of the same type. In this case we have results from five HFO-to-biomass district-heating boilers. In general, as Figure 7.2 shows, the results are quite similar. However, differences in operating conditions lead to some variation. For example, at Aardla-Tartu, the output from the multiboiler plant was switched to 86 per cent natural gas and 14 per cent HFO the year before the biomass boiler was installed. Hence, the likely baselines have lower GHG emissions, leading to lower specific emissions reduction. At Haabneeme, the biomass was 15 per cent peat, 85 per cent woodchips. Since peat is not a CO_2-neutral fuel, the specific emissions reduction is also lower. The results for Türi, Valga and Võru are more similar, the only variation being plant efficiencies.

A comparison can also be made with the coal-to-biomass district-heating projects in the Czech Republic. While a full examination of baseline uncertainty was not carried out for these projects for the reasons explained earlier, a simple comparison was undertaken between the specific emissions reduction of the projects, assuming that the pre-project situation continues for the lifetime of the project (baseline 1 for the Estonian heat-supply projects). This shows, not surprisingly, that the coal-to-biomass projects had a higher value for specific emissions reduction than the HFO-to-biomass projects (for example, $0.42tCO_2e/MWh$ for Staré Město, compared with $0.37tCO_2e/MWh$ for Türi).

Incremental Costs

Figure 7.3 summarizes the results for the incremental costs over the lifetime of the projects.

The results for the two Mustamäe projects are again not shown in Figure 7.3 because they are so small: US\$0.007 million to US\$0.032 million for

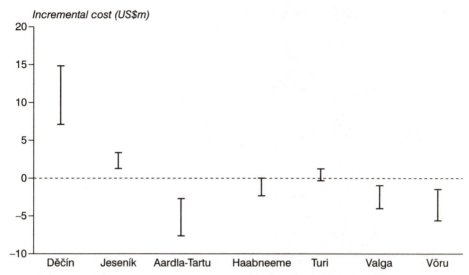

Figure 7.3 *Incremental Costs for Case Study JI Projects*

Mustamäe Vilde tee; and US$0.012 million to US$0.063 million for Mustamäe Sütiste tee 58. It is again clear from all of these results that the uncertainty is high.

The reasons for the large range are multiple. Issues such as the investment costs of the project, the difference in the fuel prices between the project and the baseline, and the timing of technology replacement in the baseline are all important.

A further point to note is that several of the projects yield negative incremental costs for some or all of the baselines considered (they are cost-savings over the lifetime). This is important since, according to a strict interpretation of economic theory, such projects could not be considered *additional* because they would have been carried out without JI. However, as we see in the next chapter, incremental costs are critically dependent upon the values used for discount rate and project lifetime. And, of course, as discussed in Chapter 3, negative incremental costs are not the only way to determine the additionality of a project.

Specific Incremental Costs

Figure 7.4 summarizes the results for the specific incremental costs over the lifetime of the projects. Again, a large range of uncertainty due to baseline choice is apparent.

Comparison between and within project types again reveals some interesting insights. To begin with, the variation between the heat-supply projects is as large as that between projects of different types. The use of natural gas at Aardla-Tartu, as well as a large variation in the price of locally sourced biomass between the projects, are the main reasons for this. Lower than expected output at Türi is also significant. Since the market for woodchips

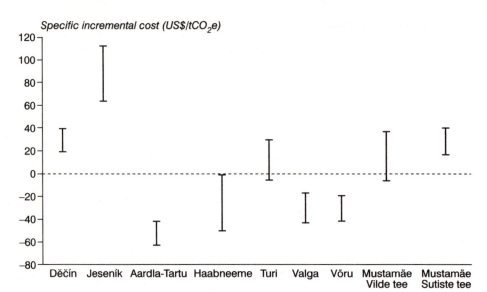

Figure 7.4 *Specific Incremental Costs for Case Study JI Projects*

was still being established in Estonia at the time that the projects were initiated, considerable price volatility occurred.

The particularly high values for specific incremental costs at Jeseník wind farm were due to errors in the design phase leading to underperformance. As a result, this range should not be considered to be general to wind energy.

The relatively high values for the two heat-demand projects at Mustamäe are surprising, since building energy-efficiency projects is often expected to save money. However, the baseline choice is particularly critical here: if the urgent building repairs are assumed to be carried out in the baseline, the projects break even, and the specific incremental cost falls to zero.

General Comments

It should be noted that, for all the JI projects studied in this chapter, we have considered it reasonable to repeatedly choose two particular baseline options:

1   the existing case continues for the technical lifetime (although we consider our assumptions on costs in this case to be somewhat optimistic); and
2   a delayed start (by ten years) is incorporated within the baseline of the JI project.

The former gives the highest estimate for emissions reduction, while the latter gives the lowest (and is equivalent to a crediting lifetime of ten years).[5] This is a useful insight since it means that an estimate of uncertainty due to baseline choice can be guided by the uncertainty in the timing of the JI project's introduction under the host country's normal development. However, as we have seen in the electricity-supply, cogeneration and heat-demand projects, uncertainty due to system interactions complicates this (as discussed further in Chapter 8).

Comparison with Framework Convention on Climate Change Reported Data

In this section we compare the estimates of emissions reduction derived for this study with those for the JI projects officially reported to the FCCC secretariat (UN FCCC, 2000) under the AIJ pilot phase. Official reports have been made for the following projects covered by this study: Aardla-Tartu, Haabneme, Valga, Võru and Děčín.

Table 7.11 details the comparison, using the upper and lower values calculated in the baseline assessment in the previous sections. Figure 7.5 illustrates this comparison.

The first point to note is that the Estonian projects have all been assessed using a short crediting lifetime. It seems that the official assessors felt it was likely that such projects may be undertaken by the host after that time and

Table 7.11 *Comparison between Estimates of Emissions Reduction Reported to the FCCC Secretariat and Those from This Study*

Project[a]	FCCC reported		This study[b]		
	Crediting lifetime years	Total emissions reduction tCO_2	Crediting Lifetime years	Total emissions reduction tCO_2e	Reasons for difference
Estonia					
Aardla-Tartu	15[c]	122,300[c]	10	89,000	error in fuel displaced;
(heat supply)			25	224,000	
Haabneme	10	124,000	10	77,000	feasibility data
(heat supply)			25	192,000	overestimated; peat not assessed;
Valga	10	64,000	10	69,000	insignificant;
(heat supply)			25	176,000	
Võru	10	114,000	10	89,000	feasibility data
(heat supply)			25	247,000	overestimated
Czech Republic					
Děčín	27	607,150	10	216,000[d]	baseline emissions
(cogeneration)			25	728,000[e]	for electricity higher

Key:
a Emissions reduction for network upgrade projects are reported separately and have not been assessed in this study.
b Values from this study are for CO_2, CH_4 and N_2O; as a result, they are slightly higher than the FCCC results which are CO_2 only.
c Revised by NUTEK following reassessment including monitoring.
d Low emissions estimate for electricity baseline.
e High emissions estimate for electricity baseline.

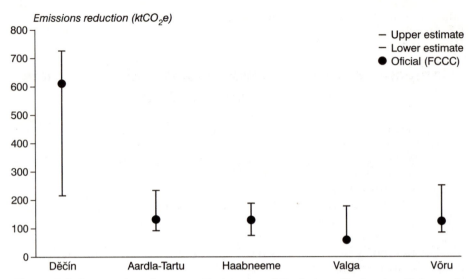

Figure 7.5 *Comparison between Estimates of Emissions Reduction Reported to the FCCC Secretariat and Those from This Study*

cannot be credited further. Consequently, all their estimates tend to be at the low end of the range found by this study. Inconsistencies tend to be because of the use of feasibility data in the official assessment. One official report (Aardla-Tartu) has been updated based on measured operating data. Its estimates for emissions reduction are consistent with those of this study, if we assume a 15-year lifetime. However, this similarity is a coincidence since there are significant differences in the data on which both estimates are based. In this study, we found that, shortly before the biomass boiler was commissioned, the plant began supplying natural gas as well as HFO. Hence, the displaced fuel in our calculations was significantly different from that in the official report.

The emissions reduction reported to the FCCC for the Czech cogeneration plant at Děčín lies towards the high end of the range of emissions reduction calculated in this study. This is because the official statistics assume a crediting lifetime of 27 years, equal to the estimated technical lifetime. (In fact, this assumption would place the project at the highest point of the range in this study, were it not for the fact that the two calculations make different assumptions about the baseline: this study assumes that the displaced electricity is generated 100 per cent by brown-coal power plants, whereas the FCCC statistics assume a constant average mix of fuels.)

The comparison presented here shows how different project assessors have made very different assumptions about the baseline (including the length of time before the JI project itself would have been undertaken) and hence come up with differing estimates for total emissions reduction. Clearly, some consistency is required in baseline setting in order to prevent this process from being biased.

Conclusions

In this chapter we have discussed the methodology used to account for emissions reduction and incremental costs of JI projects and presented some results. These assessments have been carried out at the project level – in particular, exploring the difficult issue of baseline construction.

One focus of the accounting assessment has been to examine the uncertainty associated with baseline construction. To this end, we have tried to conduct a rigorous assessment of JI projects. Not surprisingly, we have found that such an assessment is both data intensive and time consuming. Difficulties have been encountered due to a lack of data on the pre-project situation in certain circumstances.

In spite of these difficulties, we can conclude that there are generally several reasonable options for baseline choice for any given JI project. These involve the use of different technologies and fuels and the timing of changes in such factors. Such a range of baseline choice leads to a very wide variation in estimated values for emissions reduction, specific emissions reduction, incremental costs and specific incremental costs over the lifetime of the project. For emissions reduction and specific emissions reduction, we have estimated this uncertainty to be about ±45 per cent for heat-supply projects, ±55 per cent for cogeneration projects, and ±60 per cent for electricity-supply projects. For demand-side projects we have assumed a shorter project lifetime; therefore, the uncertainty in these cases is around ±35 per cent. It is important to note that these results are based on assessments which assume no changes in energy demand, fuel quality, fuel availability or technical efficiency. These estimates should be considered as minimum values for uncertainty. Consequently, we feel that, even with a detailed assessment, the large uncertainty in estimates of emissions reduction and incremental costs arising from the counterfactuality of the baseline cannot be reduced. The issue of uncertainty is revisited in Chapter 8.

This conclusion has important implications for JI, since high uncertainty in emissions reduction can be exploited to maximize credits. In Chapter 9 we discuss the potential for some form of standardization to address this problem. This would have the added benefit of reducing the transaction costs of JI.

Early in this chapter, we carried out a brief assessment to examine whether specific emissions (such as GHG emissions per unit output) can be used as the basis of a standardized method for baseline construction. We found that specific emissions can be used to represent a complex situation – for example, for the Děčín cogeneration project parameters such as electricity and heat output – and that plant and network efficiencies can be summarized in the value for specific emissions. We also carried out a comparison of specific emissions for given technologies and fuels based on standard data tables, which produced similar results to those using measured data, indicating that this sort of standardized method would be reasonable.

Finally, in this chapter we carried out a comparison between the estimates of emissions reductions reported to the FCCC for the official AIJ projects assessed in this study with the range of estimates calculated here. In general, the official values were within our ranges. However, a couple of further points are worth noting. In the projects where Sweden was the donor, the official estimates for the AIJ projects tended to be at the low end of our range due to the short crediting life chosen (10 to 15 years). But in the case where the US and Denmark were the donors (Děčín), the official estimate was at the high end of our range due to the long crediting life chosen (27 years).

Therefore, we reiterate the conclusion made above that baseline choice and crediting life (timing of introducing the JI project itself into the baseline) are critical in determining the emissions reduction attributed to a given project.

Uncertainty and Sensitivity Analysis: Methodology and case study results

S Parkinson, P Bailey, K Begg and T Jackson

Introduction

In Chapter 7, we set out the basic project-level methodology for calculating four *critical variables* (emissions reduction, specific emissions reduction, incremental costs and specific incremental costs) over the lifetime of a joint implementation (JI) project. We calculated the values of these critical variables for each of our selected case study projects against a variety of counterfactual baselines. In this chapter, we explore the robustness of other assumptions used in the analysis, employing methods of uncertainty and sensitivity analysis.

We begin by identifying the main sources of uncertainty in the accounting assessment. Next, we review the main methodologies available in uncertainty and sensitivity analysis. These methods are then used to carry out a series of analyses. The first of these analyses explores the importance of system interactions for non-separable projects. We then examine the sensitivity of critical variables to different economic accounting assumptions (such as discount rate and project lifetime). We also explore the impact of the practice of discounting emissions on the values of the critical variables. Next, we carry out a comparison between values of the critical variables based on feasibility data and those based on monitored data. Finally, we undertake a series of analyses to determine the relative importance of different sources and combinations of uncertainty.

Sources of Uncertainty

The first step in managing uncertainty in the assessment of JI projects is to identify its sources. In this chapter, we attempt to categorize such sources. Firstly, we have already noted the uncertainty associated with the *counterfac-*

tuality of the baseline. We denote this as counterfactual uncertainty. Since this was discussed in considerable detail in Chapter 7, we do not pursue it further at this point.

The second issue which directly affects the level of uncertainty in calculating emissions reduction and incremental costs is whether to base them on:

- projections of future project performance – for example, using data compiled at the feasibility stage of project execution (known as an *ex-ante* calculation); or
- measured data – for example, annual project-operating data (known as an *ex-post* calculation).

The difference between these two kinds of calculation will depend upon two main factors: firstly, whether or not the technology performs according to specification; and, secondly, whether or not demand expectations are as predicted. Obviously the *ex-ante* method is the only option which can inform an investor decision on whether to go ahead with the given project. In principle, either *ex-ante* or *ex-post* methods could be used to provide the basis for issuing credits for emissions reductions. The first method would have the advantage of investor attractiveness, given that a value for the emissions reduction (and therefore the number and price of credits issued) would be known at the start of the project. However, the second method has the advantage of being more accurate since it would be based on actual demand profiles and technology performance rather than on less certain future projections. Therefore, it is important to assess how much extra uncertainty is added by the use of feasibility data over measured data. We call this source of uncertainty *project-performance uncertainty*.

The third issue is the degree of accuracy with which the technical and financial parameters (such as output, efficiency, emission factor, investment costs and fuel costs) can be determined or measured. We call this *measurement uncertainty*.

A further issue is the background situation: the economic, political, social and environmental factors in the host country and internationally. Particularly at a project level, these factors implicitly help define projections of project and baseline performance, and hence are difficult to evaluate separately from the counterfactual and project-performance uncertainties. Exceptions to this are parameters and variables such as exogenously determined fuel prices. At a system level, further sources of *background uncertainty* can be explicitly investigated – for instance, uncertainty in the technical and financial parameters of the technologies described in the energy–economic model.

As a result, we can categorize the sources of uncertainty into four groups: counterfactual, project performance, measurement and background uncertainty. The sources of these uncertainties are summarized in Table 8.1.

From the discussion above we can see that, while the uncertainty in the project performance can be removed by monitoring the JI project, there will always be some counterfactual, measurement and background uncertainty.

Table 8.1 *Sources of Uncertainty in JI Project Accounting*

Type of uncertainty	Source
Counterfactual	Inability to determine: baseline technology/fuel; performance of baseline technology; timing of replacement/length of time-frame; equivalence of service
Project performance	Lack of knowledge of future demand profiles and project operation: zero if monitored operating data are used
Measurement	Accuracy of technical/financial data: for example, plant output; efficiency of plant/network; emission factor (fuel/technology characteristics); utilization factor
Background	Lack of knowledge of effect of future political/economic/ social/environmental factors on JI project/baseline: for example, energy system development; fuel availability/prices; air pollution regulations

Methodologies for Dealing with Uncertainty

Having categorized the sources of uncertainty into four groups, we now describe the methodologies used to decide the importance of each, and also estimate the total combined uncertainty from all four sources in the emissions reduction calculations.

There are basically three main methods to assess the uncertainty of the result of a set of calculations or a mathematical model. These are, in order of complexity: *simple sensitivity analysis, scenario analysis* and *stochastic simulation*. Scenario analysis can also be used as a way of studying a variety of options at a purely qualitative level. The three methods will first be discussed in general terms and then in terms of their applicability to the problems discussed here.

Simple Sensitivity Analysis

Simple sensitivity analysis is where some value in a mathematical model (for example, an input variable or parameter) is varied according to the limits of its perceived uncertainty to determine the effect on the model output. A researcher can then compare this with the effects on the output of other uncertain input variables or parameters and make a judgement about which of the uncertainties are most critical to the analysis.

In practice, a small number of input variables or parameters will be selected and varied, one by one, to their estimated limits of uncertainty, and the consequent effect on the output will be noted. A more thorough sensitivity analysis is achieved by varying all the input variables or parameters, one by one, to their perceived levels of uncertainty.

While simple sensitivity analysis is straightforward, there are drawbacks. The main obstacles are:

- The sensitivities of multiple outputs to parametric uncertainty are difficult to compare.
- It is very difficult to detect interaction between parameters which may lead to less accurate estimates of output sensitivity.

These problems are addressed to some extent by sensitivity analysis using stochastic simulation (see below).

Scenario Analysis

Scenario analysis is very common in the study of problems associated with climatic change (see, for example, IPCC WG III, 1996). This is where a series of options is specified, each one based on a set of assumptions about the possible values of the input variables or parameters, and the output is calculated for each option in turn. This type of analysis has the advantage of focusing on the main points of interest to the researcher, and can therefore be less time consuming than varying the inputs and parameters one by one. A more advanced version of this methodology involves estimating the probability of the occurrence of a given scenario, which can add further information about the result.

Scenario analysis can also be used to carry out a qualitative investigation. As mentioned above, a series of options can be chosen, but in this case only a qualitative assessment of the outcome of each option is specified for comparison. A simple example might be: option 1 – the power plant is built and the visual impact is high; or option 2 – the power plant is not built and there is no visual impact.

One possible drawback with this approach is that, because only a selection of input variables/parameters are examined in each scenario, there may be significant sources of uncertainty among those left out which would not be examined.

Stochastic Simulation

Stochastic simulation gives a much more detailed assessment of the effect of the uncertainty in the model inputs and parameters than do the previous two methods due to a set of assumptions (see Parkinson and Young, 1998). It does, however, require more sophisticated tools, such as a fast computer platform.

In stochastic simulation, all the parameters and inputs are defined in terms of probability distributions based on their perceived uncertainties. The model simulation is then carried out repeatedly a large number of times (several hundred to several thousand, depending upon statistical considerations), each time using parameter or input values sampled from these distributions either randomly (known as Monte Carlo sampling) or using a stratified sampling method (for example, Latin Hypercube sampling).[1] In this way, a probability distribution for each output can be produced which gives a measure of the uncertainty.

This methodology is less subjective than either of the above as it takes into account the contributions of all the parameter and input uncertainties to all the outputs, and does so simultaneously, thereby including any combined effects of groups of parameters. The major source of subjectivity here is in the estimates of the probability distributions, which is a feature present in the previous two analyses.

The results of stochastic simulation can be used to carry out more rigorous sensitivity analysis than that described above. Using conventional regression analysis to compare the sample of each parameter and input to the sample of the output, the degree of correlation can be found which gives a measure of the contribution of each parameter and input to the total uncertainty.

Application in This Study

Having defined the three methods to analyse the uncertainty in the emissions reduction and costs for a given JI project, we must now decide how to apply them in order to examine the effects of each of the four sources described earlier (counterfactual, project performance, measurement and background), including their combined effect. Most of this analysis is carried out at project level, using a discount rate of 4 per cent and a project lifetime of 25 years. However, some of the assessment is carried out at a system level and/or a different discount rate (see below).

In order to estimate counterfactual uncertainty, scenario analysis has been used. A number of scenarios have been defined for the baseline of each JI project and then a range of uncertainty for each of the critical variables can easily be found for each JI project. The results of this scenario analysis have already been presented in Chapter 7.

In order to look at the project-performance uncertainty at the project level, we again use scenario analysis. We define one scenario of project performance based on feasibility data, and another based on operating data for the first few years of the project. If we then compare the *monitored* scenario with the *feasibility* scenario, we can calculate the percentage change in, for example, the emissions reduction for each JI project.

With regard to measurement uncertainty, we use stochastic simulation. We only examine the uncertainty in the emissions reduction due to this source. We estimate the degree of accuracy with which technical parameters can be measured, based on published sources. We then define probability distributions for each of these parameters and carry out stochastic simulation to give an estimate of the uncertainty in the emissions reduction.

It is very difficult to neatly define background uncertainty, particularly since there is some overlap with project performance and counterfactual uncertainty. As a result, we only explore the effect of one specific source of background uncertainty in this study – the fuel price projections – and only the effect on incremental costs. Here, we use scenario analysis.

After looking at each source of uncertainty individually, we then look at how they combine using stochastic simulation. We only carry out this analysis for emissions rather than costs. Probability distributions for the technical variables are estimated based on the assessments above, and are described in more detail later in the chapter. We carry out three uncertainty assessments: *total*, *monitored* and *no baseline*. The first assessment (total) gives an estimate of the uncertainty in the emissions reduction due to project performance,

Table 8.2 *Summary of Uncertainty Analysis by Source and Methodology*

Method Source	Simple sensitivity analysis	Scenario analysis	Stochastic simulation
Counterfactual		✔	
Project performance		✔	
Measurement	✔[d]		✔[b]
Background[a]		✔[c]	
Combinations of above			✔[b]

Notes:
a fuel prices only
b emissions only
c costs only
d system-level assessment

measurement and counterfactual (implicitly including background) uncertainty. Monitored assessment looks only at the uncertainty due to the counterfactual and measurement sources. The final assessment (no baseline) is where we only examine the uncertainty in *emissions* rather than emissions *reduction* from a counterfactual baseline (only the effect of measurement uncertainty is assessed). Hence, we can look at the total uncertainty in the estimate of the emissions reduction, and then at how this uncertainty can be reduced through monitoring. We also carry out sensitivity analysis, based on regression analysis, to find which specific parameters contribute most towards the combined uncertainty.

It is much harder to carry out uncertainty analysis at the system level because of the size and complexity of the energy–economic model, EFOM-ENV. Therefore, we have only carried out simple sensitivity analysis on a small number of parameters.

Table 8.2 summarizes the uncertainty and sensitivity analysis used.

Project- versus System-Level Assessment

As discussed in Chapter 4, if a JI project can be considered separable from the energy system (it has no significant interactions with the system), it can be adequately assessed using a project-level analysis. However, for non-separable projects, we argued that, in theory, a system-level analysis is necessary.[2] In this section we explore that argument by carrying out a project-level analysis and a system-level analysis on three non-separable projects: Jeseník (electricity supply from wind); Lettland (electricity supply from wind); and Děčín (cogeneration from natural gas).

Such a system-level assessment requires the use of an energy–economic or bottom-up model.[3] These models are commonly used for analysing the development of energy systems both nationally and internationally. A detailed review of their use in climate change research is given in Hourcade et al (1996). In summary, they describe the network of the energy system in a given country

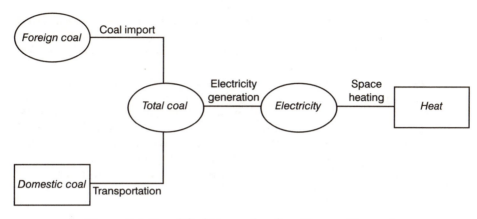

Figure 8.1 *Simplified Example of an Energy Network*

(both to supply heat and electricity) and explain how it changes subject to exogenously specified values for demand, emissions targets, etc. The underlying assumption of these models is one of cost minimization. Technologies are specified in terms of technical parameters, such as fuel type, efficiency and capacity, and financial parameters, such as investment and fuel costs.

A simple example of this structure is shown in Figure 8.1.

In this study, we carried out a review of a number of energy–economic models in order to find one appropriate to the work. On the basis of this, EFOM-ENV was selected, particularly since it has been used to assess a number of Central and Eastern European (CEE) countries, including the Czech Republic.

The Czech version of EFOM-ENV was developed under the EUR10 programme (van Harmelen et al, 1995) and is currently owned and maintained by the Czech consultancy VUPEK. A number of assumptions have been made about the Czech energy system in constructing this version, and we summarize the main ones here. Full details are given in van Harmelen et al (1995).

- Demand projections are based on gross domestic product (GDP) growth of 4.7 per cent, together with structural changes to encourage uptake of more efficient technologies.
- A very simple load curve is assumed to operate in the electricity sector, only discriminating between base load plants and peak load plants. This is particularly problematic, as we shall see later.

Using this version of EFOM-ENV, assessment was carried out of the Czech non-separable projects: Děčín (cogeneration from natural gas) and Jeseník (electricity supply from wind). In order to increase the size of the sample, we also assessed a third project – a Latvian wind farm (Lettland) – as though it were based in the Czech Republic.

The system-level assessment using EFOM-ENV was a simple comparison of two scenarios. In the first, EFOM-ENV was executed, minimizing total discounted costs and subject to Czech emissions targets (for GHGs, SO_2 and

NO_x) over the period 1990 to 2015. In the second, the JI project was inserted in 1996. Thus, the incremental costs and emissions reduction due to the project could be calculated by differencing the total discounted costs and the total emissions for the two cases.

A third scenario could have been executed such that the greenhouse gas (GHG) emissions reduction was constrained to reach that in the second scenario, but in the absence of the JI project. This would have been a more correct comparison with the second scenario, since the reduction due to the JI project would not be credited to the host country and so could not be counted towards meeting its GHG target. Unfortunately, programming problems prevented such a scenario from being executed. However, we still feel that the analysis and results presented here illustrate the issues of concern.

Jeseník

Tables 8.3 and 8.4 compare the results of assessing the Jeseník wind farm using a project- and a system-level analysis for different discount rates (dr) and lifetimes, and also for project size. This latter examination was achieved by scaling up the JI project parameters by a factor of 100.

As can be seen from Tables 8.3 and 8.4, differences are found at the system level. These mainly affect the incremental cost of the JI project rather than the GHG emissions reduction. Specifically, the main effects are as follows.

- GHG emissions reduction and specific emissions reduction calculated by the system-level and project-level analyses are very similar. The brown-coal fired power plant replaced by the JI project in both cases had similar enough characteristics that little difference was found.
- Incremental costs are significantly lower at the system level, except for the 300MW case (with a 4 per cent dr; lifetime: 20 years). The reason for this is as follows. In the system model with the JI project included, there is less need for cleaner energy sources elsewhere in the system to meet the emissions targets. Hence, less costly options are chosen by the model, partially offsetting the cost of the JI project.
- Project lifetime and discount rate significantly affect the results.
- An increase in the size of the JI project (from 3MW to 300MW, which could represent a programme of similar projects) slightly affects its interaction with the system, but again does not affect which type of plant is replaced. As a result, the specific emissions reduction (per unit output) is unchanged.

Furthermore, simple sensitivity analysis discovered that changes in the parameter values could significantly affect the system-level results. For example, a 10 per cent increase in investment costs for the baseline (the brown-coal power plant) leads to a 10 per cent increase in the GHG emissions reduction because the JI project replaces a higher fraction of the polluting plant for the same cost.

Table 8.3 *Comparison between Project- and System-Level Assessment of Emissions Reduction Variables for the Jeseník Wind Farm*

	Emissions reduction $ktCO_2e$		Specific emissions reduction tCO_2e/MWh	
	Project (baseline 2)[a]	System (EFOM)	Project (baseline 2)[a]	System (EFOM)
3MW				
10% dr, 10 years	24	26	0.90	0.99
4% dr, 20 years	48	47	0.90	0.89
300MW (100x)				
10% dr, 10 years	2400	2600	0.90	0.99
4% dr, 20 years	4800	4700	0.90	0.89

Note:
a There are some differences between the emissions factors used in the project-level analysis in Chapter 7 and those in EFOM-ENV. Therefore, in this table we have recalculated the project-level results with those factors used in EFOM-ENV.

Lettland

A similar comparison was carried out for the Lettland wind farm. As in the case of Jeseník, some system interactions have been found, but again, these mainly affect cost rather than GHG emissions. The wind farm replaces a brown-coal power plant. However, due to the lower investment cost of Lettland compared with Jeseník (CZK 58 million compared to CZK 115 million), the EFOM model found that it could still meet its emissions targets but at a lower cost by spending less on emission reduction measures in the transport sector.

Specifically, the main effects are as follows.

- GHG emissions reductions calculated at the system and project level are very similar. The plant replaced in both cases had similar enough characteristics that little difference was found.
- Incremental costs are significantly higher at the project level, particularly for a 4 per cent discount rate (dr) and a lifetime of 20 years. As for Jesenik, there is less need in the system model with the JI project included for cleaner energy sources elsewhere in the system to meet the emissions targets. Hence, cheaper options are chosen by the model.
- Project lifetime and discount rate significantly affect the results.
- The size of the wind farm does not significantly affect its interaction with the system (the farm was scaled up from its realized size of 1.2MW to 120MW, which led merely to a scaling up of the incremental cost and emissions reduction).

Lettland has also been assessed using the Russian version of the PERSEUS model (Rentz et al, 1998). In this case, the JI project was scaled up to 1000 times its size (1200MW) and assessed under similar conditions (start date:

Table 8.4 *Comparison between Project- and System-Level Assessments of Incremental Cost Variables for the Jeseník Wind Farm*

	Incremental costs US\$ million		Specific incremental cost[a] US\$/tCO$_2$e	
	Project (baseline 2)[b]	System (EFOM)	Project (baseline 2)[b]	System (EFOM)
3MW				
10% dr, 10 years	3.5	3.2	150	120
4% dr, 20 years	4.0	3.0	93	64
300MW (100x)				
10% dr, 10 years	350	320	150	120
4% dr, 20 years	400	520	93	110

Notes:
a Specific incremental costs in this table have been calculated using undiscounted emissions (on the basis of equation 7.18) because of the format of the output from the system model used in the calculation.
b There are some differences between the emissions factors used in the project-level analysis in Chapter 7 and those in EFOM-ENV. Therefore, in this table we have recalculated the project-level results with those factors used in EFOM-ENV.

1995; lifetime: 20 years; discount rate: 4 per cent) to those found in the EFOM-ENV analysis (Wietschel, personal communication). The project primarily substituted gas-fired combined-cycle plants, so the specific emissions reduction was significantly smaller.

Děčín

System-level assessment using EFOM-ENV was attempted for the Děčín cogeneration plant. In this case, the replaced plant was found to be gas cogeneration (the JI project itself). However, since it is known that the heat produced by the project will replace a brown-coal district-heating boiler, this result can be rejected. Attempts at constraining EFOM-ENV to replace the heat from such a boiler were unsuccessful, and we conclude that EFOM-ENV needs further development to carry out this task.

Summary

The comparison carried out between a system-level and a project-level analysis gave mixed results. For two of the projects, the system-level analysis did not reveal any significant difference in terms of estimated emissions reduction, although incremental costs were decreased due to 'knock-on' effects in other sectors. For the other project, the system-level results were considered unrealistic.

There are a number of points relevant to these results. The modelling of the load curve in the Czech EFOM-ENV is crude: it only discriminates between base and peak plants, which makes it particularly problematic for assessing variable sources such as wind and cogeneration. Furthermore, some of the system interactions noted were knock-on effects in sectors which, in practice, are unlikely to be affected by such projects (for example, transport). This is due to the optimizing nature of the model, which is a simplifying assumption of economic behaviour, and may be inappropriate for the project sizes considered here.

The PERSEUS model attempts to overcome some of these shortcomings by the use of more detail in the load curves and the modelling of economic behaviour. However, as we have already remarked, increasing the level of detail often increases the uncertainty involved because it introduces a larger number of uncertain parameters that have to be specified. So there is no guarantee that PERSEUS can overcome these problems. In addition, it is very difficult to realistically model non-market barriers to JI. One other problem is that collecting the detailed data for such models may be difficult, especially in countries with a low institutional capacity.

Energy–economic models were originally designed to aid national energy planning. They are now being used more and more to advise on national GHG emissions-reduction programmes. The emphasis has, therefore, always been on high-level assessment. This is supported by the points made above. Hence, in the light of the small differences between the system- and project-level analyses of emissions reduction seen here (even for simulated JI projects 100 times larger than ours), we see little justification for carrying out a system-level assessment. Of course, for very large projects, the situation may be different.

Effect of Different Accounting Frameworks

In this section we explore how different economic accounting frameworks may affect the values of the four critical variables. We examine two different accounting scenarios: *financial*, using a discount rate of 10 per cent with a lifetime equal to an amortization period of 10 years; and *social*, using a discount rate of 4 per cent together with a technical lifetime of 25 years. We have chosen these two scenarios to reflect the two commonly practised discounting methods relevant to JI as discussed in Chapters 3 and 7. The particular 10 per cent/10 year and 4 per cent/25 year combinations have been chosen so that the neglected terms, beyond the end of the lifetime, are about the same size.[4] We also look at the practice of discounting emissions under each of these scenarios.

In this section we detail results from one JI project (Děčín, cogeneration) for each of its baselines. The analysis was also carried out for Jeseník (wind) and Türi (biomass boiler). Since they are, in general, very similar to the Děčín case, they are not presented here.

Děčín

Tables 8.5, 8.6 and 8.7 show the effect of the different economic accounting frameworks on the values of critical variables for Děčín. These results illustrate that the choice of discount rate and lifetime has a large effect on the values of the critical variables.

Table 8.5 *Effect of Emissions Discounting (Using Social Costing) on Critical Variables at Děčín*

	Emissions reduction $ktCO_2e$		Specific incremental cost $US\$/tCO_2e$		Specific emissions reduction tCO_2e/MWh	
	Undiscounted	Discounted	Undiscounted	Discounted	Undiscounted	Discounted
Baseline 1	730	450	20	33	0.62	0.62
Baseline 2	560	370	13	19	0.47	0.50
Baseline 3	440	310	27	39	0.37	0.42
Baseline 4	640	400	16	25	0.54	0.54
Baseline 5	290	240	26	33	0.26	0.33

For emissions reduction, with emissions discounting, there is a fairly consistent drop of 40–60 per cent when we switch from social costing to financial costing. The specific emissions reduction tends to increase, but this is mainly due to the shortening of the lifetime to 10 years, which cuts out the low emissions baseline options which come into effect in year 11 (baselines 2, 3 and 5).

For incremental costs, there is more variation between cases because of the different make-up of each baseline. One critical aspect is the relative sizes of the investment costs and the fuel costs in the baseline. Using a high discount rate reduces the importance of the fuel costs (future costs) relative to the investment costs (present costs). Obviously, using a low discount rate emphasizes the fuel costs. The specific incremental cost generally rises with a higher discount rate because of the large fall in emissions reduction.

For the social accounting framework, emissions discounting leads to a lowering of the value for emissions reduction of 20–40 per cent, which leads to a rise in the specific incremental costs of 25–65 per cent. Emissions discounting has no effect on specific emissions reductions, so long as the baseline is constant over the project lifetime (baselines 1 and 4), since the discounting term (annuitization factor) simply cancels out of the equation.

For the financial accounting framework, baselines 1, 2, 3 and 5 become equivalent since the changes in baselines 2, 3 and 5 occur from the 11th year onwards. Consequently, the uncertainty in the baseline is significantly reduced. Emissions discounting again leads to a lowering of emissions reduction, this time by 40 per cent, resulting in an increase in the specific incremental cost of 60 per cent.

Summary

From this analysis we see that switching from a social accounting framework to a financial one (increasing the discount rate and shortening the lifetime) significantly decreases estimates of emissions reduction of JI projects and consequently increases the specific incremental costs. We also see that the practice of discounting emissions has a similar effect. While we have only presented results for one JI project, analysis of two further projects (of different types) confirms this (Jackson et al, 1999).

Table 8.6 *Effect of Emissions Discounting (Using Financial Costing) on Critical Variables at Děčín*

	Emissions reduction $ktCO_2e$		Specific incremental cost $US\$/tCO_2e$		Specific emissions reduction tCO_2e/MWh	
	Undiscounted	Discounted	Undiscounted	Discounted	Undiscounted	Discounted
Baselines						
1,2,3,5	290	180	40	64	0.62	0.62
Baseline 4	250	160	27	43	0.54	0.54

The effect of discounting emissions is particularly important since the conventional calculation for specific emissions reduction effectively discounts emissions (see equation 7.17, Chapter 7). It is clear, therefore, that without an agreed standard practice for the economic accounting framework, considerable differences will result in the calculated values for the critical variables over a range of JI project types. For example, the value of the discount rate could be changed to make a project with low specific incremental costs seem more expensive and hence qualify as a JI project when it would not otherwise have done so. The consequence of such problems is that it will not be possible to compare specific incremental costs of different JI projects; therefore, there will be no way to assess whether JI is operating as a cost-effective instrument as intended.

Another point to note from this analysis is that a shorter crediting lifetime significantly reduces the uncertainty in the baseline.

Feasibility- versus Monitoring-Based Assessment

Feasibility data are the only data available at the start of a project and are based on best estimates of future project performance (such as demand and fuel costs). Hence, the data are highly uncertain. Here, we present a comparison of the values of the critical variables calculated using feasibility data with the values of the same variables using monitoring-based operating data for nine of the JI projects.

Table 8.7 *Comparison of Incremental Costs at Děčín Using Different Economic Accounting Frameworks*

	Incremental costs US$ million (social costing)	Incremental costs US$ million (financial costing)
Baseline 1	14.9	11.4
Baseline 2	7.2	11.4
Baseline 3	12.0	11.4
Baseline 4	10.1	6.7
Baseline 5	7.7	11.4

Table 8.8 *Summary of the Comparison between Feasibility- and Monitoring-Based Assessments of Emissions Reductions for Selected JI Projects*

JI project	Emissions reduction ($ktCO_2e$)		% change	Reason for change
	Feasibility	Monitoring		
Aardla-Tartu	221	224	+1	different fuel substituted; high output (effects cancelled)
Haabneeme	338	192	−43	low demand
Türi	212	89	−58	low demand
Valga	217	176	−19	low demand
Võru	289	247	−15	low demand
Staré Město	50	33	−34	low demand
Kardašova Řečice	43	38	−12	low demand
Děčín	897	728	−19	low demand
Jeseník	217	65	−70	low output (design error)

For reasons of consistency, we have calculated the estimates of the critical variables in both cases using the same underlying assumptions (for example, discount rate, lifetime, emissions factor). In some cases this has led to different estimates from those given in the published feasibility study. This has been done so that differences in performance, for example, are detected rather than differences in assumptions.

In all cases the comparison has been carried out using baseline 1 for each project, including the social framework for economic accounting with no discounting of emissions.

Emissions Reduction

Table 8.8 summarizes the comparison between feasibility- and monitoring-based assessments of emissions reductions. As can be seen, for eight out of the nine projects the emissions reductions were overestimated in the feasibility study.

In Haabneeme, there are two reasons for the overestimation. The first is that the boiler output was much lower than expected (an average of 27GWh/year over the first four years compared to a projected 38GWh/year). The second is that 15 per cent of the fuel for the JI project is peat, which – as discussed earlier – cannot be considered a CO_2-neutral fuel.

In Türi, Valga and Võru, the reason was, again, lower-than-expected heat demand. In Türi, the actual demand was less than 50 per cent of the expected level, due mainly to local industry switching to home production of heat. As discussed earlier, the outputs of both Türi and Võru have increased beyond the low levels; but in both cases the increase has been due to network improvements carried out under other JI projects and therefore is associated with those projects.

Table 8.9 *Summary of the Comparison between Feasibility- and Monitoring-Based Assessments of Specific Emissions Reductions for Selected JI Projects*

JI project	Specific emissions reduction (tCO_2e/MWh)		% change
	Feasibility	Monitoring	
Aardla-Tartu	0.34	0.25	−26
Haabneeme	0.36	0.29	−19
Türi	0.42	0.37	−12
Valga	0.35	0.35	none
Võru	0.34	0.34	none
Staré Město	0.42	0.42	none
Kardašova Řečice	0.34	0.34	none
Děčín	0.66	0.62	−6
Jeseník	1.06	1.05	−1

Optimistic values for heat demand were also given in the feasibility study for the two Czech district-heating projects: Staré Město and Kardašova Řečice. Hence the estimates for emissions reduction were again too high.

The largest overestimation is for the Jeseník wind farm. In this case a design fault led to the output being 70 per cent lower than expected. A fire and a flood in the first couple of years compounded this problem. At Děčín, the overestimation of the emissions reduction was due to an overestimation of both the output and the efficiency of the plant, both in terms of electricity and heat.

The Aardla-Tartu boiler conversion in Estonia was the only project in this study which did not overestimate its emissions reduction (at least, that based on the monitored data from the early years of the project). Unlike the other boiler conversion projects, the expected heat demand was much higher than expected. However, the year before the biomass boiler came on line, the multiboiler plant switched to a natural gas/HFO mix. As a result, the pre-project situation (and the baselines based upon it) changed from 100 per cent HFO to 85 per cent natural gas and 15 per cent HFO. This, of course, had the effect of reducing the expected emissions reduction. Coincidentally, these two effects virtually cancelled each other out: the emissions reduction based on monitored data was 1 per cent higher than the feasibility-based value.

Specific Emissions Reduction

Table 8.9 summarizes the comparison between feasibility- and monitoring-based assessments of specific emissions reductions. It shows that in six of the nine projects, the difference between the two cases was zero or very small.

In the three cases where the difference was significant, this was either because the information on the pre-project situation had not been carefully checked (at Aardla-Tartu the fuel mix was wrong, while at Türi the boiler efficiency was incorrect) or the project fuel had changed (at Haabneeme, some peat was burned).

Table 8.10 *Summary of the Comparison between Feasibility and Monitoring-Based Assessments of Incremental Cost for Selected JI Projects*

JI project	Incremental cost (US$ million)	
	Feasibility	*Monitoring*
Aardla-Tartu	−1.4	−5.9
Haabneeme	−1.5	−0.2
Türi	−1.4	1.1
Valga	−1.1	−1.7
Võru	−0.1	−2.5
Staré Město	1.5	2.5
Kardašova Řečice	0.5	0.5
Děčín	15.2	14.9
Jeseník	2.0	2.6

Incremental Cost

Table 8.10 summarizes the comparison between feasibility- and monitoring-based assessments of incremental cost. Relative figures are not shown since they are often not meaningful when positive and negative values are being compared.

For a number of the projects, the change in the estimate for incremental cost was due to a change in fuel prices. Biomass prices, in particular, were very volatile and most changed significantly from the feasibility case. Price decreases were seen at Aardla-Tartu, Valga and Võru, whilst increases occurred at Staré Město, Haabneeme and Türi. The largest change was at Türi, where the biomass price increased from 7 Estonian kroons per gigajoule (EEK/GJ) to over 20 EEK/GJ.

Changes from the expected plant output and efficiency also affected the total fuel costs, and hence the incremental cost. Again, the change in the pre-project situation at Aardla-Tartu (from HFO to gas/HFO) and the fuel change at Haabeneeme (to a biomass/peat mix) were significant.

Few changes were found in investment costs between the feasibility and monitored cases.

Specific Incremental Cost

Table 8.11 summarizes the comparison between feasibility- and monitoring-based assessments of specific incremental cost. Again, relative figures are not shown since they are often not meaningful when positive and negative values are being compared.

The value of this critical variable is calculated from the incremental cost (Table 8.10) and the emissions reduction (Table 8.8). Since the reasons for differences between feasibility and monitoring data for these latter variables have already been discussed, Table 8.11 highlights only the most important reasons for the differences with respect to specific incremental cost.

Table 8.11 *Summary of the Comparison between Feasibility- and Monitoring-Based Assessments of Specific Incremental Cost for Selected JI Projects*

| JI project | Specific incremental cost US$/tCO2e | | Main reasons for change |
	Feasibility	Monitoring	
Aardla-Tartu	−10	−42	different fuel mix in pre-project situation
Haabneeme	−7	−1	different fuel mix in project
Türi	−10	21	increase in biomass price/ decrease in demand
Valga	−8	−15	decrease in biomass price
Võru	−0.7	−17	decrease in biomass price
Staré Město	48	119	decrease in demand
Kardašova Řečice	17	21	decrease in demand
Děčín	27	33	decrease in output
Jeseník	15	63	decrease in output due to design fault

Summary

Figure 8.2 summarizes the comparison between the estimates of emissions reduction based on feasibility data and those based on monitored operating data. JI projects which have underperformed (the values based on monitored operating data are lower than those based on feasibility data) are shown as negative.

As stated above, in all but one case the projects underperformed. In three out of the nine cases the underperformance is considerable. There are three reasons for the differences:

1 variations in demand/output;
2 variations in project fuel;
3 variations in the pre-project (and therefore the initial baseline) fuel.

As a result, we can only conclude that feasibility data are unsuitable for emission reduction calculations since it would lead to the environment objectives of JI being compromised. COWI (1996) reached a similar conclusion.

The comparison of specific emissions reduction between the feasibility and the monitored case gives a rather different picture, however. In six out of the nine projects the difference between the two cases was insignificant. In two out of the other three projects the difference would have been eliminated by more careful data collection at the feasibility stage. This result, together with the discussion above, reinforces the argument that emissions reduction estimates can be reliably calculated by using values of specific emissions reduction for a given fuel/technology, together with monitored data.

Concerning costs, the only obvious result is that there is often a large difference between costs from the feasibility case and those from the monitored case. This again emphasizes the danger of relying too heavily on feasibility

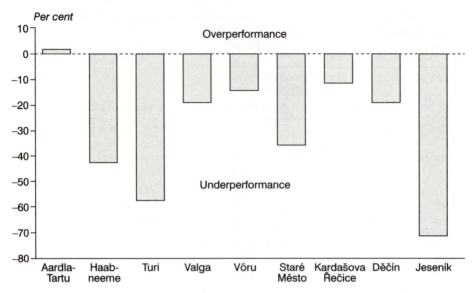

Figure 8.2 *Summary of the Comparison between Feasibility- and Monitoring-Based Assessments of Emissions Reduction for Selected JI Projects*

data. In one project, Türi, the change in costs meant that the project was no longer cost negative, and hence could not be considered as a no-regrets (negative specific-incremental costs) project. Such significant variations are particularly important if cost data from feasibility studies are used to judge the additionality of a project as discussed in Chapter 3.

It should be emphasized that much of the operating data used above were collected from site visits, which gave a better understanding of the project than would have been obtained from written descriptions alone. We recommend this approach.

Effect of Background Factors

In this section we take a brief look at the effects of changes in one of the background factors in the project-level analysis: fuel-price projections.

For two of our case study projects, Aardla-Tartu (biomass boiler) and Děčín (gas cogeneration), we carried out a comparison between the cost results of two fuel-price scenarios (both using baseline 1 and the social framework for economic accounting with no discounting of emissions). In the first scenario (which has been used by all the project-level analysis presented in this chapter), the fuel prices are held constant from the first year of the project, unless measured data were available to contradict this. In the second scenario, projected international fuel prices were used for those fuels which are not supplied from within the country (heavy-fuel oil and natural gas). These fuel prices were the same as those used by the Czech EFOM-ENV model (based on an EC price projection in 1992).

In the case of Aardla-Tartu, where the baseline is 85 per cent natural gas, 15 per cent heavy-fuel oil, and the JI project fuel is locally available biomass, the incremental cost of the project under the second fuel price scenario is 25 per cent lower than under the first scenario. In the case of Děčín, where the baseline is domestically produced brown coal and the JI project fuel is natural gas, the effect is reversed and the incremental cost of the project increases by 13 per cent under the second scenario. Clearly these changes are significant.

While the changes in incremental cost, and therefore specific incremental cost, are not negligible, they are not as large as those due to choice of baseline (see Chapter 7) or the economic accounting framework (see earlier in this chapter).

Uncertainty and Sensitivity Analysis Using Stochastic Simulation

In this section, we assess the combined effect of all four sources of uncertainty (counterfactual, project performance, measurement and background) in calculating emissions reduction. Assessment of five Estonian boiler conversion projects was carried out using a stochastic simulation package called @Risk – an add-on package for Microsoft Excel (Palisade, 1997).

As described earlier, stochastic simulation is more thorough than the sensitivity analyses carried out so far in this chapter. Model parameters and input variables are defined in terms of probability distributions rather than point values, enabling an assessment of the total uncertainty in a given output variable. Based on this, we can assess which of the four sources of uncertainty is the most important. We focus on the uncertainty in estimates of emissions reduction.

Essentially, three assessments are carried out: *total*, *monitored* and *no baseline*. In the total case, we estimate the total uncertainty due to all four sources (although, as mentioned earlier, background uncertainty tends to be subsumed within the project performance and counterfactual sources). This represents an estimate of the uncertainty in emissions reduction based on feasibility data. In the monitored case, we exclude the project performance uncertainty. If we compare this with the total uncertainty found above, we can estimate the difference in the uncertainty in emissions reduction between a monitored project and an unmonitored one, building on the assessment carried out earlier. In the no baseline case, we consider measurement uncertainty only. Therefore, a comparison between this case and the previous two will allow the uncertainty in the baseline to be highlighted.

The analysis has been carried out for all five of the Estonian boiler conversion projects (Aardla-Tartu, Haabneeme, Türi, Valga and Võru) using annual averaged data in order to simplify the work. It is assumed that these JI projects are a representative sample of Estonian biomass-fired district-heating boilers. As a result, we can use the parametric values calculated for the projects in order to construct probability-distribution functions for the analysis.

Details of the parametric uncertainties used in the total case are given in Table 8.12.[5] The uncertainties for the specific emissions s_{ji} and s_b for the JI project and the baseline respectively are calculated by taking the mean and

Table 8.12 *Uncertainties in Parameters/Variables for Estimation of Emissions Reduction Based on Feasibility Data*

Parameter/Variable	Uncertainty (66% confidence interval)
L	23 ± 1 year
s_{ji}	0.024 ± 0.031 tCO_2e/MWh[*]
s_b	0.25 ± 0.09 tCO_2e/MWh
P_o	$0.77(P_{o(f)})$ ± $0.31(P_{o(f)})$

Note: * truncated at zero

standard deviation of the values obtained in investigating baseline uncertainty in the last chapter (see Figure 7.2). While s_{ji} is representative of one fuel/technology over the time-frame (the biomass boiler), s_b is an average of possible baseline fuels/technologies. A lower value of zero is taken for s_{ji} since it is assumed that harvesting of wood will not lead to a greater uptake of CO_2 than is burned. For L, the technical lifetime, we assume that the 25 years used above is the 97.5th percentile, and therefore the 66 per cent confidence interval is 22 to 24 years. We base the probability distribution of P_o, the output of the boiler, on the comparison between the feasibility and monitored outputs of the nine projects given earlier. On average, P_o is 77 per cent of the output expected in the feasibility study, $P_{o(f)}$. Taking into account the uncertainty in this value leads to a 66 per cent confidence interval for P_o of 77 per cent ±31 per cent of $P_{o(f)}$.

Table 8.13 gives details of the uncertainties used in the monitored case. Since annual monitoring will reveal the technical lifetime exactly, there is no uncertainty in this figure. We make an assumption that this value will be 23 years (the mean value from the feasibility case). Furthermore, monitoring will reveal the output and specific emissions to within measurement uncertainty. For output, P_o, this is assumed to be ±2 per cent, whereas for s_{ji} it is project dependent (see Table 8.13); however, it is assumed to remain fairly high due to uncertainties in forest management practices. Since measurement will not reduce baseline uncertainty, this is unchanged from the feasibility case (although it is possible that this uncertainty could be reduced using baseline revision; see Chapter 9).

In the no baseline case, the lifetime is known, and the output and specific emissions of the project are known to within measurement uncertainty. In order to allow a comparison with the results from the other two cases, the plant we use here is a heavy-fuel oil boiler.

The results of the uncertainty analysis for the first two cases are given in Table 8.14, with a graphical illustration for the Valga monitored case shown as an example in Figure 8.3. As can be seen, the uncertainty in the estimate of emissions reduction is very high, roughly ±60 per cent uncertainty due to all sources, and ±40 per cent uncertainty based on annual monitoring.[6] The exception to this is the higher proportional uncertainty in the monitored case of Haabneeeme. This is a consequence of the large drop in the emissions reduction due to the realization that peat is used in the JI project: something which was not known at the feasibility stage. The magnitude of the uncertainty in the monitored case is comparable to that found in Chapter 7 for the range of

Table 8.13 *Uncertainties in Parameters/Variables for Estimation of Emissions Reduction Based on Monitored Data*

Parameter/Variable	Uncertainty (66% confidence interval)
L	23 years
s_{ji}	
Haabneeme (15% peat)	$0.08 \pm 0.04 tCO_2e/MWh$
Others	$0.01 \pm 0.06 tCO_2e/MWh^*$
s_b	$0.25 \pm 0.17 tCO2e/MWh$
P_o	$0.77(P_{o(f)}) \pm 0.02 \times 0.77(P_{o(f)})$

Note: * truncated at zero

baseline uncertainty for the boiler conversion projects. This demonstrates that the two methodologies for uncertainty assessment are compatible.

As discussed in the earlier assessment, this high uncertainty is particularly notable since these JI projects are comparatively straightforward to assess, with few system interactions, such as electricity supply or heat-demand projects. Therefore, in these latter cases we would expect the uncertainty to be significantly higher, as was found in Chapter 7.

The uncertainties in emissions *reduction* (the monitored case – that is, due to counterfactual and measurement uncertainty) are in stark contrast to the uncertainty in *emissions* (the no baseline case – that is, measurement uncertainty only), which yields uncertainties of ± 2 per cent. While it could be argued that many projects will not be able to achieve this level of monitoring accuracy, there is little doubt that this difference is very high and could be exploited to maximize credits.

The results of the sensitivity analysis for Valga are given in Figures 8.4 and 8.5. Sensitivity analyses carried out with the other four boiler projects give very similar results. As can be seen, in the total case, the contribution to the uncertainty is mainly from P_o, the boiler output, and s_b, the specific emissions of the baseline. In other words, the main sources of uncertainty arise from changing demand profiles (project performance) and counterfactual uncertainty, confirming the points made above. The contribution to the uncertainty from s_{ji} is minimal because it is much smaller in magnitude than s_b. When the project is monitored, not surprisingly, the contribution from P_o is drastically reduced.

As a result, we conclude that monitoring reduces the uncertainty in the emissions reduction by about one third, reinforcing the conclusion drawn

Table 8.14 *Uncertainty Analysis of Five JI Projects*

	Uncertainty (66% confidence limits) in emissions reduction ($ktCO_2e$)	
	Total (from all sources)	Monitored
Aardla-Tartu	101 ± 57 (57%)	103 ± 41 (40%)
Haabneeme	147 ± 84 (57%)	114 ± 60 (53%)
Türi	79 ± 46 (58%)	79 ± 31 (39%)
Valga	97 ± 55 (56%)	99 ± 40 (40%)
Võru	135 ± 80 (60%)	134 ± 54 (40%)

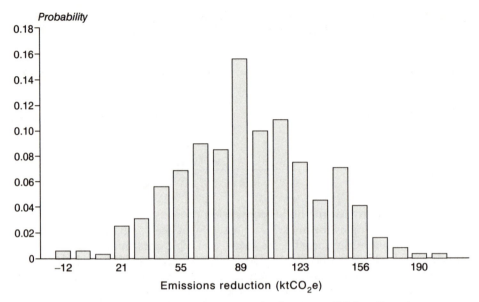

Figure 8.3 *Uncertainty in Emissions Reduction of Valga Based on Measured Data (Monitored Case)*

earlier that it is very beneficial to carry this out. However, we have also shown that the uncertainty in the baseline is an order of magnitude higher than that associated with simply measuring the *emissions* of a given plant. It should be remembered that this estimate of uncertainty has been based on a detailed assessment of separable JI projects, and hence is unlikely to be reduced. Clearly, then, if baseline construction is not carried out independently, there is scope for this uncertainty to be exploited to maximize estimated emissions reduction and therefore credits. We discuss how this might be dealt with in Chapter 9.

Conclusions

Results from this study indicate that the values of the key outputs from analysing JI projects – emissions reduction, incremental cost, specific emissions reduction and specific incremental cost – are highly dependent upon the quality of data and the assumptions made in the analysis. The detailed conclusions and recommendations are summarized below.

System Boundaries

A comparison has been carried out between project- and system-level assessments for three non-separable JI projects (the Jeseník and Lettland wind farms and the Děčín cogeneration plant).

The comparison for the wind farms found little difference in the estimates of emissions reduction, but noted some difference in costs; on the other hand,

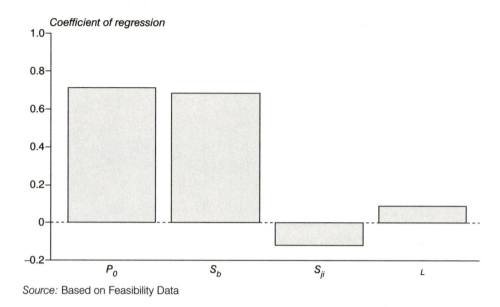

Source: Based on Feasibility Data

Figure 8.4 *Sensitivity Analysis of Emissions Reduction at Valga*

the system-level assessment of the cogeneration plant gave unrealistic results. Hence, we feel that the system-level assessment has not added any significant information to the project-level assessment in these cases. Furthermore, since we have concerns regarding the structure of the system model (in particular, simplistic assumptions regarding the load curve and economic behaviour), and regarding the high data and labour demands for its use, we do not feel that a system-level assessment (using an energy–economic model) can be justified.

However, these conclusions are based only on assessment of three small JI projects in one host country using a comparatively simplistic energy–economic model. If the JI projects were suitably large (thousands of MW), and/or a model were available for the host country with detailed modelling of the load curve, and if a similar level of detailed project data was available such that the merit order could be clearly defined, then useful information would be gained.

It should be remembered that energy–economic models have been developed for the examination of general strategies and scenarios for the energy sector. So while our analysis questions their use for individual project assessment, it does not question their usefulness in this area.

The Effect of Different Economic Accounting Frameworks

The effect of the different accounting frameworks has been explored using two scenarios: *financial*, using a discount rate of 10 per cent with a lifetime equal to an amortization period of 10 years; and *social*, using a discount rate of 4 per cent together with a technical lifetime of 25 years. The effect of emissions discounting has also been explored.

It has been found that the choice of economic accounting framework significantly affects estimates of emissions reduction of JI projects and conse-

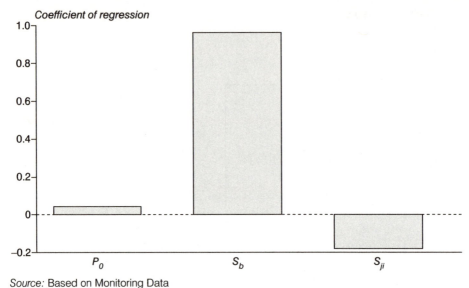

Source: Based on Monitoring Data

Figure 8.5 *Sensitivity Analysis of Emissions Reduction at Valga*

quently specific incremental costs.

Without an agreed standard practice for the economic framework, considerable differences will result in the emission and cost calculations over a range of JI project types. Therefore, it will not be possible to compare specific incremental costs of different JI projects and there will be no way to assess whether JI is operating as a cost-effective instrument as intended. The same requirement for standardized procedures applies to the construction of system baselines, and the elucidation of financial additionality criteria.

One other important observation from this analysis is that a shorter crediting lifetime significantly reduces the uncertainty in the baseline.

Feasibility- versus Monitoring-Based Assessment

For nine of the JI projects in this study, a comparison was carried out between the estimated emissions reduction and incremental cost based on: the use of project feasibility data; and monitored operating data for the first few years of project operation.

The estimates based on feasibility data, on average, overestimated the emissions reduction by 31 per cent. With three projects, these overestimates were considerable. There were three main reasons for this:

1   overestimates of project performance (for example, demand/output);
2   higher emission factors for the project fuel; and
3   lower emission factors for the pre-project (and therefore the baseline) fuel.

In many cases, the overestimates of demand occurred because of economic restructuring in the host countries: a situation very difficult to predict.

The reverse situation was encountered in comparing estimates of specific emissions reduction between the feasibility and monitored cases: in most cases the difference was negligible.

Therefore, while we can only conclude that monitored data must be used for parameters such as demand and plant output, technical parameters such as plant efficiency are likely to be close to manufacturers' specifications. This adds support to the idea that standardization of emissions-reduction accounting procedures based on standard values for specific emissions reduction is reasonable.

Background Factors

While there are many background factors that can influence the estimates of the critical variables, we chose to briefly examine one – future fuel prices – since it is well known that they are highly uncertain. A short sensitivity analysis found, not surprisingly, that assumptions concerning these prices can significantly affect the cost effectiveness of JI projects and can determine whether a project is seen to be no-regrets or not.

Uncertainty and sensitivity analysis using stochastic simulation

Four sources of uncertainty were defined at the start of the chapter: project performance, counterfactual, measurement and background. Estimates were then made of the total uncertainty in emissions reduction for heat-supply projects from all these sources using stochastic simulation.

This total uncertainty is found to be approximately ±60 per cent (66 per cent confidence interval) if the estimate of emissions reduction is based on feasibility data; however, it falls to around ±40 per cent (66 per cent confidence interval) if the estimate of emissions reduction is based on monitored operating data. This reinforces the point made above that feasibility data are not a good basis for such estimates. The uncertainty in the monitored case of ±40 per cent is comparable to that found in Chapter 7 for the uncertainty due to the counterfactual nature of the baseline.

Based on similar assumptions, we calculated an uncertainty in monitored *emissions* (rather than emissions *reduction*) of a heat-supply plant to be ±2 per cent, showing that the use of a baseline increases uncertainty by more than an order of magnitude.

These estimates are based on *separable* JI projects (negligible system interactions) which are straightforward to monitor. Therefore, for other projects which are part of a complex system or are difficult to monitor, the uncertainty can be expected to be higher.

Sensitivity analysis based on the above results identified the plant output and the specific emissions of the baseline as the most statistically significant parameters in contributing to the uncertainty in the emissions reduction. Annual monitoring considerably reduces the contribution of variability in plant output to uncertainty in the values of critical variables.

Measures for Managing Flexibility: Dealing with Complexity and Uncertainty

K Begg, T Jackson, S Parkinson, P-E Morthorst and L Nielsen

Introduction

This chapter is concerned with the institutional context of project-based flexibility mechanisms. The complexity of this context is illustrated clearly by considering a generic form of the institutional framework within which JI must operate. Figure 9.1 presents a schematic diagram of the institutional procedures which are likely to accompany the operationalization of any particular joint implementation (JI)-type mechanism. It shows that there is a need for several different accounting measures related to project feasibility, project performance and baseline assessment. It also illustrates the relevance of accreditation procedures which ensure that the emission reductions achieved by the project are appropriately credited.

This generic framework illustrates a number of the key points which we have elucidated in this book. Firstly, it is clear that the operationalization of JI implies a complex system of institutional arrangements, with feedback effects between different elements of the scheme and over time. The institutional parameters of this system include potentially different sets of institutional actors, different project-approval and auditing requirements, different project types, different regulatory safeguard measures and different accreditation procedures. Some of these parameters are clearly interrelated.

There may be some scope for simplification or *streamlining* of the institutional procedures – for instance, by avoiding excessive verification inputs to the accreditation process. The advantage of streamlined procedures is to increase flexibility in the system and to encourage investor participation; the

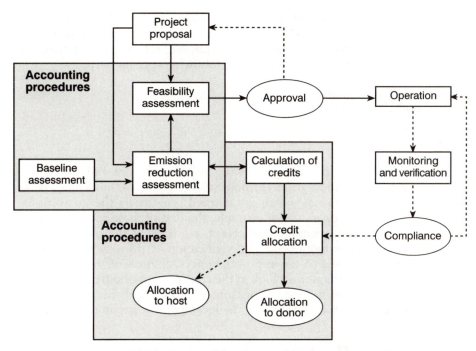

Figure 9.1 *A Generic Institutional Framework for JI*

disadvantage of streamlined procedures is to increase the potential for gaming and ultimately to risk compromising the environmental objectives of the Kyoto Protocol.

This possibility leads to a crucial observation about the management of flexibility mechanisms – namely, that each operational form of JI will perform differently against the underlying objectives defined in Chapter 3. Some operational forms will provide more security in terms of achieving environmental targets. Others will perform better in terms of economic efficiency. Each different form will have different implications in terms of equity. More heavily regulated operational forms may reduce the incentive for investors to engage in JI. Less heavily regulated operational forms may lead to emissions leakage and increased gaming, and thereby compromise the environmental objectives of the convention.

Later in this chapter, we will elucidate an approach to the management of flexibility mechanisms which entails specifying each operational form of JI (or *JI option*) in terms of a *package* of institutional measures. Some of these measures have already been incorporated, in some form, within the mechanisms of the UN Framework Convention on Climate Change (FCCC). For example, the potential for early crediting (or interim period banking) already forms a part of the institutional context set out under the clean development mechanism (CDM) under article 12 of the Kyoto Protocol. Other measures (such as baseline revision, standardization, limited crediting life and partial crediting) are still very much in the process of discussion and negotiation within the context of the FCCC.

The broad aim of these institutional measures is to facilitate the operationalization of JI in such a way as to meet the underlying objectives of environmental effectiveness, equity and economic efficiency. In particular, institutional measures are required for the following specific purposes:

- managing uncertainty;
- handling complexity;
- limiting gaming;
- incentive creation.

The measures discussed in the following sections do not fall easily into categories defined by these different objectives. Rather, we have divided the mechanisms into categories which are defined broadly by the institutional domain in which they operate. For example, the first of these categories is the broad area of baseline management. Next, we look at the importance of measures related to the monitoring and verification of JI projects. Finally, we address measures related to the appropriate accreditation of the projects. In the later stages of the chapter we look at the construction of different packages composed of groups of individual measures. Before all of this, however, we engage in an interest-group analysis of the incentives for gaming within JI.

The Incentives for Gaming

If the use of JI or the CDM as an instrument allows substantial gaming or implies severe uncertainties in measuring the emission reductions, there will be a risk that donors are given more credits than the net emission reductions implied by their investments. This means that allowing JI – in expectation of lower financial costs abroad – may have major environmental costs in terms of lower emission reductions, when compared to a situation without JI.

In this section we undertake an interest-group perspective on JI. This approach has also been adopted by Michaelowa and Dutschke (1998). These interest groups are primarily the different players who participate in a JI arrangement, including: Annex I and non-Annex I countries, donors and hosts, countries and firms, and international authorities. As we attempt to show in this analysis, each of these actors operates under a different incentive structure. In some situations, different actors in the same situation will have different incentives in relation to the project. For some such actors, under some incentive structures, there will be more incentive for gaming than under others.

An institutional framework for JI or CDM projects has not yet been developed. What these considerations illustrate is that the different interests and incentives of the agents involved must be taken into account if JI or the CDM are to operate in a fair and efficient way as a mechanism for greenhouse gas (GHG) emission reduction. The interest-group perspective proves fruitful in understanding under which circumstances a comprehensive regulation of JI or the CDM is necessary to secure environmental effectiveness, and under which circumstances the environmental effectiveness is more or less independent of the institutional framework. The analysis in this section tells us something about the way in which different agents may wish to exploit JI or the CDM if they follow their own interests, and tells something about the conflicting or mutual interests of the different agents. This analysis is therefore a first step in the direction of designing a robust institutional framework.

Table 9.1 lists the primary and secondary interests of different agents. Countries are assumed to take their reduction targets seriously. Of course, some of the motivations attributed to interest groups may not always be true. For example, some countries and some firms may view the environment as a first priority. Instead, Table 9.1 attempts to capture the interests and motivations when emissions reductions are analysed as a *free-rider* problem – namely, that the individual agent (especially the individual country) is interested in others doing something to reduce emissions because it is interested in enjoying the public fruits of the other agents' actions. Nevertheless, the individual agent does not want to pay its share of the expenses.

Table 9.1 assumes that from the free-rider perspective, only the international authorities may be expected to view the environment as their primary concern. All other agents may be expected to regard the environment only as their secondary interest.

The primary motivation for donors to participate is to fulfil their international emission-reductions commitments at costs which are as low as possible. If emission reduction costs are lower abroad, JI and the CDM give donor countries a possibility to substitute expensive emission-reduction projects at home with low-cost emission-reduction projects abroad. As a secondary benefit, some donors may try to promote their national technology and products through the JI or CDM projects in which they participate. They will wish to maximize the number of credits for their investment and uncertainty, and non-standardization in the baseline can allow scope for gaming in order to achieve this.

The primary motivation for hosts to engage in JI arrangements arises from the fact that investment funds flow into the host country. The investments in new and resource-saving – or at least emission-saving – techniques would (ideally) not have been carried out otherwise, and therefore JI and the CDM are ways to boost investments in the host countries. In the market for JI projects, host countries are interested in selling their emission reduction projects as expensively as possible. Annex I host countries are, apart from the JI financing, also concerned with fulfilling their countries' own emission reduction targets at as low a cost as possible. Therefore, Annex I host countries are interested in choosing the right projects for donor investment.

Especially big donors or hosts may be in a position to exploit their market powers on the market. This may be capitalized in the prices for the emission reduction projects. Alternatively, host firms could, for example, be forced to use the technology produced or developed in powerful donor countries.

The knowledge of primary and secondary interests and conflicting and mutual interests of the agents is valuable when designing the institutional frameworks for JI and the CDM. If the assumption behind Table 9.1 is correct – namely, that both donor and Annex I host countries are serious about their international commitments to reduce emissions – then, in principle, there will be fewer environmental problems in reallocating international reduction

Table 9.1 *Agents' Motivations to Participate in JI or the CDM*

	Primary interests	Secondary interests
International bodies	• Environment • Countries keep to their reduction commitments (to obtain the full environmental effects) • An environmentally and economically efficient emission-reduction effort (to ensure the success and credibility of the policy)	• JI as development aid • Transfer of technology
Donor countries	• Buy the emissions reduction as cheaply as possible • Keep the emission-reduction targets (to avoid a bad international reputation and to avoid possible sanctions)	• Environment • Promote national technology and products in the host countries
Host countries Annex I	• Sell emission reductions at as high a price as possible — without hindering the fulfilment of the country's own commitment at low costs (good business) • New and resource-saving techniques are introduced and financed by foreign countries/firms/industries • Sell emission reductions as expensively as possible	• Local environmental benefits
Non-Annex I	• New and resource-saving techniques are introduced and financed by foreign countries/firms/industries	• Local environmental benefits
Donor firms or industries	• Avoid the burden of national measures (fixed commitments, taxes, etc) and buy emission reductions as cheaply as possible	• Promote own products or own technology • Promote a desired environmental profile
Host firms or industries	• Sell emission reductions as expensively as possible • New and resource-saving techniques are financed by foreign countries/firms/industries (may be a competitive advantage)	• Local environmental benefits

targets between such countries. In practice, this ignores the situation where the host may not have the resources to fulfil its own commitments. Furthermore, it is clear that where countries do not take their international commitments seriously, or where non-Annex I countries are involved in the flexibility arrangements, environmental effectiveness may be diminished.

The interests of the participants will influence their attitudes to a number of issues. In particular, different situations will provide different incentives in relation to the construction of counterfactual baselines. This fact, together with the existence of a counterfactual uncertainty, which is largely irreducible, presents a significant problem for the credibility of JI and the CDM.

In the following sections, we discuss possible measures to manage these problems and suggest that one approach is to institute a framework in which a degree of standardization is combined with a number of institutional safeguards. This should be applied where there are high incentives for gaming or significant uncertainties.

Baseline Management

A good deal of the discussion in earlier parts of this book has been dedicated to the problems associated with the complexity, and sometimes irreducible uncertainty, associated with the need to establish counterfactual baselines, and the potential for gaming which this situation represents. Measures to manage these aspects are clearly critical if JI and the CDM are to be achieved successfully.

Managing Baseline Uncertainty

In Chapter 8, we defined four sources of uncertainty in accounting for emissions reduction, namely: counterfactual, project performance, measurement and background uncertainty. Using stochastic simulation, we then estimated the combined uncertainty due to all these sources for the Estonian heat-supply projects and identified the relative importance of each. Typically, the total uncertainty in estimates of emission reductions was very high, in the order of ±60 per cent. This was reduced to around ±40 per cent by using monitored data. Furthermore, in Chapter 7 we estimated that for electricity-supply projects the counterfactual uncertainty alone was as high as 60 per cent, even using monitored data.

We should emphasize that these results were produced for relatively simple projects, and used a number of simplifying assumptions which masked other potential sources of uncertainty. Therefore, it is likely that they represent a conservative estimate of the associated uncertainties. In addition, as stated previously, the large counterfactual uncertainty (that associated with defining the baseline) is, in large measure, irreducible. Nevertheless, the impact of these uncertainties can be reduced through a combination of different actions. For example, *ex-ante* projections of demand are generally unreliable as the basis for estimating emission reductions. This kind of uncertainty can be reduced by using monitored data. Moreover, the following sections discuss two specific ways of addressing the problem of counterfactuality: baseline revision and limiting the crediting lifetime.

Baseline Revision

The counterfactual uncertainty in the baseline increases considerably over time, due to unforeseeable changes in technology availability, policies, fuel prices, energy-system changes and possible leakage mechanisms. Hence, as discussed in Chapter 4, an *ex-ante* baseline projection becomes less reliable the further into the future it is used. Consequently, if this projection is revised regularly on the basis of more up-to-date information (for example, new host country policies), some of the impact of counterfactual uncertainty can be reduced. The extent of this reduction has not been quantified; but since our estimate of counterfactual uncertainty is rather high (from around ±40 per cent to as much as ±60 per cent), it is important that some attempt is made to manage its impacts.

The idea behind baseline revision is that crediting against a baseline should be done for only short periods of time. After that period of time, the baseline should be revised in the light of changes in the energy system or in the general background situation. Clearly, baseline revision should not be applied retrospectively to credits already obtained. This would increase investor risk and undermine confidence in the system. Nevertheless, revising the baseline at appropriate intervals (say every five to ten years) means that future credits (obtained for the period following the revision) are more likely to be an accurate reflection of real emission reductions.

At the point of revision, the baseline would be checked by the certifying body (for instance, the operating entity under the CDM) to ensure that it still applies for crediting over the next revision period, or whether it should be changed, or whether crediting should cease since the project would have been carried out due to developments in the host country. Increased frequency of revision (for example, every two to five years) would be called for where the environmental risks of overestimating the reductions are high, such as in situations where the potential for gaming is high and there are large uncertainties.

The detailed methodology for baseline revision is set out as part of the discussion on standardization. Baseline revision is essentially a way of maintaining the value and credibility of the credits produced. It does, however, involve additional costs and require additional resources.

Limiting crediting lifetime

Limiting the lifetime for crediting is another way of limiting the impact of uncertainties associated with future projections (particularly the baseline) and hence reduces the possibility of overestimating the emission reductions. In implementation terms, it is simpler than baseline revision to administer, since the time period for crediting would be set from the start of the project and the project would be credited for that limited period. It could also be attractive from an investor perspective since there could be more certainty over the crediting when compared with, for instance, a system which involved baseline revision. A crediting lifetime of about ten years would also coincide with amortization times used in financial investment, allowing smooth incorporation within existing systems. It has the advantage of being simple, effective and involves lower costs when compared to baseline revision. However, for long-term projects, it may not be an attractive option.

A further way of addressing uncertainty is through the discounting of credits. This is discussed under the section on accreditation procedures later in this chapter.

Baseline Standardization

The standardization of baselines offers the scope to address several of the institutional objectives outlined in the introduction to this chapter. In the first place, standardization has the benefit of streamlining institutional procedures. By this means, complexity is reduced, the process becomes more transparent, transaction costs are lowered, and JI and the CDM become more attractive to investors. Baseline standardization also avoids the possibility of manipulating the results of emission reduction calculations, and thereby reduces the scope for gaming. In this analysis, we restrict our attention to the construction of project-level baselines, and introduce one possible approach to baseline standardization which could be applied under a range of circumstances.

We begin the discussion of standardization by listing the basic elements which are required for constructing a baseline and calculating emission reductions at the project level. These were discussed in detail in Chapter 4 and have been analysed (for case study projects) in Chapters 7 and 8. The elements are:

- choice of baseline technology, fuel and timing;
- crediting lifetime;
- equivalence of energy service;
- country-level 'background' scenario;
- technical parameters;
- financial parameters;
- leakage;
- separability.

From the analysis in Chapters 7 and 8 and the above discussion, it becomes clear that there is a discrete number of parameters which can be used as a basis for standardization in energy-sector JI projects. We define four factors as:

1 country;
2 sector;
3 type (fuel/technology combination);
4 size.

Therefore, given these parameters, it is possible to calculate emission reductions for energy-sector projects using the *specific* GHG emissions (tCO_2 e/MWh), as described in Chapter 7, for both the baseline case and the JI case.

This starting point is similar to that of Luhmann et al (1997). However, our approach differs from both the default-matrix approach and the bench-mark approach described in Chapter 4. Rather, it is a hybrid approach which involves standardizing the baseline on the basis of project type, country, sector and size, but does not assume project additionality nor the indefinite validity of the baseline as happens in the bench-marking approach. The additionality of the project should be assessed separately, at the project approval stage by the use of, for example, the barrier-removal method (see Chapter 4).

Also, since the further the baseline is projected into the future, the higher the uncertainty, we advocate regular *baseline revision* at intervals of about five to ten years. This is so that any unexpected changes in, for example, the host country energy sector can be reflected in the value for the specific emissions of the baseline.[1] We should perhaps reiterate that we are advocating revisions to the baseline for the *remainder* of the JI project lifetime, not for the period preceding the revision. Alternatively, a limited crediting lifetime could be applied.

A further consequence of technological development is that there is a finite life to the validity of particular values of these specific emissions for given technologies and fuels. For example, a typical plant may become significantly more efficient over time. Standard values should also be revised frequently to reflect this development.

It should also be noted that it is possible for a JI project to change its fuel. For instance, some of the Estonian boiler projects assessed in this study are burning peat, which has a much higher emissions factor than CO_2-neutral woodchips. Hence, the specific emissions for a given JI project may need to be revised on the basis of monitoring assessments.

The following steps are suggested for implementing a standardized approach to baseline construction based on specific emissions.

Step 1: Choose the relevant baseline type

There are two criteria which can be used in selecting a baseline type:

1   Can the plant that the JI project will substitute be identified? (Only if a project is separable will this be the case.)
2   What is the crediting lifetime? For example, if a project very similar to the JI project is likely to be built by the host country after approximately ten years, the crediting lifetime should be chosen to be ten years.

On the basis of these criteria, we describe four *standardized baseline*. These different types are illustrated graphically in Figure 9.2 and are discussed in detail below.

Type 1: separable, substituted and short

The type 1 baseline is for JI projects where the substituted plant/situation is known. This can only be the case for separable projects, or for those which are part of a limited network (for example, several of the Estonian heat-supply projects discussed earlier).

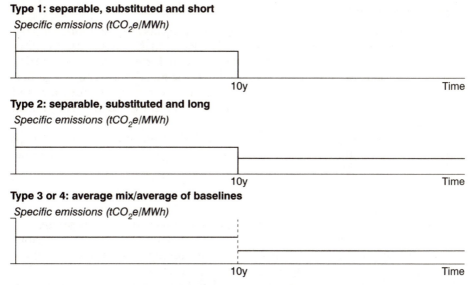

Figure 9.2 *Standardized Baseline Types*

A constant value for specific emissions is defined for a limited lifetime. The value for the specific emissions is defined as that for the substituted plant and is corrected, if necessary, to ensure equivalence of service with the JI project. The lifetime is limited to, for example, ten years because not only are projections very uncertain beyond this time period, but – more significantly – it is likely that a project similar to the JI project would have been carried out by the host anyway after that time. Of course, if the technical lifetime of the project is short, then this standard baseline is also appropriate.

Type 2: separable, substituted and long

Type 2 is also for separable (or 'limited network') JI or CDM projects where the substituted plant is known. It is the same as type 1 for the first period. After approximately five to ten years (as it becomes more likely that changes would have been made to the substituted plant in the absence of the project), the baseline becomes the mean of the specific emissions of technologies/fuels in the sector at that time, based on national energy statistics. This level either remains constant or falls based on an estimate of the annual increase in the sector's efficiency. Such an increase could be derived from historical trends in the host country or from an energy–economic model, but the use of either in a transition or developing economy can be suspect. Increased frequency of baseline revision is a more accurate way of dealing with this. After a further five to ten years, if the end of the technical life of the project has not been reached, the specific emissions are again revised based on national energy statistics.

This type is useful when it is unlikely that a project very similar to the JI or CDM project would have been carried out under host development during the technical lifetime of the project.

Type 3: average mix

Type 3 is particularly useful for non-separable projects (for example, electricity supply), where the replaced situation is hard to define explicitly. A mean specific emissions is defined for the sector in which the project is operating based on national energy statistics, following the same idea as type 2. Again, it could be constant or varying. Revision, using the latest energy statistics, would again be necessary at least every five to ten years until the end of the technical lifetime.

This type would encourage new or uncommon technologies with a high potential for reductions, whereas projects similar or worse than the average would not be favoured.

Type 4: average of baselines

Type 4 is designed to be used when the previous types are inappropriate. It is more versatile, but it requires more effort to construct it. The specific emissions of a number of different plausible baselines (technologies/fuels/timing, etc) are calculated, as well as the mean or expected value taken over the technical lifetime of the project. This assessment of baselines is created by independent analysts based upon a small number of test projects (for example, pilot AIJ – activities implemented jointly – projects) of the same type and in the same region or sector. This average (constant) specific emissions is then used for the technical lifetime of the project. However, there still needs to be a revision after approximately ten years in order to check the range of baselines. Such a revision would be more time consuming than that for the previous baseline types.

It should be noted that for all four types, conservative values for specific emissions (for particular countries, sectors, project types and sizes) are needed to counter possible leakage and gaming effects as discussed earlier. Types 2 and 3 require data on the energy system of the host country, while type 4 also needs to take into account the energy and environmental policy context in order to produce a range of reasonable baselines (similar to the methodology used in Chapter 7). However, once values for types 2, 3 and 4 are calculated and made available for a project type, size, sector and country, the results can be applied to the appropriate projects with minimum effort by investors. As mentioned above, these values will, of course, have to be updated to keep pace with technological change.

We suggest that the work required to produce these values is funded by a levy on JI and CDM projects in order to ensure that the project-based mechanisms are not subsidized from elsewhere in the convention.

Table 9.2 presents a summary of the standardized baseline types, highlighting the advantages and disadvantages of each.

It should be noted that our four standard baseline types do not include using the marginal technology – another possibility recommended in the literature (CCAP, 1998; Heister, 1999). This is because we are not convinced that arguments based on the assumption of economic efficiency are reliable in likely host countries (countries in transition, developing countries) due to lack of investment capital, lack of institutional capacity and/or political instability.

Table 9.2 *Summary of Baseline Types*

	Where applicable	Advantages	Disadvantages
Type 1	• short to medium lifetime • substituted plant is known • project types: heat supply (limited networks)	• low chance of overcrediting • number of credits relatively certain • simple	• higher chance of undercrediting if medium lifetime
Type 2	• any project lifetime • substituted plant is known at start • project types: heat supply (limited networks)	• can be used for any project lifetime	• more complex than type 1 • restricted by availability of sector data • requires some independent research
Type 3	• any project lifetime • substituted plant unknown • project types: electricity supply and demand, heat supply and demand, cogeneration	• can be used for any project type and lifetime where the substituted plant is unknown	• more complex than type 2 • requires some independent research • restricted by availability of sector data
Type 4	• any project lifetime • substituted plant unknown • project types: heat supply and demand, cogeneration, non-standard projects	• can be used for any project type and lifetime	• more complex than type 3 • requires more data from independent research • restricted by availability of data and cost of obtaining it

It should be noted that in the literature, rather than taking a constant average level for specific emissions, there are also suggestions for baselines with variation of the emission reductions over time based on energy–economic models (CCAP, 1998; Lile et al, 1998). As discussed in relation to type 2 above, we suggest that it is more accurate to address this through baseline revision. Of course, investors may prefer a projection over time and less revision.

There also remains the possibility of a potential JI or CDM project being sufficiently individual to merit the construction of a non-standardized baseline. If this is the case, such construction should be carried out (using the guidelines for the project-specific approach outlined in Chapter 4) by independent analysts to reduce the potential for gaming.

Discussion

Since, in theory, intermittent sources – such as the wind projects examined in this study – could substitute for a range of plant, an average mix for the sector level of specific emissions seems a reasonable compromise, as in a type 3 standardized baseline accompanied by the package of measures described later. Where a wind generator is used with a storage device, it is easier to identify which plant would be substituted since it would then substitute for peak load plant when required and a type 1 or 2 standardized baseline could be employed.

For a cogeneration plant, the calculation is in two parts. The heat substitution part of the calculation is relatively straightforward since heat networks tend to have straightforward, easily identified substituted plant for the baseline. Types 1 or 2 baselines are appropriate; however, where there is uncertainty in substituted plant, types 3 and 4 baselines could be used. The electricity part of the calculation faces the same problems as the wind generator: it is not always readily identifiable which plant or plants are being substituted. Here, again, a sector-average mix approach can be justified for this section of the calculation – for example, type 3.

In the case of demand-side management (DSM) projects, such as the energy efficiency project at Mustamäe, the picture can be complicated by behavioural aspects. Some compensatory device would be required in calculating energy saved by the project to account for the expected increase in demand to provide higher comfort levels. Usually, the main uncertainty is not associated with the choice of baseline technology, although there may be a question of how long the original heat-supply source would continue to operate before being replaced. Rather, the main uncertainty relates to the magnitude of the energy saved vis-à-vis the change in demand brought about by the project. At some point there may be sufficient information in the form of a data bank to be able to standardize this expected savings in energy for specific energy-efficiency measures taken (Violette et al, 1998).

The process of standardizing the construction of baselines is summarized in Figure 9.3.

Step 2: calculating the emission reductions

GHG emissions for the JI or CDM project and the baseline are calculated by multiplying the specific emissions of each by the annual output of the JI or CDM plant. This annual output should ideally be the measured output for the plant used. This aspect is extremely important in addressing the uncertainties in the calculation and is discussed below. The emissions reduction is thus the difference between the specific emissions from the baseline and the specific emissions from the project, multiplied by the measured output over the appropriate time period. This procedure assumes that the baseline technology can deliver the same energy service as the project. If this cannot be assumed (for

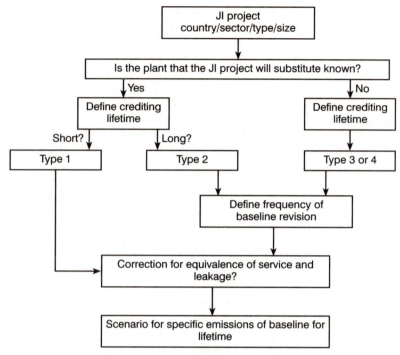

Figure 9.3 *Standardized Baseline Construction*

example, some electricity-supply projects where the utilization factors are different), then corrections should be made (Luhmann et al, 1997). As mentioned above, the specific emission figures would be valid only for a limited time and a reappraisal would be required after approximately five to ten years. For biomass plants, there are the added questions of the long-term CO_2 neutrality of the fuel source and avoiding double-counting it as a sink. These aspects would have to be incorporated as part of the reappraisal procedure for these projects.

Monitoring and Verification

Monitoring, verification and compliance procedures are critical in ensuring that flexibility in meeting GHG emission reduction targets is not achieved at the expense of the aims of the convention. As discussed in Chapter 8, emissions-reduction calculations based on feasibility data have tended to be overestimated by an average of around 30 per cent for the case study projects analysed in this study. Clearly, if this is repeated on a wider scale, basing estimates of emissions reduction on feasibility data would undermine the aims of the convention. Monitored data regarding the project output or fuel consumption should therefore be used in calculating emission reductions.

To date, most of the practical experience of monitoring has been with emissions trading schemes in the US under the Clean Air Act for a range of pollutants, including sulphur dioxide, ozone-depleting chemicals and lead. Related to this, the US Environmental Protection Agency (EPA) has devised production and consumption allowances for cost-effective compliance of the Montreal Protocol, and has a monitoring process for reporting production and import levels (Adams, 1997). Lessons for the monitoring regime can be gleaned from reviews of such schemes (see, for example, Tietenberg, 1985; Sorrell, 1994; Adams, 1997; Ellerman et al, 1997; Mullins, 1997) and from relevant regulatory documents (SCAQMD, 1994). For example, in the acid rain programme, continuous emission monitoring and electronic reporting were used, providing hourly measurements of SO_2 and NO_x emissions and with back-up systems in the event of failure. This provided confidence that participating plants were complying with their allowance allocations. However, this is an extremely expensive option and – in light of the uncertainty associated with the counterfactuality of the baseline – may not be appropriate for project-based flexibility mechanisms, especially for smaller plant. For CO_2, measurement of fuel consumption or plant output may be sufficient since well-defined emissions factors are available for a range of fuels. Spot checks on a selected number of project flue gases could be carried out if necessary for additional security.

Assessments reveal that, in the projects studied, the main reason for the large discrepancy between the expected and actual situation has been a large drop in demand due to reorganization of the energy sector in the countries concerned. However, design and operator faults, fires and flooding have also played a role. As discussed above, by eliminating performance uncertainty through monitoring the plant output, we reduce the uncertainty in heat-supply projects from 60 per cent to 40 per cent. This single simple action produces a large gain in environmental efficiency.

It therefore makes sense to suggest that emission reductions and related credits should be calculated annually based on monitoring the performance of the project. A further benefit of this practice is that it would give an incentive for the donor and host to ensure the long-term viability of the project and reduce the risk of overcrediting a project which is not performing or has failed. Furthermore, this action would entail little extra work since output, for example, can be easily measured and reported to the relevant authorities in order to calculate the appropriate number of credits. Feasibility data will, of course, still be needed to give guidance for investment decisions.

As we saw earlier in this chapter, there is an incentive for the donor (and in the case of the CDM, the host as well) to overestimate emission reductions by overreporting the output from the plant. As a result, independent verification procedures of the output data would be required. (At its most basic level, this process would ensure that the project actually exists!) The number and frequency of such checks is open to discussion, the trade-off being between the transaction costs and environmental efficiency. Verification also needs to take account of the CO_2 neutrality of a biofuel source.

Additional monitoring and verification procedures would be required to audit projects for their environmental and social effects, as discussed in Chapter 6.

Accreditation Procedures

In Chapter 2, we made the point that the AIJ pilot phase does not allow the issuing of credits to donor parties. However, the Kyoto Protocol has subsequently introduced mechanisms for crediting projects carried out both under article 6 (with Annex I hosts) and under article 12 (the CDM). In this section, we examine the specific issues which arise as a result of the crediting regimes envisaged under the protocol.

Some details have been given about the form of these regimes. Under article 6 (where the hosts have GHG targets), the credits are called emission reduction units (ERUs) and may only be awarded to JI projects for emissions reduction during the commitment period (2008–2012 inclusive). Under article 12 (the CDM, where hosts do not have targets), the credits are called certified emission reductions (CERs) and may be awarded from the year 2000 onwards. Furthermore, CDM projects are subject to a levy, which will be used to fund adaptation measures in countries particularly vulnerable to climate change.

In the following discussion, we review some of the other issues: *credit allocation*; *partial crediting*, also known as *discounting* of credits; and *early crediting*, in particular analysing its effects on total emissions reduction activity.

Credit Allocation

There are two main allocation issues:

1 Should credits be awarded only to parties to the protocol or to private entities as well?
2 Should credits be shared between the donor and host?

The Kyoto Protocol allows for private entities to be awarded credits directly if authorized by their government. From an economic efficiency perspective, allowing the participation of private entities is desirable. However, this should be weighed against their accountability under the protocol. If private entities are not properly regulated by their national governments, they may undermine the aims of the protocol.

A further issue is whether 100 per cent of the credits awarded for a JI or CDM project automatically go to the donor. It is possible that a host may contribute some of the project cost in return for some of the credits. If the host has emission targets, it may use these credits to contribute to those targets. If not, the host may sell them for foreign currency, or bank them for use against future emission targets. (The latter raises the problems of early crediting, discussed below.)

Another possible reason for credits going to the host is as compensation, should a project lead to unforeseen negative social and environmental effects. This, however, assumes that the environmental or social detriment can be compensated by monetary means, and that there are no problems of distributional equity if the credits go to the host government when the detriment is local.

Discounting of Credits (or Partial Crediting)

There are four main reasons why it might be necessary only to credit a fraction of the emissions reduction calculated by an accounting assessment. These are:

1 large uncertainty in estimates of emissions reduction;
2 negative environmental and social effects in the host due to the project;
3 to provide more incentive for domestic action by the donor;
4 early crediting problems.

We deal with the early crediting issue below. It should be kept in mind that discounting of any sort will obviously increase the price of credits.

As discussed in Chapter 8, the uncertainty associated with calculations of emissions reduction is high, and is particularly due to the counterfactual nature of the baseline. Therefore, the possibility of gaming to maximize donor credits is also high. One solution to counter this is to discount credits (Vellinga et al, 1992). Our estimate of uncertainty in emissions reduction estimates showed evidence of varying with project type. It follows that a sliding scale of 'crediting fractions' may be necessary: to prevent donor domestic action, where baselines are not necessary, from being undermined; and to provide an incentive for efforts to reduce uncertainty.

Chapter 6 made it clear that JI and CDM projects have local social and environmental effects on the host. Sometimes these effects may be beneficial; at other times, they will be detrimental. Article 12.2 of the Kyoto Protocol requires that CDM projects should assist host countries 'in achieving sustainable development'. However, even for article 6 JI, negative local effects will adversely affect future uptake of projects, in addition to being inequitable. One way of providing an incentive to limit negative effects is to discount the credits awarded to the donor, should the project become damaging.

Another reason for discounting credits is to encourage early action. Michaelowa and Schmidt (1997) suggest a novel method for GHG abatement action where credits are progressively discounted over time while, concurrently, a carbon tax is progressively increased in donor countries. Hence, early action is encouraged without undermining the incentive to invest in abatement technologies domestically.

Early Crediting

As discussed above, the Kyoto Protocol defines a commitment period which extends from 2008 to 2012 inclusive, and for which quantified emission limitation and reduction commitments (QELRCs) have been defined. For the period before 2008, no targets have been set. At the time of publication, JI projects carried out under article 6 will receive ERUs only during the commitment period, making them comparable with actions taken domestically to meet the QELRCs. However, in the case of the CDM, article 12.10 allows for CERs to be *banked* during an *interim period* (2000 to 2007 inclusive) and added to those obtained during the commitment period. This process has become known as *early crediting* (also sometimes known as interim period banking).

Clearly, the two accounting procedures are not compatible and tend to favour the CDM. The argument for the bias in accounting towards CDM actions is that it would encourage investment in emissions reduction programmes in developing countries at the earliest possible stage (see, for example, Jepma, 1998b). The problem with early crediting is that, since the emission targets have only been agreed for the period 2008 to 2012 inclusive, it is possible that credited CDM action during the interim period may be offset by uncontrolled increases in the donor country during that time.

In fact it can be shown (see Appendix 1) that the emissions reductions associated with a CDM action with a constant emissions reduction profile, and starting in 2000, count 2.6 times as much towards the QELRC target during the commitment period as does a domestic action or an article 6 JI project. Since there is no emissions target in place for the donor until 2008, it is quite possible for its domestic emissions to increase during the interim period and to offset the CDM project without penalty. Thus, it is possible for this sort of banking to lead to less total action over the whole (interim and commitment) period to meet the emissions reduction target. Indeed, it can be shown (Parkinson et al, 1999) that, for each tonne of CO_2-equivalent emissions reduction carried out in a CDM project with banking, the *total* emissions reduction needed to meet the QELRC of the donor is decreased by roughly 0.3 to 0.6 tonnes. Clearly, this could become a significant effect.

To put the scale of the problem in perspective, it has been estimated (see Appendix 1) that for the US early crediting could lead to an effective relaxation of its emissions reduction target of around 1.8 percentage points. In other words, the effective target in the US would be a 5.2 per cent reduction from 1990 levels instead of the 7 per cent agreed under the Kyoto Protocol. In the Netherlands the effective relaxation could be between 8.2 and 14.3 percentage points, leading to an effective target amounting to an increase of between 2.2 per cent and 8.3 per cent over 1990 levels instead of the 6.0 per cent cut agreed under Kyoto.

The question arises as to whether it is possible to retain the incentive for action which early crediting provides without compromising the total action needed to comply with emissions targets. In fact, one simple way would be to use partial crediting as described in the previous section, in which only a fraction of the emissions reduction is awarded credits (Parkinson et al, 1998b; 1999). The value of the 'crediting fraction' could be set such that the uncredited CDM action is equal to the emissions-reduction action lost as a result of the early crediting mechanism. Thus, partial crediting would ensure that the total action taken to meet the Kyoto targets was maintained.[2]

On the basis of an analysis of possible emissions-reduction action, it can be estimated that this fraction should be between 40 per cent and 70 per cent (Appendix 1). Since this analysis is based on rather conservative assumptions, it would be appropriate to choose a crediting fraction towards the lower end of this range. Obviously, the use of such a fraction would reduce the attractiveness of the scheme to investors. However, this should be viewed in the context that the main argument for CDM action is its low cost compared with domestic action, and therefore the increase in the price of credits resulting from the use of such a fraction may not be that significant.

Furthermore, it is important to consider this issue in a wider policy context. Currently, there is significant doubt over whether the US will ratify the Kyoto Protocol, since the US senate wants guarantees of 'meaningful participation by developing countries' over fears of economic disadvantage that ratification may cause the US (Grubb et al, 1999). Many developing countries, on the other hand, currently refuse to accept emissions targets since they argue that anthropogenic climate change is a problem caused by industrialized countries, and that current per capita emissions are considerably higher than those in developing countries – therefore, significant action should be taken by industrialized countries first. As a result, a significant amount of CDM action, with early crediting, may contribute towards a compromise.

It has been suggested that early crediting should be extended to apply also to article 6 JI (see, for example, Jepma, 1998b). Clearly, this would have the advantage of offsetting a part of the bias created by early crediting of CDM actions. However, it would lead to a significant 'tightening' of the emissions targets for Annex I host countries. For the Czech Republic, it can be shown that its effective target could be tightened by 2–3 per cent, leading to a QELRC of 10–11 per cent below base-year levels, instead of the 8 per cent cut agreed under the Kyoto Protocol (see Appendix 1).

Early crediting is also being considered as an incentive to reward early domestic action, particularly in the US. Detailed analysis by Rolfe et al (1999), however, concludes that from both an economic and environmental perspective, the use of carbon taxes and/or a domestic emissions trading scheme is more effective.

In summary, early crediting – whether for the CDM or article 6 JI – will effectively alter emissions targets in favour of the donor. This should explicitly be recognized in negotiations over these mechanisms such that all trade-offs are transparent.

Summary of Individual Measures

In the introduction we set out a number key objectives that inform the institutional measures for managing JI and the CDM. The subsequent sections have discussed specific measures in three broad categories: baseline management, monitoring and verification, and accreditation procedures. Table 9.3 summarizes these individual measures and categorizes them according to their intent (in relation to the principal objectives they are designed to meet). Table 9.4 summarizes, in particular, the measures which can be used to address specific kinds of uncertainty.

Constructing a Package of Measures

From the preceding discussion, it is clear that there is scope for using a standardized project-level approach to baseline construction which is not only more practical (and therefore increases investor attractiveness), but also reduces the potential for gaming. However, further measures are required to

Table 9.3 *Summary of Motivations for Specific Institutional Measures*

	Managing uncertainty	Handling complexity	Limiting gaming	Incentive creation
Baseline revision	✔		✔	
Limited crediting life	✔	✔	✔	
Baseline standardization		✔	✔	
Monitoring and verification	✔		✔	
Credit sharing				✔
Partial/discounted crediting	✔		✔	
Early crediting				✔

reduce the uncertainty in estimates of emissions reduction to more acceptable levels. In this section we suggest that an appropriate way to proceed is to construct *packages* of measures, which taken together address uncertainty and reduce gaming, but also maintain the attractiveness of JI and the CDM to potential investors. There are many possible combinations of the simple measures discussed above; here we give one example for a separable biomass district-heating boiler project where the substituted plant is known and the technical lifetime is long (for instance, 25 years).

We suggest one particular operational form which comprises a combination of standardization procedures with a number of institutional safeguards aimed at ensuring environmental effectiveness, in a manner consistent with providing a practical instrument which remains attractive to potential investors. The procedures are as follows:

- type 2 standardized baseline with a value for specific emissions (tCO_2e/MWh) based on conservative values;
- annual monitoring of operating data for output (plus fuel input and operating hours as a check);
- baseline revision every ten years;
- annual crediting over operating life of plant;
- verification of project existence and spot checks for confirmation of operating conditions and CO_2 neutrality of biomass, for example, every five years.

This particular operational form requires more work initially for an independent body to prepare standardized baselines, but allows more long-term projects to be assessed. It does address most concerns of an appropriate reduction in the risk of overestimating emission reductions, and it is relatively simple to put into operation. This package of measures to reduce the key uncertainties would apply whether a non-standard or simplified baseline approach was used.

The process being advocated is to adopt a simplified or streamlined approach, combined with institutional safeguards. The simplification in baseline construction yields significant returns in terms of practicality, and reduces the associated transaction costs. However, it must be combined with

Table 9.4 *Summary of Measures for Dealing with Uncertainty*

Particular uncertainties	Measures
1 Output/demand variations over time for JI project and baseline	• Monitoring (and use of monitored data in emissions accounting) • Verification by third party
2 Choice of baseline technology/fuel and timing of replacement	• Standardized baseline methodology • Baseline revision for long lifetime projects after, for example, ten years • Limited crediting lifetime • Partial crediting
3 Fuel availability and prices for project	• Monitoring • Verification by third party
4 Changes in technical parameters (efficiency, fuel quality) of JI project or baseline over time	• Conservative estimates for specific emissions for JI project and baseline • Baseline revision • Limited crediting lifetime • Partial crediting • Monitoring • Verification by third party
5 Energy-system development, indirect economic effects and changes in policy and country priorities	• Baseline revision • Limited crediting lifetime • Partial crediting
6 Leakage	• Conservative estimates for specific emissions • Baseline revision
7 Risk of failure	• Monitoring • Verification by third party

additional safeguards as detailed above. These safeguards need not involve a great deal of work but would provide large gains in environmental effectiveness. This is a win–win situation where the process for investors is streamlined but there is confidence in the emission reductions achieved. This also helps the marketability of the resulting credits.

Figure 9.4 illustrates how such a package of measures could be operationalized.

Conclusions

In this chapter we have elaborated a variety of institutional measures that could be used to operationalize flexibility mechanisms in global climate policy. The motivation for such measures is found in a variety of institutional requirements, specifically: the management of uncertainty, dealing with complexity, limiting the potential for gaming, and creating appropriate incentives to involve a wider participation in emission reduction activities.

In terms of devising operational forms of JI and the CDM which are transparent and not too complex, we have examined, in particular, the possibility

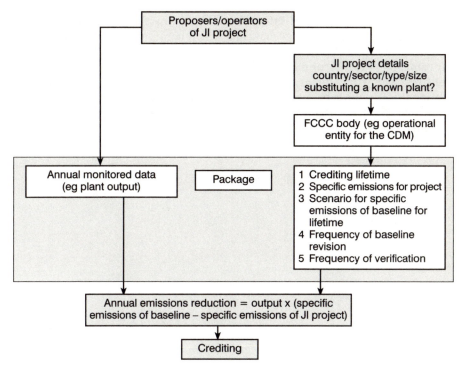

Figure 9.4 *Operationalization of a Package of Measures for JI*

of baseline standardization. We concluded that standardized baselines are appropriate in certain circumstances, provided that they are combined with measures designed to reduce the impact of uncertainty and the potential for gaming on the environmental effectiveness of JI. In particular, it has become clear that much of the uncertainty associated with the baseline cannot be reduced by the method of constructing the baseline, and additional measures are required. Such additional measures include monitoring and verification protocols, baseline revisions, partial crediting and limited crediting lifetimes.

This chapter has also examined the question of early crediting. This measure is currently incorporated within article 12 of the Kyoto Protocol (the CDM) as a means of encouraging the participation of cooperative actions between Annex I and non-Annex I parties to the convention. The analysis revealed that early crediting effectively relaxes donor country targets due to the possibility of credited action inside the interim period (2000–2007) being offset by an unpenalized increase in domestic emissions by the donor country. Extending early crediting to article 6 JI would not only extend the relaxation of donor country targets, but could also tighten host country targets, leading to problems of distributional equity. One solution to this problem is to apply a partial crediting fraction of between 40 per cent and 70 per cent to all certified emission reductions issued during the period of 2000–2012.

Finally, this chapter has discussed the development of specific packages of institutional measures designed to combine streamlined management procedures with appropriate institutional safeguards. This is an approach to the operationalization of project-based mechanisms which could, in principle, be used to ensure that flexibility in achieving emission reductions is achieved, without compromising the environmental objectives of the convention. However, it should be clear from this analysis that each package of measures, and each operational form, must be assessed on its merits against the range of objectives (outlined in Chapter 3) that inform global climate policy. This task is the subject of Chapter 10.

Evaluating Joint Implementation Options: An Illustrative Analysis

K Begg, T Jackson, S Parkinson and P-E Morthorst

Introduction

One of the principal contentions of this study is that joint implementation (JI) constitutes a variety of different institutional arrangements, each of which is defined by the values associated with a set of operational parameters. This set of operational parameters includes the nature of the actors involved, their status under the Framework Convention on Climate Change (FCCC), the scale and nature of the investments, and the degree of stringency or leniency in the institutional procedures under which each form operates. Another, equally important, observation from the work carried out in this study is that JI operates in the presence of multiple underlying objectives. These objectives include, at least, environmental effectiveness, equity, economic efficiency and investor attractiveness.

In Chapter 3, we pointed out that each operational form will perform differently against the underlying objectives. Some operational forms will provide more security in terms of achieving environmental targets. Others will perform better in terms of economic efficiency. Each form will have different implications in terms of equity. Typically, there is unlikely to be any particular operational form which maximizes performance with respect to all of the underlying objectives. So, for example, more heavily regulated operational forms may increase environmental security but reduce the incentive for investors to engage in JI. Less heavily regulated operational forms may encourage investor participation, but lead to emissions leakage, encourage gaming and thus compromise the environmental objectives of the convention.

Policy-making in a multi-attribute context such as this must typically concern itself with the problem of making appropriate trade-offs between underlying objectives when selecting and evaluating appropriate operational forms. It is our contention that the appropriate way to proceed in this situation is to engage in a structured approach to the design of flexibility mechanisms which recognizes the existence of multiple objectives, and explicitly identifies the trade-offs which occur between them.

This task is, however, rather complex. Firstly, it requires us to define individual operational forms of JI. Essentially, this must be done by specifying values for each of the operational parameters mentioned above. Next, we need to evaluate these individual operational forms of JI against each of the underlying objectives. Finally, we need a means of integrating these judgements within a consistent and coherent policy context. The objective of this chapter is to set out one possible approach to this task.

Firstly, we summarize the relevant operational parameters – many of which have been discussed in some detail in previous chapters – and specify a range of likely values for them. Next, we define eight particular operational forms of JI – which we call *JI options* – by selecting sets of values for the operational parameters which might be typical in the context of bilateral energy-sector investments under the Kyoto Protocol.[1] We then summarize briefly several potential methodologies for evaluating these options, and introduce the particular decision-analysis method that we have chosen to use in our (illustrative) evaluation. The next section illustrates the use of the selected decision-analysis methodology to evaluate the eight JI options defined earlier in the chapter according to the specified evaluation criteria.

In the final section, we discuss a proposal for defining an operational framework for JI in which the minimum requirements are met in terms of environmental effectiveness, equity and economic efficiency.

Operational Parameters for Joint Implementation

In this section we recapitulate, briefly, the parameters which define different operational forms for JI.

Actors

The discussion in this section deals, firstly, with the distinction between article 6 JI and the clean development mechanism (CDM) and, secondly, with the different levels of actors – from government to private.

Article 6 and the CDM

The major actors for article 6 JI and the CDM are slightly different. For article 6 JI, the donors and hosts are Annex I countries while for the CDM they are Annex I donors and non-Annex I hosts. For the CDM, a number of other institutions were specifically established. The executive body (EB) was set up to supervise the operation of the CDM. Other operational entities (OEs) will carry out specific regulatory tasks, such as the certification of credits.

Consideration of the Kyoto Protocol suggests that article 6 JI and the CDM probably require a different range of processes and safeguards; and that article 6 JI should be treated separately from the CDM, since in the former case both donor and host are subject to quantified emission limitation and reduction commitments (QELRCs), whereas in the latter the host is not. Theoretically, there is supposed to be an in-built safeguard for the environment where countries have targets. In practice, and certainly in the case of certain economies in transition, lower levels of institutional capacity would suggest that in some cases compliance with targets may be compromised by engaging in JI activities. For countries without targets, on the other hand, there are clear incentives for gaming or 'talking up' the baselines in order to achieve as many credits for the donor as possible. In both types of host it is important, for different reasons, to ensure that emission reductions are not overestimated.

In defining different JI options according to the actors involved, we have initially considered separate options for article 6 JI and CDM, though from the discussion above a large difference in approach may not be justified.

It has also been suggested that in order to limit gaming, baseline construction may need to be more sophisticated. From the analysis in Chapter 9, however, it follows that there is a limit to the usefulness of increased sophistication in baseline construction. It is our contention that increased stringency would be better ensured by applying certain institutional safeguards. These safeguards would both minimize gaming and decrease the bounds of uncertainty. Thus, the frequency of baseline revisions or verification checks could be increased for CDM projects, or there could be limited crediting life or partial crediting which would ensure environmental efficiency without increased institutional requirements.

National and private

The flexible nature of the proposed JI arrangements means that any number and type of actors can engage in an agreement. Within the countries, the actual players may be municipalities or they may be private companies. The situation can, of course, be even more complex in terms of numbers and combinations of investors at private and country level – as, for example, in the activities implemented jointly (AIJ) project at Děčín, which involved three US utilities, the Danish government, the Czech government environment fund and the municipality.

The importance of the actors lies in viewing them as interest groups and exploring their motivations. This has been discussed in some detail in Chapter 9, but the obvious distinction can be made that public institutions are expected to put the public interest first, compared to a private investor who will be interested mainly in maximizing profits. The implication of this distinction is that more checks and regulatory safeguards may be required when certain kinds of actors (such as the private investor) are involved in situations where the incentive for gaming is high – such as in non-Annex I host countries.

Different sets of actors therefore imply different regulatory requirements and institutional safeguards. Realistically, there will also be different priorities displayed by government agencies depending upon their own agendas; therefore, we suggest that a common set of procedures should be developed to apply equally to all national and private actors. This releases one layer of complexity, simplifying the specification of the JI process. In the following analysis, we assume that, in general, higher regulatory levels and institutional safeguards are necessary in situations where there is a high incentive for gaming.

Project Types

The project type to be implemented under JI is important for two reasons. Firstly, JI projects need to be compatible with the development priorities of the host country in which they are implemented. Secondly, the type of project determines the appropriate accounting methodology to be applied, including the baseline construction with its attendant safeguard requirements (see Chapter 9). In this respect, the geographical scale of the project, whether it is demand or supply side and whether or not it has system interactions are all important in determining the ease with which it can be regulated.

In this study we have been concerned throughout with supply- and demand-side interventions in the energy sector. Most projects in this sector are technological, which would be expected to be associated with reasonably well-documented science and with available engineering data. In practice, however, data availability is patchy and there are still uncertainties associated with the emission reduction and cost estimates – as discussed in detail in Chapters 7 and 8. Project types in less well-defined sectors and less well-developed countries are therefore liable to have even greater difficulties related to uncertainty and data availability. This is in addition to the problems inherent in the counterfactual approach to calculating emission reductions and costs: hence the expected need for increased safeguards with the CDM.

Regulatory Safeguards

The regulatory safeguards relate to how the project is implemented and how the emission reductions are calculated. Perusal of the documentation of the FCCC's subsidiary bodies (such as the subsidiary body for scientific and technological advice) indicates that the following list of safeguards is being discussed:

- project approval criteria;
- supplementarity cap;
- methodological guidelines for baseline construction, emission calculation and so on;
- baseline revision;
- limited lifetime of crediting;
- use of operating data for crediting;
- discounting emission reductions;
- verification of existence, operation and output;
- partial/discounted credits; and
- environmental and social assessment.

Many of these safeguards have already been discussed in some detail in previous chapters. The issue of supplementarity – that is, the imposition of some kind of cap on emissions trading and JI – was introduced within climate change negotiations in the language of the Kyoto Protocol. As we noted in Chapter 2, this requirement has not yet been elaborated upon and the issue remains controversial. For example, the European Union (EU) and the US have taken opposing views on the subject (Grubb et al, 1999).

Methodological guidelines, baseline revision, limited lifetime, use of operating data, monitoring and verification, credit discounting, and partial crediting are discussed in Chapter 9. The environmental and social aspects have been discussed in Chapter 6.

It will be essential, if credits are to be accrued from JI, that projects are subject at least to some minimal approval criteria. No such project-approval criteria have yet been consistently agreed upon within the policy arena. Consequently, most countries who have engaged in AIJ have tended to produce their own lists of criteria for determining the eligibility of projects. These usually are based broadly on the factors identified at the fifth Conference of the Parties (COP 5) (see UN FCCC, 1999b) and by other considerations raised either within the convention or within the Kyoto Protocol. Approval criteria which are currently applied or discussed include some – although not necessarily all – of the following factors (Michaelowa et al, 1999):

- Projects should be consistent with host country sustainable development paths.
- Projects should have host country acceptance and approval.
- Projects should provide real, measurable, long-term environmental benefits.
- Projects should be cost effective.
- Project funding should be additional to official development assistance (ODA).
- Projects should satisfy other definitions of additionality.
- Projects should be compatible and supportive of host country development priorities.
- Projects should contribute to capacity-building and transfer of environmentally sound technologies.
- There should be some provision for external verification of projects.
- There should be some provision for the identification of non-greenhouse gas (GHG) environmental impacts.
- Appropriate research and documentation of the project should be provided.

Some of these factors have already been discussed in detail in this book. Suffice it to say that the problem of defining an appropriate set of project-approval criteria for JI exemplifies the problem of trade-offs between underlying objectives. An extensive set of approval criteria would go some way towards ensuring both the equity and the environmental effectiveness of JI. However, such criteria might also increase the transaction costs associated with JI, reducing its cost effectiveness and its attractiveness to potential investors. The criteria may also interfere with host country sovereignty. The fact that there is currently no agreed set of criteria reflects these tensions. As we have remarked earlier (see Chapter 3), the question of how additionality is operationalized has important implications for equity, environmental effectiveness and economic efficiency.

Defining Joint Implementation Options

In this section, we set out a range of illustrative JI options. Each of these options is determined by allocating specific values to the operational parameters described in the previous section. In selecting these values, we have been led, in part, by the following:

- the nature of the projects examined in this study;
- the range of options applicable to the flexibility mechanisms introduced under the Kyoto Protocol;
- operating procedures, approval criteria and safeguards discussed previously.

These options are not intended to be fully comprehensive or even completely defined. Rather, they are presented here to illustrate the range of components and variables which define the JI framework. In presenting the options, we have opted for a *story-board* approach; each option is described briefly in terms of the following components:

- key characteristics (including the form of the Kyoto mechanism and the degree of sophistication of operating procedures);
- a background description (involving specification of the project types, the type of baseline, the crediting procedures, and the kinds of approval or safeguard criteria applied);
- approval-stage criteria;
- operating-stage criteria; and
- comments on the implications of the option in terms of hosts, donors and the FCCC.

The options are illustrative and are designed to incorporate degrees of institutional stringency, from very low to very high. Specific options are divided between those applicable to article 6 JI, and those applicable to the CDM. Although it is recognized that private- and public-sector actors will have different agendas, we have not differentiated between private- and public-sector project partners here, as discussed earlier. The institutional procedures specified in each option are determined, in part, by the degree of uncertainty or the potential for gaming associated with each situation. More stringent procedures can be used to offset greater uncertainty or higher incentives for gaming. Crediting regimes explored in these illustrative options have been chosen from the following:

- credits upfront, at the start of the project, calculated over the expected lifetime of the project and based on feasibility data;
- credits awarded annually based on monitored data;
- a limited crediting lifetime as in the type 1 baseline (see Chapter 9);
- discounted credits which start full but which gradually decrease over time to zero;
- partial credits to offset the problem of early crediting in the CDM or to counteract uncertainty.

Our eight illustrative options are set out in Boxes 10.1 to 10.8 below and are summarized in Table 10.1.

Box 10.1 Option 1 (Article 6 JI, simple)

Key Characteristics

This option involves article 6 JI with simple operating procedures.

Description

In this option, the project is of a standard type with standard specific-emission characteristics. Feasibility data are used to determine expected emission reductions and the baseline is taken to be a standardized baseline of type 1, with a limited (ten-year) crediting life.[2] Credits are allocated at the start of the project based on an average demand for the last five years of the old plant, so this is essentially on an historic supply basis. The certainty for investors is high. At the approval stage, the project is agreed between host and donor without the need for independent verification, and the FCCC is only informed of the transaction. There is no question of performing any environmental and social assessment.

Verification is limited to project existence. There is no need for baseline revision with the short lifetime for crediting. Although credits are allocated at the start, they can only be awarded in the compliance period.

Approval stage

This involves the following:

- approval: host and donor (notification to FCCC);
- baseline: standard (tCO_2e/MWh);
- credits calculated: demand based on average of last five years of old plant (feasibility data);
- environmental and social assessment: no.

Operation Stage

This involves the following:

- monitoring: none;
- verification: of existence;
- baseline revision: none;
- credits awarded: annually during compliance period.

Comments

The host will bear the risks if the credits are not generated by the project as expected, and the host will have to engage other measures in order to ensure that its targets are met. The host also bears the risk of the detriments to other environmental and social areas from the project. An assumption is that standard compensation procedures would apply if the project failed.

BOX 10.2 OPTION 2 (CDM, SIMPLE)

Key Characteristics

This option involves a CDM project under simple operating procedures.

Description

In this option, the project is of a standard type with standard specific-emission characteristics. The baseline is taken to be a standardized baseline of type 1, with a limited (ten-year) crediting life. In this case, unlike the article 6 JI, the credits for the project are not provided upfront, based on feasibility data. Instead, they are based on operating data but for a limited crediting lifetime in order to limit uncertainties in the baseline. Approval procedures involve a third party check on the project assessment and on the baseline. Although an environmental and social assessment is possible, none is undertaken and there is no public consultation. Credits are allocated from the start of the project and banked for the compliance period. Verification of existence and output by one spot check is the minimum check.

Approval Stage

This involves the following:

- approval: host/donor/FCCC body;
- baseline: standard (tCO$_2$e/MWh); third party approval needed;
- environmental and social assessment: no;
- local participation and consultation: no.

Operation Stage

This involves the following:

- monitoring: annual output data from operator;
- verification: of existence; one spot check for legitimacy;
- baseline revision: not necessary with limited life;
- credits calculated: based on reported output;
- credits awarded: for ten years in compliance period.

Comments

There are more checks than the article 6 JI case in order to ensure that the initial approval and baseline are set up properly. The emission reductions are also based on output, combined with a limited crediting period of ten years – which is more stringent than the regime for crediting the article 6 JI. This is designed to limit the risks of overestimating reductions. The host is not protected from additional environmental and social impacts and there is no consultation.

BOX 10.3 OPTION 3 (ARTICLE 6 JI, INTERMEDIATE)

Key Characteristics

This option is applicable to article 6 JI and incorporates a set of regulatory procedures of intermediate complexity.

Description

In this option we describe an intermediate level of regulation for a project. The approval procedure is independently vetted, as with option 2. The baseline used for assessment is of type 2, where the baseline technology is known and the baseline emissions are calculated using the standardized specific emissions for the technology. This is also subject to checking. The lifetime is the engineering life, so there is a baseline revision process after ten years.[3] The demand is taken as the output from the plant, based on annual monitored data. The emissions from the project are then calculated using the specific emissions for the technology. There is an environmental and social assessment of the impacts and public participation in the process. Verification of project existence and of the output is on a random spot-check basis. Credits are awarded annually based on reported output during the compliance period.

Approval Stage

This involves the following:

- approval: host/donor/FCCC body;
- baseline: standard (tCO_2e/MWh); third party approval needed;
- environmental and social assessment: yes (>50MW use EU-standard EIA);
- local participation and consultation: yes.

Operation Stage

This involves the following:

- monitoring: annual output data by operator;
- verification: of existence; one spot check ;
- baseline revision: every ten years;
- credits calculated: based on reported output;
- credits awarded: annually during the compliance period.

Comments

Here, the simple case has been expanded to account for equity and more environmental efficiency. The host can only give credits which are generated on the basis of monitored data; therefore, there is less risk that the host has to provide credits upfront for emission reductions which then fail to materialize. The environmental and social assessment should ensure that any adverse effects are minimized, but there is no audit of this during the operating stage, so some shared risk between donor and host remains.

BOX 10.4 OPTION 4 (CDM, INTERMEDIATE)

Key Characteristics

This option is applicable to CDM and incorporates a set of regulatory procedures of intermediate complexity.

Description

In this option we describe an intermediate level of regulation for a project. The approval procedure is independently vetted, as with option 2. The baseline is of type 2, where the baseline technology is known and the baseline emissions are calculated using the standardized specific emissions for the technology. This is also subject to checking. The lifetime is the engineering life, so there is a baseline revision process after ten years.[4] The demand is taken as the output from the plant, based on annual monitored data. The emissions from the project are then calculated using the specific emissions for the technology. There is an environmental and social assessment of the impacts and public participation in the process. Verification of project existence and of the output is on a random spot-check basis. Credits are awarded annually based upon reported output and can be banked over the whole lifetime.

Approval Stage

This involves the following:

* approval: host/donor/FCCC body;
* baseline: standard (tCO_2e/MWh); third party approval needed;
* environmental and social assessment: yes (>50MW use EU-standard EIA);
* local participation and consultation: yes.

Operation Stage

This involves the following:

* monitoring: annual output data by operator;
* verification: of existence; one spot check (host no incentive);
* baseline revision: every ten years;
* credits calculated: based on reported output;
* credits awarded: annually during engineering lifetime.

Comments

Here, the simple case has been expanded to account for equity and more environmental efficiency. The host can only give credits which are generated on the basis of monitored data; therefore, there is less risk that the host has to provide credits upfront for emission reductions which then fail to materialize. The environmental and social assessment should ensure that any adverse effects are minimized; however, there is no audit of this during the operating stage, so some shared risk between donor and host remains.

Box 10.5 Option 5 (Article 6 JI Extra)

Key Characteristics

This option is similar to option 3 and is applicable to article 6 JI with operating procedures of intermediate complexity. However, it differs significantly in the specification of baseline procedures.

Description

The main difference between this option and the intermediate case is that the baseline is based upon an average specific emission for the sector (type 3 baseline as specified in Chapter 9). Since there is no baseline revision, this will increase the uncertainty in the estimation; the uncertainty must be offset in order to ensure that the reduction in emissions is not overestimated and does not jeopardize reduction targets. The credits are therefore only given for 50 per cent of the annual output reported.

Approval Stage

This involves the following:

- approval: host/donor/FCCC body;
- baseline: standard (tCO_2e/MWh); third party approval needed;
- environmental and social assessment: yes (>50MW use EU-standard EIA);
- local participation and consultation.

Operation Stage

This involves the following:

- monitoring: annual output data by operator;
- verification: of existence; one spot check for legitimacy (host no incentive);
- credits calculated: based on reported output;
- credits awarded: annually during the compliance period at 50 per cent of total emission reduction value.

Comments

The donor has the risk of the plant operation failing to provide enough credits and therefore of not achieving the required emission reductions in the donor country. There is no audit of environmental and social effects during operation, so some shared risk between host and donor remains.

BOX 10.6 OPTION 6 (CDM, EXTRA)

Key Characteristics

This option is similar to option 4 and is applicable to the CDM with operating procedures of intermediate complexity. Like option 5, however, it differs in the specification of baseline procedures.

Description

The main difference between this option and the intermediate case is that the baseline is fixed on an average specific emission for the sector (type 3 baseline as specified in Chapter 9). Since there is no baseline revision, this will increase the uncertainty in the estimation, and this uncertainty has to be offset in order to ensure that the reduction in emissions is not overestimated and does not jeopardize reduction targets. The credits are therefore only given for 50 per cent of the annual output reported.

Approval Stage

This involves the following:

- approval: host/donor/FCCC body;
- baseline: standard (tCO_2e/MWh); third party approval needed;
- environmental and social assessment: yes (>50MW use EU-standard EIA);
- local participation and consultation.

Operation Stage

This involves the following:

- monitoring: annual output data by operator;
- verification: of existence; one spot check for legitimacy (host no incentive);
- credits calculated: based on reported output;
- credits awarded: annually during engineering lifetime at 50 per cent of total emission reduction value.

Comments

The donor has the risk of the plant operation failing to provide enough credits and therefore of not achieving the required emission reductions in the donor country. There is no audit of environmental and social effects during operation, so some shared risk between host and donor remains.

Box 10.7 Option 7 (Article 6 JI, Complex)

Key Characteristics

This option is applicable to article 6 JI, and incorporates a more complex set of operating procedures.

Description

In this JI option, we have a project described by a simple representation of specific emissions. The baseline is a standardized form but the technology is unknown; therefore, it uses type 3 or 4 baselines. It should be approved by all parties, including the FCCC. As earlier, the initial approval of the project is also subject to the independent authority of the FCCC. Annual monitored data are again used as the basis of calculating emission reductions, but more verification checks are incorporated in order to compensate for increased incentives for gaming. Baseline revision is more frequent at every five years to minimize uncertainties. An environmental and social assessment is required, as well as participation by local people. This time the impacts are audited during operation so that remedial action can be taken a minimum of five years after commissioning.

Approval Stage

This involves the following:

- approval: host/donor/FCCC body;
- baseline: standard (tCO_2e/MWh); third party approval needed;
- environmental and social assessment: yes (>50MW use EU-standard EIA);
- local participation and consultation: yes.

Operation Stage

This involves the following:

- monitoring: annual output data by operator; environmental and social audit by third party (after five years: credit penalty for non-compliance);
- verification: of existence; several spot checks of output (host no incentive);
- baseline revision: every five years;
- credits calculated: based on reported output;
- credits awarded: annually during the compliance period.

Comments

This is a tightly regulated option to limit gaming. Partial crediting was considered but not applied because the package of measures is already stringent and further penalties were not considered feasible, in practice.

Box 10.8 Option 8 (CDM, Complex)

Key Characteristics

This option is applicable to the CDM and incorporates a more complex set of operating procedures.

Description

In this JI option we have a project described by a simple representation of specific emissions. The baseline is a standardized form but the technology is unknown; it therefore uses type 3 or 4 baselines. It should be approved by all parties, including the FCCC. As earlier, the initial approval of the project is also subject to the independent authority of the FCCC. Annual monitored data are again used as the basis of calculating emission reductions; however, more verification checks are incorporated in order to compensate for increased incentives for gaming. Baseline revision is more frequent at every five years to minimize uncertainties. An environmental and social assessment is required, as well as participation by local people. This time the impacts are audited so that remedial action can be taken a minimum of five years after commissioning.

Approval Stage

This involves the following:

- approval: host/donor/FCCC body;
- baseline: standard (tCO_2e/MWh); third party approval needed;
- environmental and social assessment: yes (>50MW use EU-standard EIA);
- local participation and consultation: yes.

Operation Stage

This involves the following:

- monitoring: annual output data by operator; environmental and social audit by third party (after five years: credit penalty for non-compliance);
- verification: of existence; several spot checks of output (host no incentive);
- baseline revision: every five years;
- credits calculated: based on reported output;
- credits awarded: annually during technical lifetime and banked during the interim period.

Comments

This is a tightly regulated option to limit gaming. Partial crediting was considered but not applied because the package of measures is already stringent and further penalties were not considered feasible, in practice.

Table 10.1 *Summary of Selected JI Options*

Options	Standardization type	Crediting type	Data type	Safeguards
1 Article 6 JI, simple	std or specific project/std baseline type 1 (subst)	ten-year crediting life; full credits upfront	feasibility	• approval: host/donor • limited life • verification of existence
2 CDM, simple	specific project/std baseline type 1 (subst)	ten-year crediting life; annual full credits	operational	• approval: host/donor/ FCCC • operating data • limited life • verification of existence
3 and 4 Article 6 JI/CDM, intermediate	specific project/std baseline type 2 (subst)	ten-year reviews of baseline paid by donor; annual full credits	operational	• approval: host/donor/ FCCC • environmental and social survey • public participation • operating data • baseline revision after ten years • verification of existence and one spot check
5 and 6 Article 6 JI/CDM, intermediate extra	specific project/ std baseline combination type 3 (average over all baselines)	for technical life of plant no reviews; annual 50% credits	operational	• approval: host/donor/ FCCC • environmental and social survey • public participation • operating data • 50% credits • no revisions • verification of existence and one check

Options	Standardization type	Crediting type	Data type	Safeguards
7 and 8 Article 6 JI/CDM, complex	specific project/ std baseline type 3 or 4	five-year reviews of baseline paid by donor; annual full credits	operational	• approval: host/donor/ FCCC • baseline approval • environmental and social survey • public participation • operating data and environmental and social audit • baseline revision every five years • verification of existence and several spot checks

Key:
std = standardized
subst = substituted plant known

Methodologies for Evaluating Joint Implementation Options

This section gives a short overview of a number of approaches that could be used for evaluating the JI options. This is followed by a more detailed description of the particular decision-analysis method we have chosen to use in our illustrative assessment.

Evaluation Techniques

The central questions when considering which evaluation technique is appropriate are: what is being evaluated, why is it being evaluated and who should perform the evaluation? The appropriateness of any particular technique will depend upon the answers to these questions. There are many well-established methodologies for assessing projects, policies, plans or strategies. At the project level, environmental impact assessment (EIA) is a very commonly applied, structured technique for assessing a wide variety of environmental, social and economic impacts. Also at the project level, but not exclusively so, cost-benefit analysis is a frequently applied numerical technique of assessment from an economic perspective. In response to criticisms of using a single numerical quantity (money) in cost-benefit analysis, multi-attribute decision analysis (MADA) has been developed to allow structured numerical assessment of a project or policy. The UK Department of the Environment, Transport and the Regions (DETR) has now moved away from cost-benefit analysis to MADA.

Many practitioners of EIA at the project level have appreciated that projects do not exist independently of each other, which has led to the development of cumulative environmental assessment. CEA attempts to look at the overall impacts of a series or programme of projects. Strategic environmental assessment (SEA) has developed along similar lines as project EIA and is a means of assessing policies, plans or strategies. Another computational technique increasingly used at the policy level for such issues as climate change or acidification is integrated assessment modelling, which – in some cases – is being embedded in integrated assessment. Integrated assessment (or integrated environmental assessment, as it is sometimes called) aims to include qualitative as well as quantitative analysis in the assessment.

Perhaps the most common assessment methodology of all is the expert panel. This panel typically creates a written assessment of a particular issue and may, though does not always, use one of the methods above. Finally, there are various techniques for involving members of the public in assessments, such as citizen juries, focus groups or other types of discussion groups. These public participation techniques are sometimes combined with the expert assessment methods described above.

In summary, there are many different assessment techniques available, including hybrid methods. However, given the multi-objective nature of the problem, the uncertainty associated with it and the existence of conflicting viewpoints, the method we have chosen as the most comprehensive for gaining insights into evaluating different JI options is multi-attribute decision analysis (MADA) with decision conferencing (Phillips, 1989).

This technique is described in detail below. Its strengths are clearly set out and it must be pointed out that although an expected numerical value is produced at the end of the analysis, the main function of MADA is to provide a framework for rational analysis of a problem. By doing so it facilitates communication and understanding. The actual number obtained (which, in theory, should indicate which option is chosen) should be regarded as a starting point for further exploration of the problem, rather than an end point in itself.

Multi-attribute Decision Analysis with Decision Conferencing

Decision analysis has a long history and is one of the few assessment methodologies with a clearly validated theoretical basis. When making a decision, there is no such thing as objective choice. In all cases decisions are based on subjective choice – which is a combination of the utility or moral worth of the choice – and probability – which is the degree of belief associated with the choice. These ideas were first discussed by Bernouilli 250 years ago, and they have subsequently been developed by a number of people. In the 1930s, Ramsay argued that if you wished to make a coherent choice then you would follow the principle of coherence, and Savage (1954) encapsulated these ideas in a series of rules:

- Given two alternatives a and b, one either has a preference or one is indifferent about alternatives (a≥b).
- If a is preferable to b, and b is preferable to c, then a is preferable to c (transitivity).
- If for two alternatives most aspects are the same but one alternative has one or more aspects which are better, then this will be preferred (dominance).
- The choice will be unaffected by what the alternatives have in common (sure thing principle).

From these few rules, three theorems can be proved:

1   Probabilities exist and these are logically consistent with coherent preferences.
2   Utilities exist and the numbers represent how much you value the consequences. They are composed of subjective values and a risk attribute.
3   For rational choice, the alternative with the highest expected utility should be chosen.

Thus, the foundation for decision analysis is built on an axiomatic base. The technique helps one to be consistent. The theorems were developed into an applied technology by Raiffa (1968). Later Keeney and Raiffa (1976) introduced a multi-objective context and a new assumption that preferences were mutually independent. Under this assumption, the utility U_j for the jth consequence can be obtained by summing the utilities U_{jk} for k criteria:

$$U_j = \sum_k w_k \, U_{jk} \qquad\qquad (10.1)$$

where w_k is a weight. So, for example, in the purchase of a new car, cost and car colour can be judgementally independent criteria, and the utility of a particular model of car can be calculated by summing the (appropriately weighted) utilities of the individual criteria.

Decision analysis has two main advantages over other approaches. It has a sound foundation and it is the only theory which can incorporate uncertainty and multi-objectives.

Decision Conferencing

The decision conferencing approach involves a facilitator and analyst working with a group of 'problem owners' over a series of meetings: structuring the problem, eliciting inputs and working through the results, which may need to be refined through several iterations. These meetings are focused, interactive and task oriented.

Models are used to process the inputs as they are derived. Exploration of the sensitivities, uncertainties and areas of conflict are an important part of the analysis and can be easily accomplished using this approach. In this way, a shared understanding of the problem is developed by the group, which can lead to generation of new options, improvement of existing options and in some cases a rethink of the original strategy leading to the decision. Another strength of the combined methodology is the ability to role-play the views of other interest groups, leading to generation of negotiating positions.

Value Functions

The procedure relies on eliciting a value function from the problem owners. It represents the value attached to the option and is purely subjective.

Scales are used to look at differences in the numbers for the options scored on a given criterion, such as environmental effectiveness. The scales themselves can be of two types: ratio scales or interval scales. Ratio scales have the zero fixed and use arbitrary units. With the ratio scale, zero means the minimum acceptable level on that criterion, while the top of the scale is the maximum feasible value, which may or may not coincide with the best option performance on that criterion. If the scale is set up in this way, it can be used simply with the ratios of the numbers on the scale. With interval scales, which are used as the basis of the evaluation in this study, the top and bottom of the scales correspond to the most and least preferred options under evaluation. In this case, only the ratios of the differences between numbers are meaningful. If option A is scored at 50, then the increase in preference in moving from the option at 50 to option B at 100 is equivalent to the decrease in preference in moving from option A to option E at zero (see Figure 10.1).

Weights

Having established value scales or constructed functions for each of the individual assessment criteria, the decision-analysis methodology normally proceeds by weighting the individual criteria according to their (subjective) importance to those making the decision. The expected utility from each option is then calculated by summing the weighted values over the range of criteria – as shown in equation 10.1. For those seeking to make a coherent decision, the option with the highest utility should be chosen.

In this illustrative exercise, we have not engaged in the latter stage of the MADA methodology. We have implicitly assigned equal weights to individual criteria, but we do not calculate an overall expected utility for each option. Rather, we have used the MADA methodology to illustrate the existence of trade-offs between equally weighted individual criteria – some options score highly according to one criterion but poorly against another. The importance of these scores, in terms of the overall decision in a full-scale analysis, is determined by the relative weights assigned to the different criteria. In principle, it is possible to extend our illustrative analysis in this way to calculate an overall expected utility. However, as mentioned above, a single number answer is not the point of the analysis. Rather, the MADA process provides a means, firstly, of structuring the problem and, secondly (when used with an appropriate sensitivity analysis), of generating insights into the trade-offs involved in solving it.

Figure 10.1 *Preference Ordering on an Interval Scale*

Main Attributes of Multi-attribute Decision Analysis with Decision Conferencing.

The analysis is carried out within a social context but it does not necessarily aim to reach consensus. Rather, it is a process involving group participation which incorporates multiple perspectives and within which each individual view can be accounted for. It aims to engage the collective will in order to implement a solution and allows consideration, in a consistent manner, of a wealth of data which normally is difficult to handle and value. The analysis allows areas of opportunity to be identified, such as new or improved options, strategy reassessment and role playing either for robustness or negotiating positions. Additional benefits include the fact that the robustness of the result can be explored and uncertainties accounted for, and that the process provides an audit trail which renders the decision process transparent.

Illustrative Evaluation Using Multi-attribute Decision Analysis Techniques

The exercise conducted during this study was not a full-scale decision-analysis exercise. In particular, it did not weight the different criteria, calculate an overall expected utility for each option or carry out sensitivity analysis. Rather, the intention was to use the methodology in an illustrative fashion to show how it could provide the basis for an evaluation framework for the JI options defined above. Each JI option was scored using MADA techniques against a set of evaluation criteria based on the underlying objectives identified in Chapter 3. The evaluation exercise was carried out over two two-day sessions, facilitated by Dr Begg and involving an assessment group composed of project collaborators. Although this was not a full decision analysis, it nevertheless provided valuable insights into the evaluation process and gave a clear indication of the trade-offs between different criteria in individual options. It also indicated that the current emphasis on investor attractiveness when structuring JI mechanisms could lead to problems in using this mechanism.

Evaluation Criteria

The first step in the analysis was to define clearly the criteria against which the options were to be evaluated. These derive mainly from the objectives underlying JI, as identified in Chapter 3. In other words, we were concerned primarily with environmental effectiveness, equity and economic efficiency. In line with the discussion in Chapter 3, the question of economic efficiency was further subdivided into questions of cost effectiveness (from a social point of view) and issues of investor attractiveness. Our top-level evaluation criteria were therefore defined as:

- environmental effectiveness;
- equity;
- cost effectiveness; and
- investor attractiveness.

After considerable discussion, these criteria were disaggregated into a number of subcriteria. These are discussed in the following subsections and illustrated graphically in Figure 10.2.

Environmental effectiveness

This was defined in terms of the risk of overestimating GHG emission reductions. This criterion reflects a number of factors, including the level of uncertainty surrounding emission reduction estimates, the method used for the estimation, the incentives for gaming in a particular situation, and the number of safeguards involved in the operational procedures.

Equity

Equity considerations were discussed in terms of both donor and host countries. A major assumption was that, in view of the historical responsibility for pollution by developed countries, donor and host equity considerations should not balance.

For the donor, it was considered that equity considerations could not be provided specifically by a single JI option. The mechanism of JI itself provides the opportunity for trade, and the advantage which investors gain from that is not a function of an implementation option. The ease of access to project-based JI has to be equal for all investors, and in that sense there is an institutional implication that JI implementation options maintain this aspect. However, it is not differentiated by any one option. Thus, donor equity was not explicitly considered further in the analysis.

By contrast, it became clear that most of the country-level host factors could only be addressed in the approval criteria for JI projects or in a methodology specifically set up and adopted to take account of these goals. For example, to avoid overcommitment by the host or the use of inappropriate technology, the host needs to have some information on its energy system and proposals for a strategy for a future development path. As discussed earlier, this requires a country-level strategy.

Considerations of equity in terms of the host country appeared to be composed of various provisions in order to ensure that:

- An appropriate level of local environmental and social impact assessments are made and plans to mitigate or avoid secondary effects are put into operation.
- Local capacity-building (necessary for the proper working of the project) is incorporated.
- There is a level of local participation in the process of gaining approval for the project.

In a more complex treatment, these individual elements could define specific subcriteria. However, in this simplified analysis, they were simply regarded as contributing factors to one overriding criterion of host equity.

Cost effectiveness

The objective of cost effectiveness refers to minimization of GHG emission-reduction costs. By encouraging donors with high marginal abatement costs to invest in host countries with lower marginal costs, the objective of cost effectiveness is achieved provided that the marginal technology is chosen. The marginal technology may have a higher initial investment cost, but the rewards in emission reductions are also supposed to be higher.

In principle, the criterion of additionality should ensure cost effectiveness since it requires that the project should cost more and yield more reductions than the ordinary market choice. In practice, this is not necessarily the case and therefore each project has to be examined separately. If additionality is a basic part of the approval criteria, then how this is operationalized is key to realizing cost effectiveness. Operationalizing additionality has proved to be difficult and this has been discussed at some length in Chapter 3. The underlying reason for this difficulty is the trade-offs inherent between conflicting objectives of cost effectiveness, equity, practicality and, to some extent, the overall environmental effectiveness of the JI mechanism. Evaluating JI options under this criterion therefore rests to some extent on how additionality is addressed. However, as currently defined, the JI options do not include this aspect specifically and at this stage cannot be differentiated on this basis. The subcriterion of additionality is therefore not used explicitly in this analysis; but the discussion shows that the JI options should be redefined in order to include different additionality operationalization regimes.

At the project level, calculations have been made of the specific incremental cost of emissions reduced. As noted in Chapter 8, these costs are highly dependent upon certain assumptions and there is a degree of variability in the results. Projects may be compared provided the assumptions are the same. Generally speaking, however, there are such large uncertainties that the cost effectiveness of projects could not be judged unless some comparison with a least-cost path for both countries was available. It was decided, therefore, that cost effectiveness could only be judged if the JI framework allowed a least-cost development. This led to a disaggregation of the overall criterion in order to capture the different factors which would be involved in this least-cost development. These factors included ease of using the option and market efficiency.

Ease of using the option and low transaction costs   This reflects the fact that the cost efficiency demands market efficiency in the sense that it should be easy to develop JI projects. As a result, any aspect of a JI implementation option which facilitates this is preferable. Here, implied institutional requirements for the option of administrative procedures for approval, implementation, verification and monitoring are important. These requirements are also important in determining the transaction costs for a project. However, it should be borne in mind that as more projects are set up, so procedures are refined and the transaction costs are expected to fall.

Market efficiency   This criterion is related to quality of information and is correlated to how certain the credits are, including access to markets, institutions and price. It was felt that current options could only be distinguished on the basis of quality of information, which has been assessed under environmental efficiency. As a result, there was no further assessment on this criterion.

Investor attractiveness

This is not specifically an aim of the convention. However, it is generally acknowledged that in view of limited government funds, the success of emission reduction policies depends upon involving the private sector, which will be subject to possible fiscal measures at home in order to minimize costs to meet internal targets. Investor attractiveness was considered to depend upon both the crediting arrangements and the accounting arrangements involved in a JI option. The cost of the credits as a criterion was dropped from the analysis since this was project specific and hard to measure for the overall JI process. However, the potential amount of credits was incorporated as a subcriterion, as was the certainty involved in receiving the credits – a function of the accreditation procedures. Thus, two subcriteria were evaluated under investor attractiveness, namely:

1   potential amount of credits: the amount of credits companies could obtain for a project; and
2   certainty of credits: how certain the companies would be of obtaining the credits.

Value Tree

The final value tree used in the illustrative evaluation process is shown in Figure 10.2. The preceding discussion confirms that a good deal more complexity might reasonably be required for a complete analysis of the different options. However, for illustrative purposes, the value tree shown in Figure 10.2 will suffice.

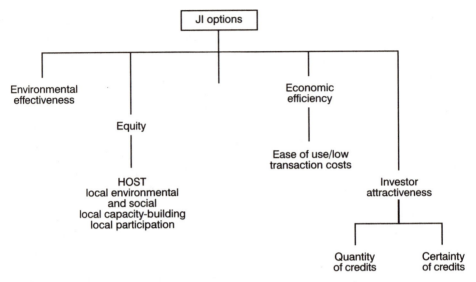

Figure 10.2 *Value Tree for Illustrative Evaluation of JI Options*

Illustrative Scoring

The next stage of this evaluation process is to score the individual JI options defined in Boxes 10.1 to 10.8 against the criteria elucidated above. It is obvious from the foregoing discussions that a comprehensive evaluation would require some redefinition of the JI options to include essential elements (such as those associated with additionality) which have been excluded from our initial assessment. Nevertheless, Table 10.2 provides an indication of how it might be possible to score the different JI options according to selected criteria. This illustrative scoring was derived in a mock decision-conferencing situation, in which a number of project collaborators from the European Commission (EC) study participated. The evaluation process itself induced considerable further discussion, which is currently the focus of continued research.

Discussion

Assuming equally weighted criteria, the illustrative scores in Table 10.2 suggest that the complex options (options 7 and 8) are the most attractive in terms of environmental effectiveness and equity compared to the others, while their main drawbacks arise from low scores in economic efficiency and investor attractiveness. Though purely illustrative, this result is plausible because of the higher transaction costs associated with complex operational procedures. Investor attractiveness also suffers in the complex options, mainly because of higher uncertainty associated with getting credits from the investment.

   The strengths of the simple options are that they are expected to have low transaction costs and are attractive to investors, particularly in terms of the certainty in getting credits. However, the article 6 JI option (option 1) fares very badly in terms of environmental effectiveness as a result of the use of

Table 10.2 *Summary of Illustrative Scores for Selected JI Options*

JI option	Environmental effectiveness	Equity	Economic efficiency	Investor attractiveness	
				Quantity of credits	Certainty of credits
1 Article 6 JI/simple	0	0	100	0	100
2 CDM/simple	75	0	80	0	80
3 Article 6 JI/intermediate	70	67	50	100	40
4 CDM/intermediate	65	67	50	100	40
5 Article 6 JI/extra	75	67	60	0	70
6 CDM/extra	75	67	60	0	70
7 Article 6 JI/complex	100	100	0	100	0
8 CDM/complex	80	100	0	100	0

feasibility data and full crediting 'upfront'. In contrast, the CDM simple option (option 2) fares well due to the use of monitored data and the restricted crediting lifetime. Both 1 and 2 perform very badly in terms of equity since they do not include provisions for ensuring host country equity in the operational procedures (such as an environmental and social assessment).

The 'extra' options (options 5 and 6) were much more balanced on all criteria except in terms of the quantity of credits. However, the importance of this depends upon the difference between the top and bottom of the scale and how much that is valued by investors. It may not, in the end, prove a problem since it is offset by a less complex option (in particular, the absence of baseline revisions). It is interesting to note that if environmental and social assessments and public participation were included in the CDM simple option (option 2), this would be roughly equivalent to the CDM intermediate extra option (option 6).

The intermediate options (options 3 and 4) seem to score reasonably well on all aspects. This appears to be a well-balanced option but does have more institutional demands (captured in terms of lower scores for 'ease of use') compared to both the simple and the extra options.

Again, we emphasize here that we have not carried out the final stages of the MADA, which involves weighting the individual criteria or carrying out sensitivity analyses. It is therefore slightly misleading to draw overly specific conclusions from the scores shown in Table 10.2. This implicitly assumes that each criterion was assigned the same weight. In reality, of course, a different weight might be attached to the criterion of environmental effectiveness than to cost effectiveness. Clearly, an extreme case – in which, for example, only the criterion of weight was deemed to be cost effective – would yield a very different evaluation of the JI options than a case where environmental effectiveness was considered important.

It became obvious during the exercise that, although we had endeavoured to define the JI options in terms of several critical criteria, it was not possible to fully assess the selected options as they stood because some elements necessary for a full assessment of equity or of overall cost efficiency were missing.

For example, the method of operationalizing additionality could not be specified. Furthermore, various sustainability aspects were neglected. These included, for example, the capacity-building capability of the host country, measures to ensure that development is in line with host country priorities, the correct pricing of credits, safeguards to prevent host countries with targets from overcommitting, and measures to ensure the implementation of appropriate technology. Such measures are related to empowering the host nations to negotiate on an equal basis with donors. Donor distributional equity is satisfied through crediting regimes, trade advantages and equal access to CDM opportunities, which flows from the transaction itself and the institutional set-up for investor attractiveness.

In order to integrate these equity and cost-efficiency aspects fully within the JI options, it is necessary to include:

- an extended set of approval criteria;
- audit and compliance procedures;
- arrangements for resources to enable the host to formulate development and energy strategies;
- operationalization regimes for additionality.

Minimum Requirements for Joint Implementation

Table 10.3 sets out a generic framework for defining JI options and illustrates the range of operational parameters which define each option. The basis for the individual components of this generic framework lies in preceding chapters in this book.

Table 10.3 also defines three further options (A, B and C) by assigning three sets of values to the operational parameters. Each of these options could be regarded as addressing the main objectives of the convention (environmental effectiveness, equity, economic efficiency) in a reasonably balanced manner. The accounting and accreditation measures are informed by the evaluation analysis carried out above, where we saw that the options which require accreditation on the basis of monitored data, and which use limited lifetimes or partial credits, are simple yet powerful methods of limiting gaming. They compare favourably in terms of environmental effectiveness with the more monitored approach of the intermediate and complex options.

Options A and B offer relatively simple frameworks, combining standardized baseline procedures with certain institutional safeguards. These options could be applied to short-term article 6 JI and CDM projects. Option C includes more stringent safeguards, including baseline revision and stricter verification protocols, and could be applied to longer-term CDM projects. On the basis of the experience gained during this project, these options are most likely to be effective in achieving goals of environmental effectiveness, equity and economic efficiency.

Table 10.3 *Generic Framework for Defining JI Options*

Stage	Component	Alternatives	Option A	Option B	Option C
Approval stage					
	1 Approval criteria	Restricted set[5]			
		Extended set[6]	✔	✔	✔
	2 Operationalization of additionality	Pragmatic			
		Barrier	✔		
		Restricted project set			
		System model baseline			
		None; but take other measures in order to compensate			
		Combination of above			
	(new)	Appropriate technology in line with sustainable path		✔	✔
	3 Independent project approval		✔	✔	✔
	4 Independent baseline approval		✔	✔	✔
Accounting stage					
		Complex model			
	5 Baseline	Project partial model			
		Simplified baseline + safeguards	✔	✔	✔
	6 Data	Annual Monitored Feasibility	✔	✔	✔
	7 Safeguards	Monitored data	✔	✔	✔
		Baseline revisions			✔
		Verification protocols	✔		✔
		Limited lifetime	✔		
		Discounting reductions/credits			
		Non-compliance procedures			
Crediting stage					
		Upfront			
	8 Regimes	Annually on monitored data	✔	✔	✔
		Sliding scale			
		Partial crediting for CDM to offset banking			
		Partial/discounted crediting to offset uncertainties		✔	
Auditing stage					
	9 Regimes	Existence only			
		Existence plus one spot check of operation	✔	✔	
		Existence plus several spot checks			✔
		Existence plus spot check/s plus environmental and social audit			

Conclusions

In this chapter we have explored the development of a holistic evaluation framework for JI. The basis for this framework rests on recognizing two critical factors: firstly, that JI operates in the context of multiple underlying objectives; and, secondly, that there exists a large number of different operational forms of JI (or JI options) that are defined by assigning different values to key operational parameters. Eight illustrative options have been defined.

Typically, each option will perform differently against the underlying objectives. Some options – for instance, those incorporating stronger environmental safeguards – will perform better in terms of the environmental objectives of the convention; others will prove more attractive to investors. In general, such situations are characterized by the need to make trade-offs between different objectives. Partly because of this fact, partly because of the sheer operational complexity involved, and partly because of the existence of irreducible uncertainties in the assessment, the evaluation of JI options becomes a demanding task requiring a relatively sophisticated assessment methodology.

This chapter has demonstrated that MADA could be one way of proceeding in the face of this complexity. We have carried out an illustrative MADA evaluation of each of the eight selected options, and indicated how each of them might be expected to perform against the underlying objectives. Though illustrative, our evaluation shows clearly how the trade-offs between different objectives involved in designing JI may be made explicit. Appropriate institutional frameworks are essential if JI is to satisfy the demands made on it in the policy arena.

In particular, although some institutions (such as the executive board) have been defined under article 12 for the CDM, there are currently no appropriate institutions set up for implementation of article 6 JI. The continuation of the AIJ pilot phase (decided at COP 5) offers a clear opportunity to rectify this situation. It would also be appropriate to redesign institutional elements of the existing AIJ structure – such as the uniform reporting format – in order to make them applicable to the Kyoto mechanisms. In doing so, however, it will be vital to recognize the range of underlying objectives, including environmental effectiveness and equity, and to design appropriate procedures to safeguard these objectives. Table 10.3 indicates some of the minimum requirements for this task.

The methodology set out in this chapter highlights the fact that there are many operational forms for JI-type mechanisms. For example, there are over 3000 theoretical permutations of the set of parameters shown in Table 10.3. Though complex to manage, this multiplicity also allows some flexibility in the provision of safeguards. Different combinations of measures can be used to ensure particular objectives. More stringent safeguards in the accounting framework can offset less stringent safeguards on accreditation, or vice versa.

The exercise set out in this chapter has illustrated that it is necessary to define clearly each operational form of JI from start to finish. Only by doing so is it possible to identify the trade-offs between underlying objectives, and if necessary to design specific measures within the option to ensure that an appropriate balance is achieved between environmental effectiveness, equity and economic efficiency. The procedure illustrated here offers the potential to move the debate on flexibility mechanisms forwards. Rather than arguing over whether or not such mechanisms are fair and efficient, this methodology allows us to design each option to make sure that they are.

Appendix 1

Analysis of Crediting Regimes

Introduction

In Chapter 9 we outlined how early crediting (also know as *interim period banking*), as specified under article 12.10 of the Kyoto Protocol, might undermine the objectives of the Framework Convention on Climate Change (FCCC). In this appendix, we give the detailed justification for these arguments.

As we have discussed, the Kyoto Protocol defines a *commitment period*, which extends from 2008–2012 inclusive, for which emission reduction targets (known as quantified emission limitation and reduction commitments, or QELRCs) have been defined. For the period before 2008, no targets have been set. At the time of publication, JI projects carried out under article 6 will receive emission reduction units (ERUs) only during the commitment period, making them comparable with the QELRCs. However, in the case of the CDM, article 12.10 allows for certified emission reductions (CERs) to be banked during an *interim period* (2000–2007 inclusive) and added to those obtained during the commitment period.

Clearly, the two accounting procedures are not compatible and tend to favour the CDM. Furthermore, since the emission targets have only been agreed for the period 2008–2012 inclusive, it is possible that credited CDM action during the interim period may be offset by uncontrolled increases in the donor country during the interim period. Consequently, such early crediting could lead to a reduction in the total action needed over the whole period to meet the target, potentially compromising the objectives of the protocol.

There are two perspectives on this. The first (see Parkinson et al, 1998b; 1999) is that some form of compensatory mechanism is necessary to prevent early crediting from reducing the overall action. The second perspective (see Jepma, 1998b) argues that the banking of credits is beneficial because it encourages early CDM action, and this extra action would balance or even outweigh any relaxation in the QELRC targets. Hence, it is argued that banking of credits should be extended to ERUs under article 6. This second argument is augmented by the recent work of Kammen and Kinzig (1998), who stress the need for early action and even suggest that CDM emission reductions should be credited twice (to the donor and the host) so long as a minimum of 50 per cent of action is taken domestically by the donor.

In this appendix, we summarize the analysis put forward by Parkinson et al (1999), which was carried out as part of this study. The analysis examines possible crediting regimes under the Kyoto Protocol which could apply to joint implementation (JI) under both articles 6 and 12. Particular focus is given to the early crediting issue.

The remainder of the appendix is set out as follows. Firstly, we define and examine the banking issue; then we carry out an analysis of the *banking* and *no banking* regimes, and explore a possible way to make them compatible. Next, we attempt to estimate the size of the impact of early crediting in relation to the QELRC targets. Finally, we discuss the conclusions of the work in the context of the ongoing climate change negotiations.

The Banking Issue

JI, as currently written in the Kyoto Protocol, has its roots in emissions trading (Jackson et al, 1998). Under emissions trading regimes (for example, the US Clean Air Act), tradeable permits can be gained when, for example, a power plant achieves reductions greater than its target. These permits can then be sold to others who do not meet their targets, or *banked* for future use or sale. Such banking is considered necessary to help increase cost effectiveness (Tietenberg, 1985). Therefore, it is not surprising that banking is considered necessary in the context of JI.

However, it should be recognized that banking for JI, as is allowed in the CDM under article 12.10 of the Kyoto Protocol, is not equivalent to banking under previous emissions trading regimes. The reason for this is that emissions targets have not been defined for the whole period during which CDM credits (CERs) can be awarded. To illustrate this, we give an example in terms of emissions reduction from a CDM project. Banking of credits leads to a situation as shown in Figure A.1, assuming that the project yields a constant annual emissions reduction and runs from the start of 2000 to the end of 2012. E_p are the annual greenhouse gas (GHG) emissions of the project, while $e_{r,p}$ are the annual emissions reduction from a counterfactual baseline.

It can be seen that, under article 12.10, the emissions reduction of a CDM project with a constant emissions-reduction profile, and starting in 2000, counts 2.6 times as much towards the QELRC target as does a domestic or article 6 JI project.[1]

Since there is no emissions target in place for the donor during the interim period, it is quite possible for its domestic emissions to increase and offset the CDM project without penalty. Thus, it is possible that this sort of banking will lead to less total action being carried out over the whole period (interim and commitment) to meet the emissions target. It is only goodwill on the part of the donor in controlling emissions that will prevent this total action from being reduced. Effectively, this could be seen as a *relaxation* of the emissions target. It is important to contrast this with the intended purpose of flexibility mechanisms, which is to allow a redistribution of emission reductions between countries without affecting the overall target.

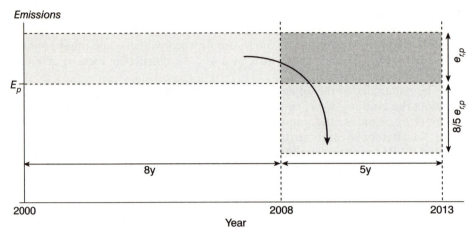

Figure A.1 *Banking Credits for a CDM Project*

The argument for this accounting bias is that it encourages GHG emissions-reduction programmes to start earlier in developing countries than without banking (Jepma, 1998b). Since a number of these countries are developing fast, it is argued, the maximum cost savings can be made by early introduction of, for example, renewable energy. Such extra action, they argue, would offset the effective relaxation of the Annex I country targets. The same argument can also be applied to article 6 JI with the transition economies of Central and Eastern Europe and the former Soviet Union. Hence, this line of reasoning leads to the conclusion that early crediting should be introduced for JI projects hosted by these countries as well.

However, a simple analysis of this situation shows up some shortcomings in this argument. In Figure A.2, we illustrate a likely evolution of the emissions reduction due to a series of CDM projects, over the period 2000–2012 inclu-

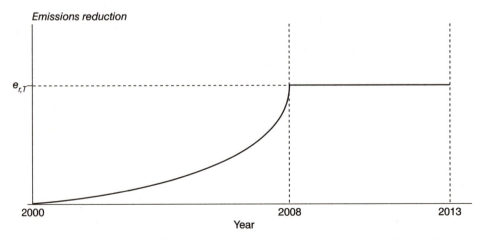

Figure A.2 *Emissions Reduction under a Crediting Regime with No Banking*

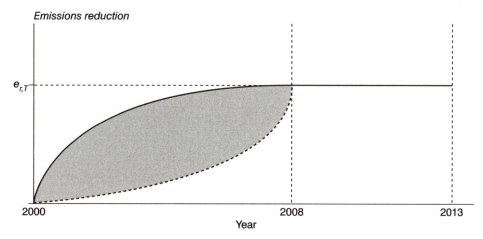

Figure A.3 *Emissions Reduction under a Crediting Regime with Banking*

sive, if no banking were to be allowed.[2] We assume that the donor has identified a level of annual emissions reduction, $e_{r,T}$, due to CDM action, that it needs in order to meet its target. To begin with, in the early years of the interim period, the amount of emissions reduction is small due to the lack of credits available. As we get closer to the commitment period, so the level increases quite rapidly in anticipation of credits from 2008 onwards. The level during the commitment period is assumed to be constant (at a value of $e_{r,T}$) because, according to article 3.7, the emissions during this period will be averaged.

If we assume, next, that banking is permitted, as envisaged under article 12.10, then the incentive to invest early is present and we see a much faster rise (see Figure A.3). The net gain in total emissions reduction from the no banking case (see Figure A.2) to the banking case (see Figure A.3) is shown by the light grey shading.

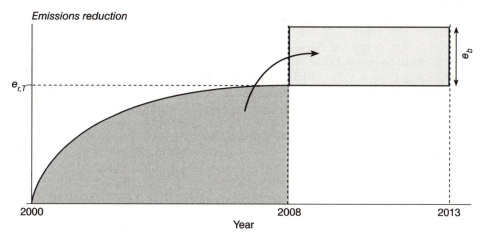

Figure A.4 *The Effect of Banking Emissions Reduction from CDM Action*

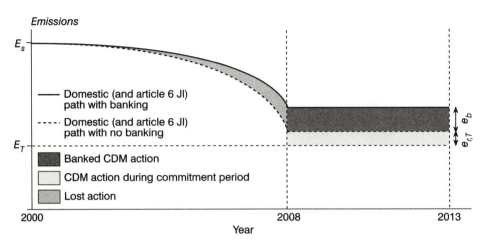

Key:
E_S = donor country emissions in 2000
E_T = donor country emissions target
e_b = annually averaged banked CDM emissions reductions
$e_{r,T}$ = annually averaged emissions reduction of CDM programme during commitment period

Figure A.5 *Emissions Reduction Paths of a Donor Country (Domestic and Article 6 JI) under Banking and No Banking Scenarios for the CDM*

However, as shown in Figure A.4, the larger dark-grey area can be banked for use during the commitment period, and hence less domestic (or article 6 JI) action is needed during this time. But, as is argued, this banked CDM action could have been offset by uncontrolled increases domestically in the donor during the interim period. Therefore, the replaced domestic and article 6 JI action could be lost (the target is still effectively *relaxed*, as discussed before). The level of relaxation is e_b, where e_b is the total banked CDM emissions reduction averaged over the commitment period.

Furthermore, this relaxation in the target will not only mean that less domestic and article 6 JI action is needed during the commitment period, but also that less is needed during the interim period, as is shown in Figure A.5.

It could be argued that, because early crediting leads to more CDM action earlier (see Figure A.5), a higher level of CDM emissions reduction during the commitment period ($e_{r,T}$) will be achieved. However, since banking effectively relaxes the overall target, the incentive actually works in the opposite direction: more early CDM action leads to less being needed during the commitment period ($e_{r,T}$ is likely to be lower). Parkinson et al (1999) discuss this point further.

Calculating and Compensating for Lost Action

Can we quantify this *lost action* due to early crediting? At its simplest level, the lost action, L_T, can be expressed as the sum of the losses in action during the interim period, $L_{CDM,I}$ (see Figure A.5), and the commitment period, $L_{CDM,C}$ (see Figure A.4), minus the increase in CDM action during the interim period (see Figure A.3). Therefore:

$$L_T = L_{CDM,I} + L_{CDM,C} - I_{CDM} \qquad (A.1)$$

Parkinson et al (1999) attempt to quantify this amount, based on a number of linear assumptions made in relation to Figures A.1 to A.5, and estimate that this lost action is between 30–60 per cent of the total CDM action. In essence, this means that, for each tonne of CO_2 equivalent emissions reduction carried out in a CDM project with banking, the *total* emissions reduction needed to meet the QELRC of the donor (domestic, article 6 JI and CDM over the whole period) is decreased by roughly 0.3 to 0.6 tonnes. Clearly, this is a significant effect. It should be noted that this is a conservative estimate because of the nature of the assumptions made (see Parkinson et al, 1999).

Is it possible to retain the incentive for early action by crediting during the interim period without compromising the total action needed to comply with emissions targets? One simple way is that of *partial crediting* (see Chapter 9), where only a fraction of the emissions reduction is awarded credits. The value of this *crediting fraction, c*, should be set such that the uncredited CDM action is equal to the lost action. To calculate c in the above situation, we therefore have:

$$T_{CDM}(1 - c) = L_T \qquad (A.2)$$

where T_{CDM} is the total CDM action over the whole period. Since L_T is between $0.3T_{CDM}$ to $0.6T_{CDM}$, the crediting fraction, c, becomes 40–70 per cent. This means that, in order to ensure that the total emissions reduction under the CDM with early crediting is as large as that without, only 40–70 per cent of the CDM emissions reduction should be credited.

It is interesting to note that a previous analysis of this issue (Parkinson et al, 1998b) under different assumptions calculated a value for the crediting fraction of 56 per cent, in the middle of the range calculated here.

Scale of the Impact

In this section, we attempt to estimate what might be the effective level of relaxation in a country's QELRC target due to early crediting of CERs under article 12, as discussed above. For this we use a review of estimates of the potential size of the CDM market (Vrolijk, 1999) and look at the Annex I countries, the US, the Netherlands and the Czech Republic.

Vrolijk gives a range of estimates of the size of the global CDM market from 67 to 723MtCe/y (megatonnes of carbon equivalent per year): that is, 245 to 2650MtCO$_2$e/y. If we assume that the US share of the market is approximately 10 per cent, then its CDM programme would be 25 to 265MtCO$_2$e/y. Using the analysis from Parkinson et al (1999) and taking the US target as 4597MtCO$_2$e/y – a 7 per cent cut from the 1990 level of 4943MtCO$_2$e/y (UN

FCCC, 1995a) – this leads to a range of 0.4–7.5 per cent for the relaxation of the US emissions target (the effective target would reduce to between a 6.6 per cent cut and a 0.5 per cent increase).

It should be kept in mind that the high estimate of $2650MtCO_2e/y$ for a global CDM programme is approximately half the size of the current US emissions. It seems unlikely for a market this big to grow in the next eight years. Indeed, the bottom-up economic analysis carried out by Vrolijk gives an upper estimate of only $210MtCe/y$ or $769MtCO_2e/y$. If we take this value and again assume a 10 per cent US market share, the relaxation is approximately 1.8 per cent (the US target becomes a 5.2 per cent cut).

Even more significant is the case of the Netherlands. Vrolijk discusses a level of CDM activity during the commitment period of around $6MtCe/y$ or $22MtCO_2e/y$. Again, following the methodology of Parkinson et al (1999), and taking into account the 1990 GHG emissions of the Netherlands ($215MtCO_2e$ for CO_2, CH_4 and N_2O; see UN FCCC, 1995c), we find a relaxation of between 8.2 per cent and 14.3 per cent. This changes the Dutch target from a 6.0 per cent cut (as agreed under the EU burden-sharing scheme) to between a 2.2 per cent increase and an 8.3 per cent increase.

As discussed earlier, it has also been argued that early crediting should be introduced for article 6 JI. There is a critical difference between this case and the case of the CDM, due to the presence of emissions targets for the host. As stated in articles 3.10 and 3.11, any credits (ERUs) earned from a JI project will not only count towards meeting the emissions target of the donor, but will tighten the target of the host. As a result, if ERUs are given for action during the interim period, this tightening will be significantly increased.

Again, using the analysis of Parkinson et al (1999), we can look at the situation for article 6 JI. In this case we use, as an example, the Czech Republic as host and the US as donor. We assume a global article 6 JI market of the same size as that estimated by Vrolijk for the CDM ($769MtCO2e/y$) and again estimate a 10 per cent US share. If we then assume that 5 per cent of this is carried out in the Czech Republic, we find an extra tightening of 2–3 per cent of the 1990 level. Since the Czech target is a cut of 8 per cent, the new target during the commitment period becomes a cut of 10–11 per cent. It is important that this level of *extra tightening* of the Annex I host countries' targets is fully appreciated and discussed at an international policy level.

Discussion

In this appendix we have explored early crediting: the banking of credits during an interim period with no emissions targets. The main problem with this concept (which is enshrined in article 12 of the Kyoto Protocol) is that any credits issued for emissions reduction achieved outside a target period may be offset by less action elsewhere during this time without penalty. When these credits are then banked for use in complying with a target, they can offset other action. Hence, the total amount of emissions reduction needed to meet the target is less. Effectively, this can be seen as a relaxation of the emissions target. This is unlike the intended purpose of flexibility mechanisms, which is to allow a redistribution of emission reductions between countries without affecting the overall target.

In the particular case of early crediting for the CDM, this directly leads to emissions reduction counting up to 2.6 times as much in the commitment period as that carried out under article 6 JI or as domestic action. However, it is important to realize that early crediting of article 6 JI and domestic action, as a way to equalize the mechanisms, would compound rather than alleviate the problem and, as discussed above, possibly relax the Kyoto Protocol targets further.

Here, we have summarized an analysis (Parkinson et al, 1999) which estimates how much less action would be needed to meet the QELRC targets due to the presence of early crediting. We have found that, for each tonne of CO_2-equivalent emissions reduction carried out in a CDM project with early crediting, the total emissions reduction (domestic, article 6 JI and CDM over the whole period) needed by a donor country to meet its target is decreased by roughly 0.3 to 0.6 tonnes. Based on estimates of the size of the global CDM market, this could lead to effective relaxation of donor country QELRC targets. We estimated that for the US, this could be in the order of 1.8 per cent (from a 7.0 per cent cut to a 5.2 per cent cut from 1990 levels), and for the Netherlands, of between 8.2–14.3 per cent (from a 6.0 per cent cut to between a 2.2– 8.3 per cent increase from 1990 levels).

We also carried out an estimate for the corresponding tightening of the emissions targets for Annex I host countries should early crediting be extended to article 6 JI. For the Czech Republic, we estimated that their target could be tightened by an amount in the order of 2–3 per cent (from an 8 per cent cut to a 10–11 per cent cut from 1990 levels).

We suggested that, while early crediting gives incentives for early CDM action, it should not be fully credited. Therefore, we proposed that a *crediting fraction* should be applied to CDM credits to maintain the total action needed to meet the targets. On the basis of some analysis of possible emissions-reduction action, we estimated that this fraction should be between 40 per cent and 70 per cent. We believe that this analysis has been based on conservative assumptions, hence we recommend using a value towards the lower end of this range. Obviously, the use of such a fraction would reduce the attractiveness of the scheme to investors. However, this should be viewed in the context that the main argument for CDM action is its low cost compared with domestic action, and the increase in the price of credits resulting from the use of such a fraction may not be that significant.

It is important to consider this issue in a wider policy context. Currently, there is significant doubt over whether the US will ratify the Kyoto Protocol, since the US senate wants guarantees of 'meaningful participation by developing countries' over fears of economic disadvantage that ratification may cause the US (see, for example, Grubb et al, 1999). Many developing countries, on the other hand, currently refuse to accept emissions targets since they argue that anthropogenic climate change is a problem caused by industrialized countries, and current per capita emissions are considerably higher than those in developing countries. Therefore, significant action should be taken by industrialized countries first. As a result, a significant amount of CDM action, with early crediting, may contribute towards a compromise. Whether such a compromise, with the effective relaxation in Annex I countries' targets, is acceptable is a decision which needs to be made.

Policy discussion has also revolved around the introduction of early crediting for article 6 JI. As we have discussed, this will effectively result in an extra tightening of Annex I host countries' targets (building on the argument made concerning this sort of banking for the CDM). This extra tightening is unlikely to be acceptable to these countries unless they gain significant local benefits from the early article 6 JI action.

In summary, early crediting – whether for the CDM or article 6 JI – will effectively alter emissions targets in favour of the donor. This should be recognized explicitly in negotiations concerning these mechanisms so that all trade-offs are transparent.

Notes

Chapter 1

1   Article 4.2 contains only a non-binding target for stabilization of emissions at 1990 levels by the end of the decade.
2   For a detailed guide and assessment of the Kyoto Protocol, see Grubb et al, 1999; for a more personal view of the decade of negotiations leading up to the protocol, see Leggett, 1999; for a detailed history of the IPCC, see Agrawala, 1998a&b.
3   The gases included in the basket are carbon dioxide (CO_2), methane (CH_4), nitrous oxide (N_2O), hydrofluorocarbons (HFCs), perfluorocarbons (PFCs) and sulphur hexafluoride (SF_6).
4   For most countries the base year is taken as 1990.
5   The term incremental cost – which is discussed in greater detail in Chapter 3 – refers to the difference in cost between the emission reduction project and the provision of the same energy service in the baseline.
6   Indeed, this chapter summarizes an analysis of the early crediting of CDM action, described in more detail in Appendix 1, which concludes that under this regime, for every tonne of emissions reduction carried out in the CDM, between 0.3 and 0.6 tonnes of emissions reduction action are 'lost' elsewhere in the trading system.

Chapter 2

1   This chapter is based on a paper originally published in a special issue of the *International Journal of Environment and Pollution* (Jackson et al, 1998).
2   In principle, open JI could include arrangements between countries, neither of whom had QELRCs – although in this case it is difficult to see how there would be any incentive for the donor to engage in the relationship.
3   The term *leakage* refers to the situation in which emissions reduction activities are less effective because secondary impacts from the investment lead to increased emissions elsewhere in the global system (see Chapter 4 for a more detailed discussion).
4   These countries are essentially those subject to QELRCs.
5   Nevertheless, indirect emissions leakage outside the borders of the two countries is still possible (see following text).
6   The term *cherry-picking* (sometimes also called *cream-skimming*) refers to the situation where donors exploit the cheapest emission-reductions options, leaving only the more expensive options available to the host country. These cheaper options are sometimes referred to as *low-hanging fruit*.

7   Aside from the fact that the pilot-phase activities could not formally claim credit for emission reductions achieved.

Chapter 3

1   The percentages specified for each party are set out in Annex B of the protocol. The overall goal of these commitments is to reduce emission levels by Annex I parties during the commitment period by 5 per cent over 1990 levels.
2   The cost comparison is assumed to be made in such a fashion that it accounts for the difference in cost in providing the same service from the respective options.

Chapter 4

1   That is to say, from a perspective *before* the abatement project is implemented.
2   That is to say, from a perspective some time *after* the abatement project has been implemented.
3   The capacity installed for the two plants may not be identical. How this problem is treated is addressed in detail for the relevant JI projects in Chapter 7.
4   Some researchers (for example, CCAP, 1998) use the terms bottom-up and top-down baseline, where we have used the terms project-level and system-level baseline. Since their terminology is already in use for describing different kinds of energy models, we feel it would be confusing to use it here.
5   The term 'dynamic' has also been applied to baselines which change over time – for example, to take account of expected improvements in system efficiency with time. However, this is not the way we use it in this book.

Chapter 5

1   The information in these summaries has been abstracted from more detailed assessments in Jackson et al (1999).
2   When this project started, the Swedish National Board for Industrial and Technical Development (NUTEK) was the project partner involved. In 1998, the Swedish National Energy Administration (STEM) was set up and took over this responsibility.

Chapter 6

1   This is in accordance with section 20 of the National Nature Conservation Regulations.
2   In the context of the CDM, a set of sustainability indicators and new approval criteria were recently suggested at COP 5 (Thorne and La Rovere, 1999) for incorporation within a generally applicable approval-criteria set. However, the suggestion was dismissed by policy-makers, since approval procedures are the domain of the individual host countries and agreeing indicators would be difficult at COP level.

Chapter 7

1   Also known as the *lower heating value*, this is unit amount of heat produced by the combustion of a given fuel having subtracted the heat consumed in the vaporization of any volatiles in the fuel.
2   This is a large assumption and therefore we explore alternatives in Chapter 8.
3   This estimated 'real energy consumption' (NUTEK, 1995) could have occurred because of a higher availability of heat from the district-heating network – 'high heat supply from network' examples.
4   Interestingly, there is a difference here between the standard methodology (with implied discounting of emissions) and the methodology given by equation 7.18. In the latter case, the reduction in crediting life (from baseline 1 to baseline 5) increases the specific incremental cost by 30 per cent.
5   It is interesting to note that both these baseline choices have been used in project assessments reported to the FCCC (UN FCCC, 2000).

Chapter 8

1   Latin Hypercube sampling is mathematically more complicated, but requires significantly fewer samples to be taken to yield a useful result.
2   Indeed, for a large-scale project, we pointed out that a macro or country-level assessment may be justified.
3   Bottom-up models are so named to contrast them with top-down macroeconomic models.
4   To explain, let us assume we have annual costs of US$10 per year for the foreseeable future. Using a discount rate of 10 per cent and a lifetime of 10 years, the neglected term in year 11 is US$3.50, whereas in the case of a 4 per cent discount rate and a 25-year lifetime, the neglected term in year 26 is US$3.61: that is, they are similar.
5   The uncertainties given are expressed in terms of a 66 per cent confidence interval following the standard format now used by the Intergovernmental Panel on Climate Change (see, for example, IPCC, 1999). It should be noted that the values of the uncertainties here differ from those reported in the original study (Jackson et al, 1999), which were calculated using 95 per cent confidence intervals.
6   As noted in footnote 5, these results differ from those presented in the earlier study (Jackson et al, 1999) because the earlier results were based on 95 per cent confidence intervals, whereas the ones presented here are based on 66 per cent confidence intervals.

Chapter 9

1   This has been called a *dynamic* baseline (see Chapter 4).
2   It is interesting to note that Rolfe et al (1999), in a detailed analysis of early crediting regimes at a national level, argue that partial crediting, in combination with other measures (such as a cap on credit creation), is necessary if such schemes are pursued.

Chapter 10

1   These are simplified options: only some of the possible components are examined in detail and these relate mainly to the accounting and accreditation processes.
2   The ten-year crediting life is taken as being approximately one half the technical lifetime of most heat-supply projects.
3   The ten-year revision period was chosen on the basis that this is long enough for significant change to occur. For example, the Danish energy strategy for 1990–2000 used coal as the reference technology, but this is now taken as gas.
4   See footnote 3.
5   The restricted approval criteria are those set up at COP 1 under decision 5/CP.1 on the AIJ pilot phase. They include: additionality, financial additionality, compatibility with national priorities, host approval, and the need to produce real, long-term, measurable reductions in GHGs.
6   An extended set of approval criteria would be based on the restricted set but with additional critical aspects, such as requirements to carry out environmental and social assessment of projects. It would include public participation and sustainability indicators to ensure that projects contribute to capacity-building and to the transfer of environmentally sound technologies.

Appendix

1   For a project starting later, the factor of 2.6 will be reduced until it reaches 1.0 if the project starts in 2008.
2   Note that the vertical axes in Figures A.2, A.3 and A.4 refer to emissions *reduction*, while in Figures A.1 and A.5 the vertical axes refer to emissions.

References

Adams, D (1997) *Greenhouse Gas Controls: The Future of Tradeable Permits*, Financial Times Publishing, London

Agrawala, S (1998a) 'Context and Early Origins of the Intergovernmental Panel on Climate Change', *Climate Change*, vol 39, pp605–620

Agrawala, S (1998b) 'Structural and Process History of the Intergovernmental Panel on Climate Change', *Climate Change*, vol 39, pp621–642

Ahuja, D (1993) *The Incremental Cost of Climate Change Mitigation Projects*, Working Paper no 9, Global Environmental Facility, Washington, DC

Ardone, A, W Fichtner, M Wietschel and O Rentz (1997) 'A Techno-Economic Approach to Obtain Comparable Baselines for Joint Implementation', International Workshop on Activities Implemented Jointly, Leipzig, 5–6 March 1997

Arnstein, S R (1969) 'A Ladder of Citizen Participation', *AIP Journal*, July, pp216–224

Arrhenius, S (1896) 'On the Influence of Carbonic Acid in the Air upon the Temperature of the Ground', *Philosophical Magazine*, vol 41, p237

Arrow, K J, W R Cline, K-G Maler, M Munasinghe, R Squitieri and J E Stiglitz (1996) 'Intertemporal Equity, Discounting and Economic Efficiency', Chapter 4 of IPCC WG III *Climate Change 1995: Economic and Social Dimensions of Climate Change*, J P Bruce, H Lee and E F Haites (eds), Working Group III of the Intergovernmental Panel on Climate Change, Cambridge University Press, Cambridge

Bailey, P D, G A Gough, K Millock and M J Chadwick (1996) 'Prospects for the Joint Implementation of Sulphur Emission Reductions in Europe', *Energy Policy*, vol 24(6) pp507–516

Bailey, P and T Jackson (1999) 'Joint Implementation for Controlling Sulphur in Europe and Possible Lessons for Carbon Dioxide' in S Sorrell and J Skea (eds) *Pollution for Sale: Emissions Trading and Joint Implementation*, Edward Elgar, Aldershot

Banuri, T, K-G Maler, M Grubb, H K Jacobson and F Yamin (1996) 'Equity and Social Considerations', Chapter 3 of IPCC WG III *Climate Change 1995: Economic and Social Dimensions of Climate Change*, J P Bruce, H Lee and E F Haites (eds), Working Group III of the Intergovernmental Panel on Climate Change, Cambridge University Press, Cambridge

Barrett, S (1992) 'Reaching a CO_2 Emission Limitation Agreement for the Community: Implications for Equity and Cost Effectiveness', *European Economy*, vol 1, special issue on *The Economics of Limiting CO_2 Emissions*, DGII, CEC

Barrett, S (1994) 'The Strategy of Joint Implementation in the Framework Convention on Climate Change', paper for UNCTAD, London Business School, London

Begg, K G, S D Parkinson, T Jackson, P-E Morthorst and P Bailey (1998) 'Accounting and Accreditation of Joint Implementation under the Kyoto Protocol', paper presented at the AWMA Second International Speciality Conference – Global

Climate Change: Science, Policy and Mitigation/Adaptation Strategies, Crystal City Hyatt Regency Hotel, Washington, DC, 13–15 October

Bisset, R (1988) 'Development of EIA methods' in P Wathern (ed) *Environmental Impact Assessment*, Unwin Hyman, London

Bohm, P (1997) *Joint Implementation as Emission Quota Trading – an Experiment among Four Nordic Countries*, Nordic Council of Ministers, Copenhagen

Bowles, R T (1981) *Social Impact Assessment in Small Communities: an Integrative Review of Selected Literature*, Butterworths, Toronto

Burdge, R J (1989) 'Utilizing Social Impact Assessment Variables in the Planning Model', *Impact Assessment Bulletin*, vol 8, pp85–99

Carter, L (1997) 'Modalities for the Operationalisation of Additionality', paper presented at UNEP/German Federal Ministry of the Environment, International Workshop on Activities Implemented Jointly, Leipzig, 5–6 March

Catlow, J and C G Thirwell (1976) *Environmental Impact Analysis*, Department of the Environment, London

CCAP (1998) 'Meeting minutes of the JI Braintrust Group', Holiday Inn, Old Town Alexandria, US, 18–19 February; produced by Centre for Clean Air Policy, US

Chadwick, M J (1990) 'Air pollution' in J Pasztor and L A Kristoferson (eds) *Bioenergy and the Environment*, Westview, Boulder, Colorado

CNE (1994) *Joint Implementation from a European NGO Perspective*, Climate Network Europe, Brussels, Belgium

Coherence (1991) *Cost-effectiveness Analysis of CO_2 Reductions Options*, report for the CEC, DGXII, Brussels

Colombo, C, A Artola, C Gervarsi, G Haq and I Melaki (1996) *An Analysis of Environmental Impact Studies of Installations for the Disposal of Toxic and Dangerous Waste in the EU*, EUR Report 16389, EC Joint Research Centre, Ispra, Italy

CORINAIR/EMEP (1996) *Atmospheric Emission Inventory Guidebook*, first edition, G McInnes (ed) European Environment Agency, Copenhagen, Denmark

COWI (1996) *Joint Implementation of Commitments to Mitigate Climate Change: Analysis of Five Selected Energy Projects in Eastern Europe*, COWI, Denmark

Denisov, N B, R A Mnatsakanian and A V Semichaevsky (1997) 'Environmental Reporting in Central and Eastern Europe: A Review of Selected Publications and Frameworks', UNEP/DEIA/TR.97-6, GA/205031-97/1 and CEU/50-97.1, United Nations Environment Programme, Nairobi and Central European University, Budapest

DFI (1983) *An Overview of the Generalized Equilibrium Modeling System*, Decision Focus Inc, California

EBRD (1996) *Environmental Procedures*, European Bank for Reconstruction and Development, London

EC (1997) 'Council Conclusions on Climate Change', 3 March 1997, European Commission, Brussels

EEA (1996) *Guidelines for the Data Collection for the Dobris+3 Report*, European Environment Agency, Copenhagen

EEA (1999) *Environment in the European Union at the Turn of the Century*, European Environmental Agency, Copenhagen

ELI (1997) *Transparency and Responsiveness: Building a Participatory Process for Activities Implemented Jointly under the Climate Change Convention*, Environmental Law Institute, US

Ellerman, A, R Schmalensee, P L Joskow, J P Montero and E M Bailey (1997) *Emissions Trading under the US Acid Rain Program: Evaluation of Compliance*

Costs and Allowance Market Performance, MIT Center for Energy and Environmental Policy Research, Cambridge, MA

Ellis, J and M Bosi (1999) 'Options for Project Baselines', OECD/IEA information paper, International Energy Agency/Organization for Economic Cooperation and Development, Paris

ENDS (2000) 'EU Backs First Kyoto Trading Scheme', *Ends Daily*, 29 March 2000, Environmental Data Services, London

ETSU/COWI (1994) *Comprehensive Energy Sector Study and Integrated Energy Pricing/ Taxation Study for the Czech and Slovak Republics*, final report, Czech Republic, Sector Report 5: Electricity Sector, ETSU, UK; COWI, Denmark

EVA (1994) *Möglichkeiten der Energieeffizienzsteigerung in Tschechien*, Energie Verwertungsagentur (EVA), Vienna, Austria

Eyre, N, T Downing, R Hoekstra, K Rennings and R S J Tol (1999) 'ExternE – Externalities of Energy', vol 8: *Global Warming*, European Commission, Luxembourg

FEARO (1986) *Initial Assessment Guide*, Federal Environmental Assessment Review Office, Ottawa

Fishbone, L G, G Giesen, G Goldstein, H A Hymmen, K J Stocks, H Vos, D Wilde, R Zolcher, C Balzer and H Abilock (1983) *User's Guide for MARKAL (BNL/KFA Version 2.0): A multi-period, linear-programming model for energy systems analysis*, IEA International Systems Analysis Project, BNL 51701, Brookhaven National Laboratory and Kernforschungsanlage Julich

Flavin, C and O Tunali (1996) 'Climate of Hope: New Strategies for Stabilizing the World's Atmosphere', Worldwatch Paper 130, Worldwatch Institute, Washington, DC

Fleming, D (1997) 'Tradable Quotas: setting limits to carbon emissions', paper 11, the Lean Economy, Newbury: Elm Farm Research Centre

Førsund, F R (1993) 'Sulphur Emission Trading', working paper, Department of Economics, University of Oslo, Oslo

Førsund, F and E Nævdal (1994) 'Trading Sulphur Emissions Quotas: third party constraints', working paper, Department of Economics, University of Oslo, Oslo.

Fritsche, U (1994) *The Problems of Monitoring and Verification of Joint Implementation*, in CNE *Joint Implementation from a European NGO Perspective*, Climate Network Europe, Brussels, Belgium

Gallopin, G C (1997) 'Indicators and Their Use: information for decision-making' in B Moldan and S Billharz (eds) *Sustainability Indicators*, Wiley, Chichester

Ghosh, P and A Das (1993*) UNEP GHG Abatement Costing Studies: India Country Study*, Tata Energy Research Institute, New Delhi, India

Gielen, D J and T Kram (1997) 'The MARKAL Model for Environmental Accounting in Energy and Material Systems', paper presented at the conference From Paradigm to Practice of Sustainability, Leiden, the Netherlands, 21–23 January

Glasson, J (1995) 'Socio-economic Impacts 1: overview and economic impacts' in P Morris and R Therival (eds), *Methods of Environmental Impact Assessment*, UCL Press, London

Glasson, J, M J Elsom, D van der Wee and B Barrett (1987) 'The Socio-economic Impact of the Proposed Hinkley Point C Power Station', Power Station Impacts Team, Oxford Polytechnic, Oxford

Glasson, J, R Therivel and A Chadwick (1994) *Introduction to Environmental Impact Assessment*, UCL Press, London

Goffman, J and D J Dudek (1998) 'Credit for Early Reductions: a proposal for voluntary incentive-base program', paper presented at the AWMA Second International

Speciality Conference – Global Climate Change: Science, Policy and Mitigation/ Adaptation Strategies, Crystal City Hyatt Regency Hotel, Washington, DC, 13–15 October

Gough, G A, P D Bailey, B Biewald, J C I Kuylenstierna and M J Chadwick (1994) 'Environmentally targeted objectives for reducing acidification in Europe', *Energy Policy*, vol 22(12), pp1055–1066

Grohnheit, P-E (1996) *Energy Tariff Project – Latvia: Development and Application of Energy Models*, Riso National Laboratory, Roskilde, Denmark; p20–23

Grohnheit, P-E (1996) *Scenario Tools for the EFOM Model*, Riso National Laboratory, Denmark

Groscurth, H M, T Bruckner and R Kummel (1995) 'Modeling of Energy-Services Supply Systems', *Energy*, vol 20(9), pp941–958

Grubb, M (1989) *Negotiating Targets*. Royal Institute of International Affairs, London

Grubb, M, C Vrolik and D Brack (1999) *The Kyoto Protocol – A Guide and Assessment*, Royal Institute of International Affairs and Earthscan Publications Ltd, London

Hamilton, L D (1982) 'Comparing the health impacts of different energy sources' in *Health Impacts of Different Sources of Energy*, International Atomic Energy Agency, Vienna

Hamilton, L D (1984) 'Health and environmental risks of energy systems' in *Risks and Benefits of Energy Systems*, International Atomic Energy Agency, Vienna

van Harmelen, T, H de Kruijk, A Stoffer and M Maly (1995) *Strategies for Reducing Emissions and Depositions in Central and Eastern European Countries: The Case of the Czech Republic*, Project no 7141, ECN-Petten, the Netherlands

Hargrave, T and N Helme (1998) 'Considerations in the Design of an Early Reductions Trading Program', paper presented to AWMA Second International Speciality Conference – Global Climate Change: Science, Policy and Mitigation/Adaptation Strategies, Crystal City Hyatt Regency Hotel, Washington, DC, 13–15 October

Heister, J (1999) 'Baselines for GHG Reductions: Issues and Options', paper presented at the Workshop on Baselines for the CDM, Tokyo, Japan, 25–26 February

Henneke, B, G Hirshberg and M C Trexler (1998) 'Early Crediting Action: the imperative and the CEO CAST proposal', paper presented to AWMA Second International Speciality Conference – Global Climate Change: Science, Policy and Mitigation/Adaptation Strategies, Crystal City Hyatt Regency Hotel, Washington, DC, 13–15 October

Hoibye, G (1997) 'Designing a Trading Scheme for Norway', paper presented at the International Workshop on Tradable Permits, Quotas and Joint Implementation, April 1997, University of Sussex, Sussex

Holland, M, J Berry and D Forster (eds) (1999) 'ExternE – Externalities of Energy', vol 7, *Methodology, 1998 Update*, European Commission, Luxembourg

Hourcade, J C, R Richels and Robinson J (1996) 'Estimating the Costs of Mitigating Greenhouse Gases', Chapter 8 of IPCC WG III *Climate Change 1995: Economic and Social Dimensions of Climate Change*, J P Bruce, H Lee and E F Haites (eds), Working Group III of the Intergovernmental Panel on Climate Change, Cambridge University Press, Cambridge

IEA/OECD (1997) *Activities Implemented Jointly; Partnerships for Climate and Development*, Energy and Environment, Policy Analysis series, International Energy Agency/Organization for Economic Cooperation and Development, Paris

IIED (1998) *Directory of Impact Assessment Guidelines*, International Institute for Environment and Development, London

Inhaber, H (1976) *Environmental Indices*, Wiley, New York

IPCC (1996) *Revised IPCC Guidelines for National GHG Inventories, Volume 3: GHG Inventory Reference Manual*, IPCC/UNEP/OECD/IEA, IPCC, Bracknell, UK

IPCC (1999) *Aviation and the Global Atmosphere*, a special report of Working Groups I and III of the Intergovernmental Panel on Climate Change, Geneva

IPCC WG I (1996) *Climate Change 1995: The Science of Climate Change*, J T Houghton, L G Meiro Filho, B A Callander, N Harris, A Kattenburg, K Maskell (eds), Working Group I of the Intergovernmental Panel on Climate Change, Cambridge University Press, Cambridge

IPCC WG III (1996) *Climate Change 1995: Economic and Social Dimensions of Climate Change*, J P Bruce, H Lee and E F Haites (eds), Working Group III of the Intergovernmental Panel on Climate Change, Cambridge University Press, Cambridge

Jackson, T (1991) 'Least-cost Greenhouse Planning – supply curves for greenhouse gas abatement', *Energy Policy*, vol 19(1), pp35–47

Jackson, T (1995) 'Joint Implementation and Cost-effectiveness under the Framework Convention on Climate Change', *Energy Policy*, vol 23(2), pp117–138

Jackson, T (1997) *Power in Balance – Energy Challenges for the 21st Century*, Friends of the Earth, London

Jackson, T and P Bailey (1997) 'Transboundary Initiatives for Controlling Sulfur and Possible Lessons for CO_2', *International Journal of Environment and Pollution*, vol 8 (1/2), pp37–49

Jackson, T, K Begg and S D Parkinson (1998) 'The Language of Flexibility and the Flexibility of Language', *International Journal of Environment and Pollution*, vol 10 (3/4), special issue, *EU Climate Policy: the European Commission policy/research interface for Kyoto & beyond*, pp462–475

Jackson, T, K Begg and S D Parkinson (eds) (1999) *Accounting and Accreditation of Activities Implemented Jointly*: Final Report to DGXII, contract no ENV4-CT96-0210, Centre for Environmental Strategy, University of Surrey, Guildford

Jepma, C (ed) (1995) *The Feasibility of Joint Implementation*, Kluwer Academic Press, Dordrecht

Jepma, C (1998a) 'Kyoto Protocol and Compatibility', editorial in *Joint Implementation Quarterly*, vol 4(1), p1

Jepma, C (1998b) 'Banking – editor's note', *Joint Implementation Quarterly*, vol 4(2), p1

Joskow, P L and D B Marron (1993) The Cost of Energy Efficiency, *Science*, vol 262, pp319–321.

Keeney, R L and H Raiffa (1976) *Decisions with Multiple Objectives: Preferences and Value Trade-offs*, J Wiley and Sons, Chichester

King, W (1993) *The Incremental Costs of Global Environmental Benefits*, working paper no 5, Global Environmental Facility, Washington, DC

Kinzig, A P and Kammen, D A (1998) 'National Trajectories of Carbon Emissions: Analysis of proposals to foster the transition to low carbon economies', *Global Environmental Change*, vol 8(3), pp183–208

Klaassen, G (1995) *Trading Sulphur Emission Reduction Commitments in Europe: a Theoretical and Empirical Analysis*, The International Institute for Applied Systems Analysis, Laxenburg, Austria

Kleinschmidt, V, N Schauerte-Lüke and R Bergman (1994) 'Rahmankonzept für Windkraftanlagen und – parks im Binnenland: ein Beispiel aus Nordrhein-Westfalen', *Natur und Landschaft*, vol 1, pp9–18

Kopp, R J and J W Anderson (1998) 'Estimating the Costs of Kyoto: how plausible are the Clinton Administration's figures?' http://www.weathervane.rff.org/features/feature034.html (21 October 1998)

Lefevre, T, N C Thanh, B D Thanh and S Acharya (1995) *Energy-Environment Planning in Developing Countries – EFOM-ENV Methodological Guide*, RAS/92/071, Programme for Asian Cooperation on Energy and the Environment (PACE-E), Asian Institute of Technology, Bangkok

Leggett, J (1999) *The Carbon War – Dispatches from the End of the Oil Century*, Penguin Press, London

Lehtila, A and P Pirila (1996) 'Reducing Energy Related Emissions: using an energy systems optimization model to support policy planning in Finland', *Energy Policy*, vol 24(9), pp805–819

Lile, R, M Powell, M Toman (1998) *Implementing the Clean Development Mechanism: Lessons from US Private-Sector Participation in Activities Implemented Jointly*, Discussion Paper 99-08, Resources for the Future, Washington, DC

Löfstedt, R E, K Sepp and L Kelly (1996) 'Partnerships to Reduce Greenhouse Gas Emissions in the Baltic', *Environment*, vol 38(6), pp16–20

Luhmann, H J, L Bakker, C Beuermann, M Fischedick, P Hennicke and H E Ott (1997) *Joint Implementation – Project Simulation and Organisation*, report prepared for the German Federal Environment Ministry, Wuppertal Institute for Climate, Environment and Energy, Wuppertal, Germany

Matsuo, N (1999) 'Proceedings of Workshop on Baselines for the CDM', New Energy and Industrial Technology Development Organization/Global Industrial and Social Progress Research Institute, Tokyo, Japan, 25–26 February

Maya, S (1994) 'Joint Implementation: Cautions and Options for the South', paper presented at the International Conference on Joint Implementation, Gröningen, the Netherlands, June

McInnes, G (ed) (1996) *Atmospheric Emission Inventory Guidebook*, first edition, European Environment Agency, Copenhagen, Denmark

Michaelowa, A (1996) 'Incentive Aspects of Joint Implementation of Greenhouse Gas Reduction', *Mitigation and Adaptation Strategies for Global Change*, vol 1, pp95–108

Michaelowa, A (1998) 'Joint Implementation – the Baseline Issue: Economic and Political Aspects', *Global Environmental Change*, vol 8 (1), pp81–92

Michaelowa, A, and M Dutschke (1998) 'Interest Groups and Efficient Design of the Clean Development Mechanism under the Kyoto Protocol', *International Journal on Sustainable Development*, vol 1, pp24–43.

Michaelowa, A and H Schmidt (1997) 'A Dynamic Crediting Regime for Joint Implementation to Foster Innovation in the Long Term', *Mitigation and Adaptation Strategies for Global Change*, vol 2, pp45–56

Michaelowa, A, K G Begg, S D Parkinson and R Dixon (1999) 'Interpretation and Application of UNFCCC AIJ Pilot Project Development Criteria', Chapter 3 in R Dixon (ed) *The UN Framework Convention on Climate Change Activities Implemented Jointly (AIJ) Pilot: Experiences and Lessons Learned*, Kluwer Academic Publishers, Dordrecht

Moldan, B and S Billharz (eds) (1997) *Sustainability Indicators*, SCOPE Report 58, Wiley, Chichester

Morris, P and R Therivel (eds) (1995) *Methods for Environmental Impact Assessment*, UCL Press, London

Morthorst, P-E (1993) *The Cost of CO$_2$ Reduction in Denmark: methodology and results*, Risø National Laboratory, Denmark

Mullins, F (1997) 'Lessons from Existing Trading Systems for International GHG Emission Trading', OECD Information Paper, Organization for Economic Cooperation and Development, Paris

Munasinghe, M, P Meier, M Hoel, S W Hong and A Aaheim (1996) 'Applicability of Techniques of Cost-Benefit Analysis to Climate Change', Chapter 5 in IPCC WG III *Climate Change 1995: Economic and Social Dimensions of Climate Change*, J P Bruce, H Lee and E F Haites (eds), Working Group III of the Intergovernmental Panel on Climate Change, Cambridge University Press, Cambridge

Munn, R E (1979) *Environmental Impact Assessment*, Scope Report 5, second edition, John Wiley and Sons, Chichester

MZP CR (1997) *Statistical Environmental Yearbook of the Czech Republic*, Prague

NUTEK (1995) *Mustamäe – an energy efficiency project in residential buildings at Vilde tee, Estonia*, Swedish National Board for Industrial and Technical Development, Stockholm

NUTEK (1996) *Mustamäe: Results and analysis of energy efficiency projects implemented in 1992–1996, Estonia*, Swedish National Board for Industrial and Technical Development, Stockholm

OECD (1994) *Environmental Indicators. Indicateurs d'environnement. OECD Core Set*, Organization for Economic Cooperation and Development, Paris

OECD (1996) 'Environmental Indicators for Environmental Performance Reviews', discussion paper, Group on the State of the Environment, Organization for Economic Cooperation and Development, Paris

O'Riordan, T and R D Hey (eds) (1978) *Environmental Impact Assessment*, Saxon House, Farnborough

Pachauri, K (1994) 'The Economics of Climate Change: A Developing Country Perspective', in *The Economics of Climate Change*, proceedings of an OECD Conference, Paris, pp171–179

Palisade Corporation (1997) *@RISK: Risk Analysis and Simulation Add-In for Microsoft Excel or Lotus 1-2-3*, Palisade Corporation, Newfield, New York

Parikh, J (1994) 'Joint Implementation and Sharing Commitments: A Southern Perspective', in N Nakicenovic et al (eds), *Integrative Assessment of Mitigation, Impacts and Adaptation*, IIASA, Laxenburg, Austria

Parikh, J and S Gokarn (1993) 'Climate Change and India's Energy Policy Options', *Global Environmental Change* vol 3, pp276–292

Parkinson, S D, K G Begg and T Jackson (1999) 'JI/CDM Crediting under the Kyoto Protocol: Does Interim Period Banking help or hinder GHG emissions reduction?', *Energy Policy*, vol 27(3), pp129–136

Parkinson, S D, K Begg, P Bailey, T Jackson and P-E Morthorst (1997) 'Accounting and Accreditation for Activities Implemented Jointly under the FCCC and the Sulphur Protocol', paper presented at the Conference on Science and a Sustainable Society, Roskilde, Denmark, 26–29 October

Parkinson, S D, K Begg, P Bailey and T Jackson (1998a) 'Accounting and Accreditation of Activities Implemented Jointly', paper presented at the second European Society for Ecological Economics Conference, Geneva, March

Parkinson, S D, K Begg and T Jackson (1998b) 'An Exploration of Possible Crediting Regimes for the Clean Development Mechanism', paper presented to the workshop on Dealing with Carbon Credits after Kyoto, Callantsoog, The Netherlands, 28–29 May

Parkinson, S D and P C Young (1998) 'Uncertainty and Sensitivity in Global Carbon Cycle Modelling', *Climate Research*, vol 9, pp157–174

Pearce, D (1995) in C Jepma (ed) *The Feasibility of Joint Implementation*, Kluwer Academic Press, Dordrecht

Phillips, L D (1989) 'Requisite Decision Modelling for Technological Projects' in C Vlek and G Cvetkovich (eds) *Social Decision Methodology for Technological Projects*, Kluwer Academic Publishers, Dordrecht, pp95–110

Puhl, I, T Hargrave and N Helme (1999) 'Options for Simplifying Baseline Setting for Joint Implementation and Clean Development Mechanism Projects', paper presented at the Workshop on Baselines for the CDM, Tokyo, Japan, 25–26 February

Raiffa, H (1968) *Decision Analysis*, Addison-Wesley, Reading, MA

Renn, O and T Webler (1992) 'Anticipating Conflicts: public participation in managing the solid waste crisis', *Gaia,* vol 2, pp84–95

Renn, O, T Webler and P Weidemann (eds) (1995) *Fairness and Competence in Citizen Participation: Evaluating Models for Environmental Discourse*, Kluwer Academic Press, Dordrecht

Rentz, O, M Wietschel, A Ardone, W Fichtner and M Gobelt (1998) *The Efficiency of International Co-operation in Mitigating Climate Change: analysis of joint implementation and emission allowance trading for the Federal Republic of Germany, the Russian Federation and Indonesia*, Institute for Industrial Production (IIP), University of Karlsruhe, Germany

Rolfe C, A Michaelowa and M Dutschke (1999) *Closing the Gap: A Comparison of Approaches to Encourage Early Greenhouse Gas Emission Reductions*, HWWA Report 199, HWWA-Institut fur Wirtschaftsforschung-Hamburg, Germany

Roos, A L (1992) *EFOM-ENV/GAMS Interface – User's Guide*, Netherlands Energy Research Foundation (ECN), Petten. ECN-I-92-037

Savage, L J (1954) *The Foundations of Statistics*, New York, Wiley

SCAQMD (1994) '*Reclaim* Program Summary: A Market Incentive Air Pollution Reduction Program for Nitrogen Oxides and Sulfur Oxides', Los Angeles South Coast Air Quality Management District, Los Angeles, CA

Schwarze, R (2000) 'Activities Implemented Jointly: another look at the facts', *Ecological Economics*, vol 32(2), pp255–267.

SEI (1993) *Long-Range Energy Planning System – LEAP, overview for version 94.0*, Stockholm Environment Institute, US

Shopley, J B and R F Fuggle (1984) 'A Comprehensive Review of Current Environmental Impact Assessment Methods and Techniques', *Journal of Environmental Management*, vol 18, pp25–47

Skea, J and S Sorrell (eds) (1999) *Pollution for Sale: emissions trading and joint implementation*, Edward Elgar, Aldershot

Smith, A (1994) *Energy Modelling with Environmental Constraints*, Decision Focus Inc, Washington, DC

Sorrell, S (1994) *Pollution on the Market: the US experience with emissions trading for the control of air pollution*, STEEP Special Report no 1, Science Policy Research Unit, University of Sussex, Brighton

Statistics Norway (1995) 'Indicators of the State of the Environment in Nordic Countries', mimeo, Statistics Norway, Oslo

Stockholm Konsult (1994) *Demonstration of Energy Saving Potential in Estonian Apartment Blocks*, Stockholm Konsult/Energy and Environment, Stockholm

Swedish Ministry of the Environment (1994) *The Swedish Experience – Taxes and Charges in Environmental Policy*, Swedish Ministry of the Environment and Natural Resources, Stockholm

Therivel, R and M R Partidario (1996) *The Practice of Strategic Environmental Assessment*, Earthscan Publications Ltd, London

Therivel, R, E Wilson, S Thompson, D Heaney and D Pritchard (1992) *Strategic Environmental Assessment*, Earthscan Publications Ltd, London

Thorne, S and E L La Rovere (1999) 'Criteria and Indicators for the Appraisal of Clean Development Mechanism Projects', paper presented at COP 5, Helio International

Thornton, K W (1993) 'Sensitivity Analysis and Simulation Experimentation' in P C Young (ed) *Concise Encyclopaedia of Environmental Systems*, Pergamon Press, Oxford, UK, pp532–534

Tietenberg, T H (1985) *Emissions Trading: An Exercise in Reforming Pollution Policy*, Resources for the Future, Washington, DC

UNCSD (1996) *Indicators of Sustainable Development – Framework and Methodologies*, United Nations Commission on Sustainable Development, New York

UNECE (1994) *Protocol to the 1979 Convention on Long-Range Transboundary Air Pollution on Further Reduction of Sulphur Emissions*, United Nations Economic Commission for Europe, Geneva

UNECE (1995) *Joint Implementation under the Oslo Protocol*, EB.AIR/WG.5/R.57, report by the chairman of the open-ended group of experts, United Nations Economic Commission for Europe, Geneva

UNEP (1994) *UNEP Greenhouse Gas Abatement Costing Studies, Phase 2, Appendix: Guidelines*, UNEP Collaborating Centre on Energy and the Environment, RNL, Denmark

UNEP/CEU (1997) *Environmental Reporting in Central and Eastern Europe: a Review of Selected Publications and Frameworks*, UNEP/DEIA/TR.97-6, GA/205031-97/1, and CEU/50-97.1, United Nations Environment Programme, Nairobi and Central European University, Budapest

UN FCCC (2000) *Activities Implemented Jointly – uniform reporting format*, official website of the Climate Change Secretariat http://www.unfccc.de/program/aij/aij_urf.html (30 March 2000)

UN FCCC (1999a) *Report of the Conference of the Parties on its Fifth Session*, part 2, Decision 11/CP.5, official website of the Climate Change Secretariat http://www.unfccc.de/resource/cop5.html (30 March 2000)

UN FCCC (1999b) *Report of the Conference of the Parties on its Fifth Session*, part 2, Decision 1/CP.5, official website of the Climate Change Secretariat http://www.unfccc.de/resource/cop5.html (30 March 2000)

UN FCCC (1998) *Report of the Conference of the Parties on its Fourth Session*, part 2, Decision 1/CP.4, official website of the Climate Change Secretariat http://www.unfccc.de/resource/cop4.html (30 March 2000)

UN FCCC (1995a) *Executive Summary of the National Communication of the USA*, official website of the Climate Change Secretariat http://www.unfccc.de/resource/docs/nc/usa01.htm (30 March 2000)

UN FCCC (1995b) *Executive Summary of the National Communication of the Czech Republic*, official website of the Climate Change Secretariat http://www.unfccc.de/resource/docs/nc/cze01.htm (30 March 2000)

UN FCCC (1995c) *Executive Summary of the National Communication of The Netherlands*, official website of the Climate Change Secretariat http://www.unfccc.de/resource/docs/nc/nld01.htm (30 March 2000)

USIJI (1996) *Activities Implemented Jointly: First Report to the Secretariat of the UN FCCC*, paper no DOE/PO-0048, USIJI Secretariat, Washington, DC

USIJI (1998) *Activities Implemented Jointly: Second Report to the Secretariat of the UN FCCC*, vol 1, USIJI Secretariat, Washington, DC

Villanueva, L (1993) *UNEP GHG Abatement Costing Studies: Venezuela Country Study*, Ministry of Energy and Mines, Caracas, Venezuela

Violette, D, S Ragland and F Stern (1998) 'Evaluating Greenhouse Gas Mitigation through DSM Projects: Lessons Learned from DSM Evaluation in the United States', World Bank, Washington, DC

Vrolijk, C, (1999) 'The potential size of the CDM', *Global Greenhouse Emissions Trader*, vol 6 (February), pp2–4, UNCTAD, Geneva

VUPEK (1996) *Energy Statistical Yearbook of the Czech Republic 1995*, VUPEK, Prague

Vellinga, P, T Hanisch, R Pachauri and D Schmitt (1992) *Criteria and Guidelines for Joint Implementation of Commitments*, paper for INC V, 19 February 1992, New York

Wathern, P (ed) (1988) *Environmental Impact Assessment: Theory and Practice*, Unwin Hyman, London

Wietschel, M, O Rentz, A Ardone, W Fichtner and M Goebelt (1998) 'Final Report on 'Efficiency of Cross Country Co-operation on Climate Change Mitigation: Analysis of Joint Implementation under an Emissions Trading Regime for the German Federal Republic, the Russian Federation and Indonesia', IIP, Karlsruhe

Woerdmann, E (2000) 'Implementing the Kyoto Protocol: why JI and CDM show more promise than international emissions trading', *Energy Policy*, vol 28(1), pp29–38

Wolf, C P (ed) (1974) *Social Impact Assessment*, Sage, Beverley Hills

Woodward, R T and R C Bishop (1995) 'Efficiency, Sustainability and Global Warming', *Ecological Economics*, vol 14, pp101–111

World Bank (1991) *Environmental Assessment Sourcebook: Volume I, Policies, Procedures and Cross-Sectoral Issues*, World Bank Technical Paper no 139, World Bank, Washington, DC

Yamin, F (1993) 'The Framework Convention on Climate Change: The Development of Criteria for Joint Implementation', FIELD working paper, Foundation for International Environmental Law and Development, London

Yelland, J (1998) Statement of Janet Yelland, Chair of the Council of Economic Advisors, to the US House of Representatives Committee on Government Reform and Oversight, Subcommittee on National Economic Growth, Natural Resources and Regulatory Affairs, 19 May

Index